Philip C. Almond is Professor Emeritus of Religion at the University of Queensland, and is internationally respected for his work on religion and the history of ideas, especially during the English Enlightenment. His ten previous books include *Heaven and Hell in Enlightenment England, Adam and Eve in Seventeenth-Century Thought, Demonic Possession and Exorcism in Early Modern England, The Witches of Warboys* (I.B.Tauris, 2008), *The Lancashire Witches* (I.B.Tauris, 2012) and *The Devil: A New Biography* (I.B.Tauris, 2014).

The discouerie of witchcraft,

Wherein the lewde dealing of witches and witchmongers is notablie detected, the knauerie of coniurors, the impietie of inchantors, the follie of soothsaiers, the impudent falshood of cousenors, the infidelitie of atheists, the pestilent practises of Pythonists, the curiositie of figurecasters, the vanitie of dreamers, the beggerlie art of Alcumystrie,

The abhomination of idolatrie, the horrible art of poisoning, the vertue and power of naturall magike, and all the conueiances of Legierdemaine and iuggling are deciphered: and many other things opened, which haue long lien hidden, howbeit verie necessarie to be knowne.

Heerevnto is added a treatise vpon the nature and substance of spirits and diuels, &c: all latelie written

by Reginald Scot Esquire.

1. Iohn. 4, 1.

Beleeue not euerie spirit, but trie the spirits, whether they are of God; for manie false prophets are gone out into the world, &c.

1584

England's First Demonologist

Reginald Scot &
'The Discoverie of Witchcraft'

Philip C. Almond

I.B.TAURIS
LONDON · NEW YORK

New paperback edition published in 2014 by I.B.Tauris & Co. Ltd
6 Salem Road, London W2 4BU
175 Fifth Avenue, New York NY 10010
www.ibtauris.com

Distributed in the United States and Canada
Exclusively by Palgrave Macmillan
175 Fifth Avenue, New York NY 10010

First published in hardback by I.B.Tauris & Co. Ltd in 2011

Copyright © 2011, 2014 Philip Almond

The right of Philip Almond to be identified as the author of this work has been asserted by him in accordance with the Copyright, Designs and Patent Act 1988.

All rights reserved. Except for brief quotations in a review, this book, or any part thereof, may not be reproduced, stored in or introduced into a retrieval system, or transmitted, in any form or by any means, electronic, mechanical, photocopying, recording or otherwise, without the prior written permission of the publisher.

ISBN: 978 1 78076 963 9
eISBN: 978 0 85773 218 7

A full CIP record for this book is available from the British Library
A full CIP record is available from the Library of Congress

Library of Congress Catalog Card Number: available

Typeset in Goudy Old Style by GS Typesetting Services

To Pat

'The fables of Witchcraft have taken so fast hold and deepe root in the heart of man, that fewe or none can (nowadaies) with patience indure the hand and correction of God. For if any adversitie, greefe, sickness, losse of children, corne, cattell, or libertie happen unto them; by & by they exclaime uppon witches. As though there were no God in Israel that ordereth all things according to his will; punishing both just and unjust with greefs, plagues, and afflictions in maner and forme as he thinketh good.'

Reginald Scot, *The Discoverie of Witchcraft*

'A fascinating book on a fascinating subject.'
— *The Historical Association*

'Philip Almond's commentary on *The Discoverie of Witchcraft* has offered us valuable insights into early modern Protestant thought regarding the demonic realm.'
— *Journal of British Studies*

'An excellent, easy to read, reasonably sophisticated introduction to Reginald Scot's *Discoverie of Witchcraft*. A welcome book which provides a valuable introduction to one of the most puzzling texts of the early modern period.'
— *Ecclesiastical History*

'If you're interested in the history and import of Scot's work, Professor Almond's work will be invaluable.'
— *The Magic Circular*

Contents

Acknowledgements	ix
Chapter One: 'The Discoverie of Witchcraft'	1
The Book	1
Noblesse Oblige	9
Motivations and Methods	13
The Bible, the Book, and the Books	21
Chapter Two: Witchcraft	25
Apocalypse Soon	25
A Witch in Brenchley	26
Evil and Providence	29
The Witches of Windsor	35
The Witches of St. Osyth	40
Witches, Deluding and Deluded	49
Mad and Melancholic Imaginings	60
Chapter Three: Demonology	71
Demonological Foundations	71
The Demonic Pact	78
On Sabbatical Travels	89
Animal Transformations	99
Sex and the Devil	104

Chapter Four: Magic   117
    Poisons and Potions   117
    Pythonists and Ventriloquists   121
    The Pythonist of Endor   127
    Miracles, Oracles, and Apparitions   130
    Reading the Stars   136
    Divining and Dreaming   139
    Guessing Upon Uncertain Toys   141
    Of Enchanters, Priests, and Physicians   145
    Magic, Angelic and Demonic   155

Chapter Five: Philosophy and Religion   163
    Natural Magic   163
    Secular Enchantments   168
    'Of the Art of Alchumystrie'   173
    A Devilish and Spiritual Discourse   177
    The Secret Sadducee?   182
    Carnal and Spiritual Men   187
    The Spiritual Demonologist   190

Notes   193
Bibliography   229
Index   241

Acknowledgements

This work was undertaken in the Centre for the History of European Discourses at the University of Queensland. This Centre and this University have continued to provide a congenial, stimulating and, more often than one can hope to expect, an exciting context in which to work. For this, I am indebted in particular to Professor Peter Cryle, the Director of the Centre, to Professor Ian Hunter, Australian Professorial Fellow in the History of Political Thought, and to the postdoctoral fellows of the Centre, all of whose dedication to their work has provided much encouragement to my own. The work was also made possible by funding from the Australian Research Council. I am grateful to them for their support.

This book is dedicated to my partner Patricia Lee. She has always been willing to endure my reading of the text to her as it was written, and has provided much helpful criticism.

CHAPTER ONE

'The Discoverie of Witchcraft'

The Book

In 1597, King James VI of Scotland published his *Daemonologie*. It was a work that he was moved to write by his belief in what he called 'The fearefull aboundinge at this time in this countrie, of these detestable slaves of the Devill, the Witches or enchaunters.'[1] James himself had been the target of a plot by alleged witches in Scotland in 1590–1, so it is little wonder that his mind was focused on witchcraft in this period. And it is not surprising that he felt that he needed to quell the doubts of many 'that such assaults of Sathan are most certainly practized, & that the instruments thereof, merits most severely to be punished.'[2] For James, one of the chief instigators of scepticism about witchcraft was Reginald Scot, 'an Englishman,' wrote James, who 'is not ashamed in publike print to deny, that ther can be such a thing as Witch-craft: and so mainteines the old error of the Sadducees, in denying of spirits.'[3]

Reginald Scot had published his work on witchcraft some thirteen years before, in 1584. As the title of Scot's work makes clear, with the exception of natural magic, Scot was critical not only of the possibilities of witchcraft but also of the whole panoply of matters occult, divinatory, and esoteric:

> *The discoverie of witchcraft, wherein the lewde dealing of witches and witchmongers is notablie detected, the*

> *knaverie of conjurors, the impietie of inchantors, the follie of soothsaiers, the impudent falsehood of cousenors, the infidelitie of atheists, the pestilent practices of Pythonists, the curiositie of figurecasters, the vanitie of dreames, the beggerlie art of Alcumystrie, The abhomination of idolatrie, the horrible art of poisoning, the vertue and power of naturall magike, and all the conveiances of Legierdemaine and juggling are deciphered: and many other things opened, which have long lien hidden, howbeit verie necessarie to be knowne. Heereunto is added a treatise upon the nature and substance of spirits and divels, &c.*

The work as a whole was comprised of some four hundred and eighty-eight pages in sixteen Books and two hundred and forty-nine chapters. This was supplemented by 'A Discourse Upon Divels and Spirits' of some seventy-one pages in thirty-four chapters.[4] It was England's first major work on demonology and witchcraft and it was unashamedly and unapologetically sceptical. But paradoxically, the comprehensive account of magic, witchcraft, and legerdemain contained in *The Discoverie of Witchcraft* fostered European demonologies in England, helped the spread of indigenous witchcraft traditions, and inaugurated the English tradition of secular magic and conjuring.

There is a tradition that King James VI of Scotland, on his accession to the English throne in 1603, the same year in which his *Daemonologie* was published in England, ordered all copies of *The Discoverie of Witchcraft* to be burnt. Although James was prone to burning books as demonstrations of his theological and political agenda, the evidence for his burning Scot's work is not strong. And it is highly unlikely that he did so.[5] Still, the development of the tradition is evidence of the influence of Scot and the awareness from an early period of the radical nature of the position adopted by him, both by those who were opposed, and by those who were sympathetic to it. As Thomas Ady noted in 1656 in his *A Candle in the Dark*, this book 'did for a time make great impression in the Magistracy, and also in the Clergy,' though,

'The Discoverie of Witchcraft'

he went on to say, since that time England had shamefully fallen from the truth contained within it.[6] And John Webster in his *The Displaying of Supposed Witchcraft* some twenty years later named Scot and the German physician Johann Weyer as the two persons who so 'strongly opposed and confuted the many wonderful and incredible actions and power ascribed unto Witches' that loads of 'unworthy and unchristian scandals' were cast upon them.[7]

Thomas Ady and John Webster were the first two English writers openly to defend Scot. But he clearly had supporters, albeit more reticent ones, in later Elizabethan and early Stuart England. Thus, for example, in 1593 the poet Gabriel Harvey in his *Pierce's Supererogation* declared, 'Scotte's discovery of Witchcraft dismasketh sundry egregious impostures, and in certaine principall chapters, & speciall passages, hitteth the nayle on the head with a witnesse...'[8] In the same year, Thomas Nashe indirectly defended it in his *Foure Letters Confuted*.[9] In 1601, as sceptical of the claims of those possessed by devils as of those who exorcised them, the Anglican clergymen John Deacon and John Walker endorsed Scot's opinion that the witch of Endor, far from conjuring the spirit of Samuel to appear before Saul, was nothing but a trickster.[10] Samuel Harsnett, as doubtful of the authenticity of demoniacs and as sceptical of those who reputed to cure them as his Anglican colleagues Deacon and Walker, borrowed material (though without citing Scot) from *The Discoverie of Witchcraft*.[11] William Shakespeare drew on Scot for his depiction of the witches in *Macbeth*, as did the playwright Thomas Middleton in his portrayal of 'The Witch' in the tragi-comedy of the same name.

Still, his critics were much louder than his supporters. There were more of them, and they included the major English demonologists. Thus for example, in 1587 in England's second work on witchcraft, *A Discourse of the Subtill Practises of Devilles by Witches and Sorcerers*, George Gifford clearly had Scot in mind when he declared his intention to provide 'an Aunswer unto divers frivolous Reasons which some doe make to prove that the Devils did not make those Aperations in any bodily shape.'[12] William Perkins objected to Scot's suggestion that, if witches worked wonders, it was through divine rather than demonic power.[13] John Cotta in his *The Triall of Witch-craft* in 1616, accused him of confusing witches and tricksters.[14] *The Discoverie of Witchcraft* was as important a point of reference for confutation for Richard Bernard in his *A Guide to Grand-Jury Men* in 1627,[15] as it was for support for Francis Hutchinson in his sceptical *An Historical Essay Concerning Witchcraft*.[16] And there can be little doubt that the ever credulous Joseph Glanvill had Scot in mind in his adoption of the neo-Platonic account of the 'vehicles of the soul' to argue that demons had bodies of air in order to counter Scot's rejection of the possibility of demonic bodies.[17]

As a consequence of its comprehensiveness, *The Discoverie of Witchcraft* was also an invaluable source of information on magic, demonology, witchcraft, spirits, divination of many kinds, and legerdemain. In the course of its production Scot had mined a vast array of contemporary and ancient sources. At the beginning of the work, he listed two hundred and twelve Latin, and twenty-three English authors whose views he quoted, analysed, and criticised.[18] His writing probably began in 1580 after the publication of Jean Bodin's *De la Démonomanie des Sorciers* (On the Demonomania of Sorcerers) in that year. And he continued to read fresh works right up until shortly before he completed the work. Thus, for example, Scot writes of the treatise of Leonardus Vairus on fascination as 'now this present yeare 1583. newlie published.'[19]

He undoubtedly had some help, notably from Abraham Fleming. It is now recognised that Abraham Fleming was the editor of the 1587 posthumous edition of Holinshed's *Chronicles*. He was a publishing entrepreneur, and for the decade before the publication of the *Chronicles* he had been involved with at least fifteen publishing houses in a variety of roles – poet, translator, editor, compiler, indexer, and corrector.[20] It was to Holinshed's *Chronicles* that Scot was to contribute one of the three extant pieces of writing by him about which we know.[21] This was a long account of the rebuilding of Dover Harbour, one of the great feats of Elizabethan engineering. Reginald Scot had been involved in this project, along with his cousin Sir Thomas Scot to whom he addressed one of four prefatory epistles at the beginning of *The Discoverie*, and the mathematician Thomas Digges.[22] It was probably Abraham Fleming who was the recipient of a now missing letter by Scot about his cousin Sir Thomas Scot. This was cited by Francis Peck in his *Desiderata Curiosa* (Curious Desiderata) in 1732 as 'An Epitaph upon the Death of the famous & renowned Knight Sir *Thomas Scot*... with divers Historical Notes. The whole written by Mr. *Reynold* [sic] *Scot* (Authour of *the Discovery of Witchcraft*) & sent, as thought, to be inserted in the late new Edition of *Holingshed*; but not permitted. A curious Thing.'[23]

In *The Discoverie of Witchcraft*, Fleming is regularly credited with the translation from Latin of much poetry from the Classical poets – Virgil, Ovid, Lucretius, for example and others – into English. Thus, we find some twenty-eight times 'Englished by Abraham Fleming' or a variation of this in the margins of the text. And the importance of Fleming's contribution is reinforced by the playful presence in the list of foreign and English authors of the exotic-sounding anagram 'Gnimelf Maharba.' Certainly, both Fleming and Scot shared an anti-Catholic fervour. As we will explore more closely later, they may have also shared other decidedly more unorthodox theological views.

The publication history of *The Discoverie of Witchcraft* can be quickly noted. The responsibility for the publication of the work was taken by Scot himself. No record of it appears in the formal index of printed works of the period, the Registers of the Company of Stationers. We can reasonably assume that Scot expected only trouble from any attempt to do so. The name of the printer William Brome, usually on the title page of any work, occurs at the end of the book with no date and no address other than London (though we know from a comment within *The Discoverie of Witchcraft* that his shop was in St. Paul's churchyard.) An abbreviated Dutch translation, O*ndecking van Tovery*, was made in 1609 by Thomas Basson, an English printer living in Leiden at the time. A revised version was published by his son G. Basson in 1637, also in Leiden.

Another edition of *The Discoverie of Witchcraft*, published in 1651, had a different title page from the original edition of 1584, one that was more likely to attract the eyes of the book buying public. For, in comparison to Scot's original title which suggested that there were such things as witches who dealt 'lewdly', this title suggested that there were no witches, and that old, sad, and ignorant people were the innocent victims of the machinations of the witch-hunters. And it is directed at readers far more sceptical of the legitimacy of the judicial processes involved in witchcraft prosecutions than those of Scot's time.

> *Scot's Discovery of Witchcraft: Proving The common opinions of Witches contracting with Divels, Spirits, or Familiars; and their power to kill, torment, and consume the bodies of men women, and children, or other creatures by diseases or otherwise; their flying in the Air &c. To be but imaginary Erronious conceptions and novelties; Wherein Also, the lewde unchristian practices of Witchmongers, upon aged, melancholy, ignorant, and superstitious people in extorting confessions, by inhumane terrors and tortures is notably detected.... With many other things opened that have long lain hidden: though very necessary to be known for the undeceiving of Judges, Justices, and Juries, and for the preservation of poor, aged, deformed, ignorant people; frequently taken, arraigned, condemned and executed for Witches, when according to a right understanding, and a good conscience, Physick, Food, and necessaries should be administred to them.*

It was a marketing ploy that worked, for there was a second printing of this edition in the same year, and a further one in 1654.[24]

A third edition of *The Discoverie of Witchcraft* appeared in 1665. It appeared with a different title page from both the first

'The Discoverie of Witchcraft'

and second editions though it promoted the same message as the previous edition. There were, however, two significant additions to the text of this edition, by an unknown author,[25] which were announced on the title page. Although there is ambiguity on the page, the careful reader would have concluded, correctly, that these additions were not from the hand of Scot. The first was an additional 'excellent Discourse of the *Nature* and *Substance* of Devils and Spirits',[26] the second an additional nine chapters inserted at the beginning of Book fifteen.[27] As we will see in more detail later, both of these countered the overall message of the work. For they focused on the description of and the conjuring and invoking of ghosts, demons, and spirits, and they assumed the truth of that which Scot had wished to demonstrate as trickery. In short, in form and content, they belong to the genre of the *grimoire*, and were no doubt used as such by later generations of Scot's readers.

Indeed, we can gain some insight into the use of Scot's book for divinatory or conjuring purposes from an account by the Essex Justice Sir William Holcroft of the prosecution in 1687 of Ann Watts, a fortune teller from London who had been sleeping rough in the woods of one of Holcroft's neighbours. In her possession were a number of books, no doubt the tools of her trade, among which there were said to be two works by the magician Cornelius Agrippa. One of these was probably the 1650 English translation by James Freake in 1531–3 of Agrippa's *De occulta philosophia libri tres* (Three Books of Occult Philosophy).[28] The other was most likely the 1655 English translation by Robert Turner of the *Fourth Book of Occult Philosophy*, spuriously attributed to Agrippa and first published in Latin in 1567.[29] This work also contained selections from other magical texts, notably the *Heptameron or Magical Elements* (1496) spuriously attributed to Peter de Abano, and the anonymous *Arbatel of Magick* (1575). Ann Watts also possessed a copy of one of John Gadbury's almanacs, and most importantly a copy of Scot's *The Discoverie of Witchcraft*, probably the 1665 edition, which she no doubt used for spells, tricks, and conjurations. Holcroft ordered all of these works burnt. It is ironic that Scot's book, reputedly burnt by King James I for its sceptical approach, was eventually burnt for its utility as a source book for magic.[30]

While the encyclopedic and comprehensive nature of the first edition could lead a later editor to add to its attraction as a source book for aspiring practitioners of 'spiritual magic', *The Discoverie of Witchcraft* also provided an impetus for the growth of 'secular magic.' As Simon During remarks, 'because Scot distinguishes sleight of hand so carefully from magic, his book clears a space within which conjuring tricks (in the modern sense) may be dissociated from the popular magic nostrums and natural magic effects to which they are allied in contemporary trickbooks.'[31] Chapters twenty-two to thirty-four of Book thirteen in *The Discoverie of Witchcraft* were devoted to the explication of conjuring tricks, from very simple tricks with balls, money, laces, knives, or cards, to the very complex such as 'the decollation of John Baptist.' This last was an illusion performed by a Kingsfield of London in which the head of an apparently decapitated boy came to life on a platter. Scot may well have seen this performed at Bartholomew Fair in 1582.[32] He was probably also reliant for his information on conjuring from a Frenchman, resident in London, named John Cautares, whom he recommended to his readers. According to Scot, he was 'in conversation an honest man.' He was not a full time professional magician but laboured 'with the sweat of his browes,' and had 'the best hand and conveyance... of anie man that liveth this daie.'[33]

Certainly, this section of *The Discoverie of Witchcraft* added to its marketability. William Brome, the printer of *The Discoverie of Witchcraft* must have thought so. He was in the retail conjuring business. From his shop in St. Paul's churchyard, Scot informs us, he sold such items as a book in which apparently blank pages were transformed into pages 'painted with birds, then with beasts, then with serpents, then with angels, &c.'[34] Brome's marketing *nous* was justified. For a version of Book thirteen from chapter twenty-two onwards, with some deletions and additions, was published in 1612 under the title *The Art of Jugling or Legerdemaine* by Samuel Rand and reprinted in 1614. This work segued into *Hocus Pocus Junior. The Anatomy of Legerdemain.* First published in 1634, it was re-published another seven times in the course of the seventeenth century.[35]

Noblesse Oblige

Whatever the purposes for which later publishers and readers may have used *The Discoverie of Witchcraft*, Scot's motivation for his work was clear. In the prefatory letter to Sir Roger Manwood, Scot described his work as 'in the behalfe of the poore, the aged and the simple.' It was a sentiment he expressed in his first work in 1574, *A Perfite Platforme of a Hoppe Garden, and Necessarie Instructions for the Making and Mayntenaunce thereof.*[36] This work, declared Scot, was intended for 'Countrie people', those 'placed in the frontiers of povertie.'[37] And it was a theme that he reiterated in his contribution to Holinshed's *Chronicles,* not least in his careful account of the wages and conditions under which the labourers worked on Dover Harbour, and in his sympathy for the rituals created by the labourers themselves.[38] It was the poor and powerless, and poor older women in particular, he wrote, who were the most open to accusations of witchcraft, and the least able to defend themselves:

> [T]hey, which are commonlie accused of witchcraft, are the least sufficient of all other persons to speake for themselves; as having the most base and simple education of all others; the extremitie of their age giving them leave to dote, their povertie to beg, their wrongs to chide and threaten (as being void of any other waie of revenge), their humour melancholicall to be full of imaginations, from whence cheeflie proceedeth the vanitie of their confessions; as that they can transforme

themselves and others into apes, owles, asses, dogs, cats, &c: that they can flie in the aire, kill children with charmes, hinder the coming of butter, &c.[39]

Scot's *Discoverie of Witchcraft* was not only motivated by a concern for the most likely candidates for witchcraft accusation but also directed towards those whom he believed had a moral obligation to ensure that they were not unjustly persecuted. At the beginning of the book there are three prefaces addressed to four men. All of them were, like Scot, from the county of Kent. Added to these, there is one general preface 'to the readers'. The first of these prefaces was addressed to Sir Roger Manwood, chief baron of the Exchequer, the second to Scot's cousin Sir Thomas Scot. These prefaces were strategically intended, for each of the addressees had juridical responsibilities and they were two of the most powerful and well-connected men in Kent.[40] From them, Scot hoped for legal support. The third Preface was to 'his loving friends' John Coldwell, Dean of Rochester (later Bishop of Salisbury) and William Redman, Archdeacon of Canterbury (later Bishop of Norwich). From them Scot sought support for the divinity and philosophy 'whereupon the groundworke of my booke is laid.'[41]

Scot's admonition to Sir Roger Manwood was imbued with the idea of the godly magistrate who, like the deity, is both a just judge and a merciful father. Manwood was, according to Scot, someone who was 'by nature wholly inclined, and in purpose earnestly bent to releeve the poore, and that not only with hospitalitie and alms, but by diverse other devises and waies tending to their comfort... even as a verie father to the poore.'[42] And it was from the judiciary, and those set in authority more generally, that Scot sought a compassionate response. 'For (God knoweth),' he wrote, 'manie of these poor wretches had more need to be releeved than chastised; and more meete were a preacher to admonish them, than a gailor to keepe them; and a physician more necessarie to helpe them, than an executioner or tormentor to hang or burne them.'[43]

'The Discoverie of Witchcraft'

This sense of the kindness and compassion to which the noble are obliged is illustrated by Scot with an exemplary tale from Girolamo Cardano's *De Rerum Veritate* (On the Truth of Things, 1557), one which emphasised the steps which could be taken to manage the melancholic delusions of witches. According to this, one Barnard, a poor but diligent servant, much valued by his master, was persuaded that he was a witch and that he knew all things and could do anything. Although he was condemned to be burnt as a witch, he preferred to lose his life rather than renege on his conviction that he had supernatural powers. His master, believing that this was a conviction that arose from melancholy, obtained a stay of execution of twenty days. During this time,

> [H]is maister bountifullie fed him with good fat meat, and with foure egs at a meale, as also with sweet wine: which diet was best for so grosse and weake a bodie. And being recovered so in strength, that the humor was suppressed, he was easily woone from his absurd and dangerous opinions, and from all his fond imaginations; and confessing his error and follie, from the which before no man could remoove him by anie persuasion, having his pardon, he lived a good member of the church, whome otherwise the crueltie of judgement should have cast awaie and destroied.[44]

Though he no doubt viewed himself as one who owed obligations rather than one to whom obligations were owed, at the time of the writing of *The Discoverie of Witchcraft*, Reginald Scot himself was not a wealthy man. In 1584, he was clearly financially reliant on his cousin Sir Thomas Scot, 'being of your house, of your name, & of your bloud; my foot being under your table, my hand in your dish, or rather in your pursse.'[45] Much of the wealth he had accrued by the time of his death on 9 October 1599 was the consequence of that which his second wife had brought to the marriage. As he concluded in the will that he had written only some twenty-four days earlier, on 15 September 1599, 'greate is the trouble my poore wief hath had with me, and small is the comforte she hath receyved at my handes whome if I had not matched with all I had not dyed worth one groate.'[46]

Although we know the date of Scot's death, the year of his birth is uncertain. He was probably born in or before 1538 at Scott's Hall in the village of Smeeth, near Ashford in Kent.[47] He was the first son of Richard Scot, himself the son of Sir John Scot, and his wife Mary, the daughter of George Whettenal, sheriff of Kent. His father died before 1544, and his mother married Fulke Onslow, clerk of the Parliaments, dying before him on 8 October 1582.[48] According to Anthony Wood in his *Athenae Oxonienses*, he entered Hart's Hall in Oxford University around 1555 at about the age of seventeen, though he did not complete a degree.[49] On 11 October 1658, at Braybourne in Kent, he married Jane Cobbe, daughter of Thomas Cobbe of Aldington. It was at this time that, Anthony Wood informs us, 'he gave himself up solely to solid reading, to the perusing of obscure authors that had by the generality of scholars been neglected, and at times of leisure to husbandry and gardening.'[50] There is no doubt that Scot had access to a fine library. We have no evidence to this effect, but it is not unreasonable to assume that it was that of his cousin Sir Thomas Scot.

Reginald Scot and his wife Jane had one daughter, Elizabeth, probably born around 1574, who married Sackville Turnor of Tablehurst in Sussex. Elizabeth and Sackville had one daughter, Cisley. We do not know when Jane Scot died, but we can assume that, at the time of writing *The Discoverie of Witchcraft*, and financially dependent on Sir Thomas Scot, he had not married his second wife Alice, a widow with a daughter Marie by her former husband who brought land holdings in Aldington, Ruckinge, and Sellindge to the marriage.[51]

Contemporary records point to a number of positions occupied by Scot over the course of his life. He had been active as a

'The Discoverie of Witchcraft'

surveyor in the construction of the sea walls at Romney, a work that led to his engagement in the Dover Harbour project. From 1586-7, he was collector of subsidies for the district of Shepway in south-eastern Kent. In the 1580s, he was employed as a manager by his cousin Sir Thomas Scot. In 1588, he was one of thirteen captains of untrained foot soldiers and 'trench mayster' or engineer assembled at Dover in expectation of the Spanish Armada. He was Member of Parliament for New Romney in 1588-9.

Scot refers to himself on the title page of *The Discoverie of Witchcraft* as 'Esquire' (and was elsewhere designated 'armiger'). This might have meant that he was a Justice of the Peace, and that consequently his interest in issues of witchcraft and justice was more than that of an interested amateur. There is little doubt that Scot had personal experience of witchcraft trials. And we know that he visited local witches to investigate their recruiting tactics and their techniques and sent others to do the same:

> Hereof I have made triall, as also of the residue of their coosening devices; and have beene with the best, or rather the woorst of them, to see what might be gathered out of their counsels; and have cunninglie treated with them thereabouts: and further, have sent certeine old persons to indent with them, to be admitted into their societie.[52]

But there is no evidence within *The Discoverie of Witchcraft* or elsewhere that he ever had a judicial role. Moreover, the term 'esquire' carried such a variety of meanings in Elizabethan England that, in the absence of any other evidence, we should probably take his self-description as meaning 'a country gentleman' which, after all, is exactly what he was.

Motivations and Methods

What was it that motivated Scot to embark on his study of witchcraft, demonology, and magic, and eventually to write *The Discoverie of Witchcraft*? The direct motivation for his interest was no doubt the prosecution of witches both in Kent and elsewhere in England of which he was personally aware. We know that between 1565 and 1584, the year of the publication of *The Discoverie of Witchcraft*, there were fourteen prosecutions for witchcraft in Kent, ten of which were for bewitching persons to death, two just for bewitching people, and two for causing the deaths of animals by witchcraft. Of these fourteen accused, nine were found guilty, and five not guilty. Of the ten accused of causing deaths, four were found not guilty, three were found guilty and placed on remand, and three were executed by hanging. All of those charged were female.[53]

These prosecutions were the consequence of an apparent moral panic about witches and witchcraft which led to the Elizabethan statute on witchcraft in 1563, in the fifth year of the reign of Queen Elizabeth. This statute, in its turn, both legitimated and increased the panic. The legislation against witchcraft enacted in 1542 during the reign of Henry VIII had lain dormant since its repeal in 1547 in the first year of the reign of Edward VI. But with the accession of the Protestant Elizabeth to the throne in late 1558, those Protestants who had fled abroad returned. And it is not unfeasible to suggest that they brought with them a concern for what they would have seen as the two main threats to the creation of a godly Protestant commonwealth, Catholicism and witchcraft. And as we will see later, for Reginald Scot, the defects of both were the same.

John Jewel was one of these Marian exiles who returned from the Continent early in Elizabeth's reign, and was appointed Bishop of Salisbury in mid-1559. Later that year he visited the West Country and was struck, not only by the continuation of Catholic practices, but by the proliferation of witchcraft. While he found the people well disposed towards religion, 'It is however hardly credible,' he wrote to Peter Martyr on 2 November 1559 on his return to London, 'what a harvest, or rather what a wilderness of superstition, had sprung up in the darkness of the Marian times.

'The Discoverie of Witchcraft'

We found in all places votive relics of saints, nails with which the infatuated people dreamed that Christ had been pierced, and I know not what small fragments of the sacred cross. The number of witches and sorceresses had every where become enormous.'[54] It was a theme he developed in a sermon before the Queen during the winter of 1559-60:[55]

> [I]t may please your grace to understand, that this kind of people (I mean witches and sorcerers) within these last few years are marvelously increased within this your grace's realm. These eyes have seen most evident and manifest marks of their wickedness. Your grace's subjects pine away even unto the death, their colour fadeth, their flesh rotteth, their speech is benumbed, their senses are bereft. Wherefore your poor subjects' most humble petition unto your highness is, that the laws touching such malefactors may be put in due execution. For the shoal of them is great, their doings horrible, their malice intolerable, the examples most miserable... these be the scholars of Beelzebub, the chief captain of the devils.[56]

To suggest that Jewel and other returning exiles were responsible for introducing Continental notions of witchcraft, and particularly the notion of the compact between Satan and the witch, goes far beyond the evidence. Jewel's sermon is focused on maleficium – harm inflicted by occult means – rather than any diabolical deals, as is the Elizabethan witchcraft statute of 1563. The new law re-established witchcraft as a crime rather than establishing it as a heresy. And ironically, as I will later argue, it is Scot who is primarily responsible for introducing Continental notions into England.

But it is not unfeasible to suggest that Elizabethan Protestantism did define itself, in general terms, in opposition to both Catholicism and witchcraft. Between them, for English Protestants, no great gulf was fixed. For witches and sorcerers used forms of magic that made use of sacred objects and texts – as did priests. It was a hammer against Catholics that Scot was to use continually in *The Discoverie of Witchcraft*. This perceived link between sorcery and Catholicism was confirmed when a group of Essex Catholics attempted to use sorcery against the Queen in 1561. And it was this event which no doubt motivated the enactment of the statute against witchcraft in 1563 in order to make possible the prosecution of such acts against the stability of the State.[57] As the preamble to the Act declared, since the repeal of the Henrician legislation in 1547,

> [M]any fantastical and devilish persons have devised and practiced invocations, and conjurations of evil and wicked spirits, and have used and practiced witchcrafts, enchantments, charms and sorceries, to the destruction of the persons and goods of their neighbours and other subjects of this realm, and for other lewd intents and purposes contrary to the laws of Almighty God, to the peril of their own souls, and the great infamy and disquiet of this realm.[58]

Under this 'Act against Conjurations, Inchantments and Witchcrafts', the penalty for damage caused to persons or their property by witchcraft was one year's imprisonment and being pilloried for six hours once in every quarter of that year for the first offence. For any subsequent infraction, an offender faced the death sentence. The penalty for murder by witchcraft was death.

Reginald Scot was familiar with a number of the trials that occurred as a result of the prosecutions that began with the enacting of this statute, and especially of those that occurred in his county of Kent. He knew, for example, of the arraignment of Mildred Norrington, a Kentish woman, in 1574, and her conviction for fraudulently pretending to be possessed by the Devil.[59] As we will see in more detail later, he knew the stories of Elizabeth Barton the Maid of Kent, of the Dutchman at Maidstone in Kent, of the trial of Margaret Simons from Brenchley in Kent, and of the restoration to health of Ade Davie, another Kentish woman. He was also familiar with several pamphlets that dealt with the

'The Discoverie of Witchcraft'

prosecution and execution of four witches at Windsor in 1579.[60] But he was clearly most moved by the prosecution and execution of witches at St. Osyth in Essex in early 1582. An account of this was published in the same year under the title, *A True and Just Recorde, of the Information, Examination and Confession of all the Witches, taken at S.Oses in the Countie of Essex: Whereof some were Executed, and other some Entreated according to the Determination of Lawe.*

For Scot, the St. Osyth's trial represented the tyrannical cruelty of the witch-hunters in England. And Scot was in little doubt that the accused were both set up and 'verballed' by Brian Darcy (or Darcey), the presiding magistrate, victims of his lurid imaginings:

> Now, how *Brian Darcies* he spirits and shee spirits, Tittie and Tiffin, Suckin and Pidgin, Liard and Robin, &c: his white spirits and black spirits, graie spirits and red spirits, divell tode and divell lambe, divels cat and divels dam, agree herewithall, or can stand consonant with the Word of GOD, or true philosophie, let heaven and earth judge. In the meane time, let anie man with good consideration peruse that booke published by W.W. and it shall suffice to satisfie him in all that may be required touching the vanities of the witches examinations, confessions and executions.[61]

In *his* pursuit of witches, Darcy was motivated by Continental accounts of witchcraft, not merely as matters of *Maleficium* but of heresy, blasphemy, and idolatry: 'al the conference, al the experimentes, finally the attemptes, proceedinges and conclusion of Sorcerers, Witches, and the rest of that hellish liverie, are meere blasphemers against the person of the most high God; and draw so neere to the nature of idolatrie (for they worship Sathan, unto whom they have allegiaunce) that they are by no meanes to be exempted from the suspition of that most accursed defection, nay rather they are guiltie of apparaunte apostasy...'[62]

The vehemence of his pursuit of witches was the consequence, or so he saw it, of a commission of the Queen for the apprehending of as many witches as there were to be found in England. And this commission was itself the result of a visitor to the Queen from November 1581 to February 1582 who was in the company of the Duc d'Alençon. 'There is a man of great cunning and knoweledge,' declared Darcy to one of the suspects, Elizabeth Bennet, on 22 February, 'come over lately unto our Queenes Majestie, which hath advertised her what a companie and number of witches be in Englande: whereupon I and other of her Justices have received Commission for the apprehending of as many as are within these limits.' This was none other than the French jurist and demonologist, Jean Bodin, author in 1580 of *De la Démonomanie des Sorciers*.[63] We know that he addressed Queen Elizabeth on the issue of toleration. Whether he did so on the issue of witchcraft is another question. Brian Darcy for one believed that he had. Now he was a devotee of the *Démonomanie*. He had read it, believed it, and absorbed its message. And his account of the witches at St. Osyth is imbued with its spirit.[64]

We do not know whether Reginald Scot had come across the *Démonomanie* of Jean Bodin before he read of it in Darcy's telling of the witches at St. Osyth. More than likely, it had previously crossed his path in the several years between its publication and Darcy's account. But what is certain is that the *Démonomanie* was one of the main works that motivated Scot to put pen to paper. With around fifty marginal references to it throughout *The Discoverie of Witchcraft*, it functioned for him as one of his two main sources for demonological theory.

Notes in the margins of *The Discoverie of Witchcraft* to Bodin's *Démonomanie* are only exceeded by those to that most famous of all early modern demonologies, the *Malleus Maleficarum* (The Hammer of Witches) of the Dominican inquisitors, Heinrich Kramer (Institoris) and Jacob Sprenger.[65] It was the first printed handbook of witchcraft and witch-hunting. By 1584, when Scot's

'The Discoverie of Witchcraft'

The Discoverie of Witchcraft was published, it had been through twelve Latin editions in Germany and France between the year of its first publication 1486 and 1523, was reprinted twice in Venice in 1574 and 1576, with three further editions in 1580 and 1582 in Protestant Frankfurt, and another in Lyons in 1584.[66] Scot was no doubt crucial in increasing the reading public in England for both the *Démonomanie* and the *Malleus Maleficarum*.

The third key source for Scot was the *De Praestigiis Daemonum* (On the Tricks of Devils), first published in 1563.[67] It was one of the two works, the other being Scot's *The Discoverie of Witchcraft*, which motivated King James VI to write his *Daemonologie*. It was a work which Sigmund Freud saw as one of the ten most significant works of all time, not least because according to Freud witchcraft was reduced by Weyer to a psychopathology. According to Weyer, witches were either the victims of superstitious priests or ignorant doctors, or they were the dupes of the Devil. Melancholic, silly, and senile, witches either deluded themselves or were deluded by the Devil. Weyer moved the blame from witches themselves to others. Scot, as we will see, accepted Weyer's belief that witches were deluded. But he did not agree that they were so, or could ever be so, as the result of the activities of demons. In the end, he was far more radical than Weyer.[68]

Scot's *The Discoverie of Witchcraft* is littered with extracts from Weyer.[69] But Weyer's main contribution to the work of Scot lay neither in Weyer's theory of witchcraft, nor in the passages in Weyer upon which Scot drew, but in the role it played in the structure of Scot's book.

Weyer began the second book of his *De Praestigiis Daemonum* with a discussion of Old Testament names for magicians of ill repute and poisoners. He had noticed that, in any discussion about the activities of witches, 'men soon offer the testimony of scriptural passages containing the term "magician," or "evil-doer," or "enchanter", or "poisoner," or even "juggler"... They then affirm that these terms denote, without distinction of meaning, the women who are commonly called "witches" or "wise women."'[70] He had noticed too that the Greek and Latin versions of the Old Testament differed on the meaning of the Hebrew terms as they occurred in the original Hebrew version of the Old Testament. So he consulted Belgian Hebrew scholar, Andreas Masius, who illuminated for him the meaning of seven Hebrew words relating to magic which he had identified in the Old Testament: *Chasaph* (female – *Mecassepha*), *Kasam*, *Onen*, *Nahas*, *Habar*, *Ob*, and *Iidoni*, as well as the generic term *Hartummin* which he identified with the 'enchanters' of Pharaoh.

For Weyer, the women 'who are commonly called "witches" or "wise women"'[71] were able to be classified under these terms. But for Scot, those identified as witches by the criteria of the *Démonomanie* and the *Malleus Maleficarum* were in a category outside of these terms. That is to say, for Scot, the witches of the demonologists did not make any appearance in the Bible. Moses, declared Scot, defined only four kinds of impious couseners or witches, of which 'our witchmongers old women which danse with the fairies, &c; are none.'[72]

Nevertheless, Scot's four kinds of Mosaic witches did include eight of the nine categories of magician listed by Weyer:

> The first were *Praestigiatores Pharaonis* [Weyer's *Hartummin*], which (as all divines, both Hebrues and others conclude) were but cousenors and jugglers, deceiving the kings eies with illusions and sleights; and making false things to appear as true: which nevertheles our witches cannot doo. The second is *Mecasapha*, which is she that destroieth with poison. The third are such as use sundrie kinds of divinations, and hereunto perteine these words, *Kasam*, *Onen*, *Ob*, *Idoni*. The fourth is *Habar*, to wit: when magicians, or rather such, as would be reputed cunning therein, mumble certeine secret words, wherin is thought to be great efficacie.[73]

'*The Discoverie of Witchcraft*'

On the face of it, Scot had not followed Weyer as closely as one might have expected for he omitted from his above list Weyer's category of *Nahas* (the art of augury). However, Scot did devote Book eleven of *The Discoverie of Witchcraft* to a discussion of *Nahas* subsequent to his discussion of *Onen* (the interpretation of dreams) in Book ten. His omission of the term *Nahas* in the passage above can therefore only be put down as a 'clerical error', something which was not uncommon in Scot's work.[74]

Be all that as it may, Scot's strategic intention in this adaptation of Weyer is clear. And importantly, it was a notably Protestant one. First, it was to separate the activities of those who may be termed 'witches' in the Bible from the activities attributed to them by the demonologists and the witch-hunters. And second, therefore, it was to deny any Biblical legitimacy to their construction of witchcraft as a Christian heresy. Thus, by his use of Weyer, Scot wanted to demonstrate that there was no relation between the demonological understanding of witchcraft and the variety of Biblical understandings of the occult world, all of which were indiscriminately labelled witchcraft by the demonologists. And, despite the mass of detail collected by Scot, this intention is clearly discernible in the structure and shape of *The Discoverie of Witchcraft*.

The Bible, the Book, and the Books

In the first five books of *The Discoverie of Witchcraft*, Scot set out to analyse and criticise the demonologists' construction of witchcraft and to provide alternative explanations for the phenomena associated with it. Consequently, the first book set out his social theory for the origins of witchcraft and witchcraft accusations. In the second book, he provided an account of the judicial procedures by means of which the convictions of those accused of impossible crimes were achieved. The next three books were devoted to an attack on the core components of Continental demonology – the Satanic compact between the witch and the Devil, the witches'

Sabbath and their transportation to it, sex with the Devil, and transformations of witches into the forms of animals and especially into wolves.

The next ten books are based upon the nine Biblical categories noted above: *Chasaph* (poisoning) in Book six; *Ob* (ventriloquism) in Book seven; *Kasam* (divination) in Book nine; *Onen* (divination by dreams) in Book ten; *Nahas* (augury) in Book eleven; *Habar* (inchantments) in Book twelve; *Hartummin* (magicians) in Book thirteen; and *Iidoni* (demonic and angelic magicians) in Book fifteen, with an interlude in Book eight to discuss the cessation of miracles, and a summary of his arguments in Book sixteen.

This structure was strategic rather than serendipitous. And it accomplished three things. In the first place, it enabled Scot to demonstrate that the demonologists misinterpreted the Biblical evidence. Witches such as the demonologists had constructed had no existence in the world of the Bible, just as they did not exist as constructed by them in Scot's world. As he concluded at the end of Book five,

> Sometimes they are called witches in common speech, that are old, lame, curst, or melancholicke as a nickname. But as for our old women, that are said to hurt children with their eies, or lambs with their lookes, or that pull downe the moone out of heaven, or make so foolish a bargaine, or doo such homage to the divell; you shall not read in the bible of any such witches, or of any such actions imputed to them.[75]

Second, it allowed Scot, for the benefit of his Protestant readers, to gather under these various Biblical terms the whole array of past and contemporary occult activities from the Biblical, Classical, and his own worlds. And third, as a consequence, it made it possible for him to demonstrate that all of these had no supernatural basis, were fraudulent, and were capable of explanation without recourse to the realm of spirits, whether angelic or demonic. It led

'The Discoverie of Witchcraft'

him in Book sixteen to be able to present a final definition of witchcraft: 'Witchcraft is in truth a cousening art, wherin the name of God is abused, prophaned and blasphemed, and his power attributed to a vile creature.'[76] It was a definition which enabled him to conclude:

> All wisemen understand that witches miraculous enterprises, being contrarie to nature, probabilitie and reason, are void of truth or possibilitie. All protestants perceive, that popish charmes, conjurations, execrations, and benedictions are not effectuall, but be toies and devises onelie to keepe the people blind, and to inrich the cleargie. All christians see, that to confesse witches can doo as they saie, were to attribute to a creature the power of the Creator. All children well brought up conceive and spie, or at the least are taught, that juglers miracles doo consist of legierdemaine and confederacie. The verie heathen people are driven to confesse, that there can be no such conference betweene a spirituall divell and a corporall witch, as is supposed.[77]

In sum, the first sixteen Books of *The Discoverie of Witchcraft* were strategically intended to demonstrate that there are no good reasons to believe in supernatural magic, trafficking with the Devil, and the daily intervention of God, angels, and demons in human affairs.

In 'A Discourse upon divels and spirits' which followed Book sixteen, Scot set out to show why there could not – logically could not – be such interaction between the material and spiritual realms. It was an argument that went to the impossibility of the embodiment of spirits of any kind. But the Discourse was more than this. For as I will argue in the final chapter of this work, Scot was not the naturalist sceptic that he has been perceived to be for the better part of the last four hundred years. Rather, Scot's *The Discoverie of Witchcraft* was derived from a critique of witchcraft that was based upon a theology of Spirit. It was a theology that entailed that he was one of the few truly spirit-filled men who could perceive the work of the Devil. And he found it in the activities of the witch-hunters and demonologists. Thus, as I hope to show, the title of this work, *England's First Demonologist*, is no mere metaphor.

CHAPTER TWO

Witchcraft

Apocalypse Soon

Reginald Scot lived in apocalyptic times. As John Dove eloquently put it towards the end of the sixteenth century, '[The world] is not onely in the staggering and declining age, but, which exceedeth dotage, at the very upshot, and like a sicke man which lyeth at deaths doore, ready to breathe out the laste ghaspe.'[1] The closer the end approached, the more it was believed Satan raged. For the Devil knew, it was firmly held, that his reign was coming to an end, and that in the eschatological kingdom brought in by the second coming of Christ, his ultimate and final defeat was inevitable. Thomas Cranmer, commenting on the petition in the Lord's Prayer 'Thy kingdom come' was doing no more than expressing the common belief of the times: 'the devyll in this latter tyme doeth dayly more and more rage against the true churche and people of God, forasmuche as he perceyvethe, that hys kyngdome draweth to an end, and a shorte tyme remayneth untyll the day of judgemente come, and his everlastynge damnation.'[2] And it was consequently no surprise to most that the Devil's servants, the witches, were in such abundance, for they were the agents on earth of his cosmic rage.

According to Scot, the world was now so overrun with the belief in witchcraft and its power that those in need fled from God to the Devil, and from the physician to the witch, in search of comfort, counsel, or cure. And witches were rife, or at least were believed to be. As Scot reported, 'I have heard (to my greefe) some of the ministerie affirme, that they have had in their parish at one instant, xvii. or xviii. witches: meaning such as could worke miracles supernaturallie.'[3] Scot, like his contemporaries, accepted that he was living in the end times. But it was not the increase in demonic activities that he saw as one of the signs of this. Rather it was *the credulous increase in belief in witchcraft and the activities of the Devil and his minions* that he saw as evidence of the imminent return of Christ. For Scot, it was not the heresy of witchcraft which was on the increase, but rather the heresy of false belief in it. And he paraphrased Scripture to make the point: 'And in the latter time some shall depart from the faith, and shall give heed to spirits of errors, and doctrines of divels, which speake lies (as witches and conjurers doo) but cast thou awaie such prophane and old wives tales.'[4]

A Witch in Brenchley

The credulity of the people, and especially of the clergy, was a common theme in Scot's writing. And the first story that he told in *The Discoverie of Witchcraft* of the supposed witchcraft of Margaret Simons, and our only account of this case, not only reinforced his critique of credulity, but gives us an insight into the robust relationships between clergy and villagers in the early modern village. In this case, the village was Brenchley in Kent, some eight miles east of Tunbridge Wells and about thirty miles west of Scot's home village of Smeeth. Scot was sufficiently interested in the case to have travelled to the area to interview the vicar of the parish John Ferrall, and a number of other villagers about the affair.

In 1581, Margaret Simons, the wife of John Simons, was arraigned for witchcraft at the Assizes in Rochester at the instigation of John Ferrall and a number of others. As far as Scot was concerned, Ferrall who was as ignorant of his faith as she whom he had accused, had brought this charge maliciously. Ferrall's son was apprenticed to Robert Scotchford, a clothier. While passing by Margaret's house one day, this 'ungratious boie' was barked at by Margaret's dog, leading him to draw a knife and chase the dog to her door. Margaret abused him, he responded in kind, and a long argument took place. Five or six days later, he fell ill, and the conflict between the boy and Margaret's dog was recalled. The vicar, sufficiently proud to think that God would not so punish his son directly, and sufficiently credulous to consult local witches, concluded that Margaret had bewitched his son. The boy was cured after Ferrall had gone to a witch, so he informed Scot, to seek a cure for him.

John Ferrall then upped the ante by claiming that Margaret had also bewitched him to the effect that he could no longer speak in the Church when he needed to do so. When Scot questioned Margaret Simons on this, she in turn went on the attack. She affirmed that, although his voice was naturally hoarse and low, it was true that his voice often failed him, especially when he tried to speak loudly. She had a different explanation for this: 'But sir, said she, you shall understand, that this our vicar is diseased with such a kind of hoarsenesse, as divers of our neighbours in this parish, not long since, doubted [feared] that he had the French pox; & in that respect utterly refused to communicate with him.'[5] So, far from meekly accepting the vicar's claims against Margaret, at least some of her friends had mounted a concerted attack against the vicar's moral standing in the parish, accusing him of having contracted syphilis. Margaret may well have galvanised her friends in her support. Taking decisive action in defence of themselves was not unheard of among those accused of witchcraft.[6]

Even within the highly flexible and fluid understanding of the relations between symptoms and diseases in early modern medicine, hoarseness was not then considered to be one of the more obvious signs of syphilis. However, it was probably this very fluidity and flexibility that motivated Ferrall medically to attempt to re-establish his moral reputation among his parishioners. On the advice of his clerical superior, he had procured from two physicians in London a certificate to the effect that his hoarseness proceeded from a disease in the lungs. He read the certificate to his whole congregation, though we do not know whether they were convinced by it. What we do know is that, having been arraigned on 3 July 1581 on charges of having bewitched Ferrall's fourteen-year-old son, and far more seriously (though Scot does not mention it) of the capital crime of bewitching to death Agnes Champe of Brenchley,[7] the jury found Margaret Simons innocent on both charges. Her acquittal was much to Scot's surprise. Not inappropriately, he remarked that 'the name of a witch is so odious, and hir power so feared among the common people, that if the honestest bodie living chance to be arraigned therupon, she shall hardlie escape condemnation.'[8]

Although Scot did not do so, we can read behind the story to a context of contested authority between the clergy and villagers. Scot strongly hinted at the personal animus against Margaret Simons that motivated the village vicar. And the vicar needed to invoke London physicians to restore his reputation among his parishioners. But Scot read the story predominantly as emblematic of a mentality created by belief in a world in which the everyday and the supernatural continually collided – a mentality that was inculcated in childhood:

> But in our childhood our mothers maids have so terrified us with an ouglie divell having hornes on his head, fier in his mouth, and a taile in his breech, eies like a bason, fanges like a dog, clawes like a beare, a skin like a Niger, and a voice roaring like a lion, whereby we start and are afraid when we heare one crie Bough [Boo]: and they have so fraied us with bull beggers, spirits, witches, urchens, elves, hags, fairies, satyrs, pans, faunes, sylens, kit with the cansticke, tritons, centaurs, dwarfes, giants, imps, calcars, conjurors, nymphes, changlings, *Incubus*, Robin good-fellowe, the spoorne, the mare, the man in the oke, the hell waine, the firedrake, the puckle,

Tom thombe, hob gobblin, Tom tumbler, boneles, and such other bugs, that we are afraid of our owne shadowes: in so much as some never feare the divell, but in a darke night...[9]

Evil and Providence

Scot did not deny the reality of witches. He was, after all, a Biblicist. The mention of the word 'witch' in the Scriptures was more than sufficient to convince him of their existence. But he did deny the attribution to witches of those powers which belong only to God. Thus to have ceded to them the powers of life and death was to go against the doctrine of divine providence – that God alone determined the length of our lives and the numbers of our days. And Scot did not deny the more difficult aspect of the doctrine of divine providence in acknowledging that God alone was responsible for all human sufferings. Nor would Scot cede to witches the power to do good, for this too went against the providential creation within the natural world of all those things necessary to remedy sickness or grief: 'Neither hath God given remedies to sicknes or greefes, by words or charmes, but by hearbes and medicines; which he himselfe hath created upon earth, and given men knowledge of the same; that he might be glorified, for that therewith he dooth vouchsafe that the maladies of men and cattell should be cured., &c.'[10]

Scot's scepticism about witchcraft was then, at least in part, grounded in the doctrine of divine providence, and in the conviction that the belief in witchcraft was a failure of genuine faith. The opening words of *The Discoverie of Witchcraft* attest to the centrality of the doctrine of providence in Scot's own critique of witchcraft: 'The fables of Witchcraft have taken so fast hold and deepe root in the heart of man, that fewe or none can (nowadaies) with patience indure the hand and correction of God. For if any adversitie, greefe, sickness, losse of children, corne, cattell, or libertie happen unto them; by & by they exclaime uppon witches. As though there were no God in Israel that ordereth all things according to his will; punishing both just and unjust with greefs, plagues, and afflictions in maner and forme as he thinketh good.'[11]

Scot's scepticism was, as we will see, far more pronounced than that of any of his contemporaries. But his view that to look to witchcraft rather than divine providence was a failure in piety was far from an original one among his Protestant contemporaries in England. It was a failure of belief in divine providence, declared Essex vicar Ralph Walker, that led to the 'vile and damnable practice of many, who for the curing of themselves, saving of their cattell, or finding of that which is lost, will presently forsake God, & have recourse unto the divell by his servants the witches.'[12] The Essex vicar George Gifford noted in his *A Dialogue concerning Witches and Witchcraftes* that the belief that misfortunes would disappear were there no witches was to fail to 'understand the high providence of almighty God which is over all.'[13] So Scot's doctrine of providence was a mainstream Protestant one.

Still, while Scot shared a firm belief in divine providence with his fellow believers, his view of what this meant for the powers of devils and witches was a unique one. His strategy was to suggest a binary opposition between the powers of God and the powers of witches. This was intended to ensure that the assertion of the former entailed the denial of the latter. In so doing, he was cutting through the complex negotiations within contemporary theology and demonology on power-sharing between God, the Devil, and witches. And he was not averse to pointing out the apparent incoherencies of the demonologists in variously ascribing *maleficia* to the witch and her charms, to a corporeal or spiritual demon, to the Devil's making the witch believe in the illusions created by him, and to uncertainty whether it was the Devil acting with God's permission, by his licence, or by his appointment, or God himself was the direct cause.[14]

In English Protestant theology, the Puritan Essex vicar George Gifford's account of these relationships was typical. Gifford's core idea was that, though nothing could occur without God's permission, God on occasion allowed Satan through the witch to bring misfortune on people to test their faith or to punish them for their sins. Satan and the witch were thus merely the means by which God's love and justice were administered: 'If thy sinnes have provoked God, and the enemie doth touch thy body or thy goods, fall downe and humble thyselfe with fasting and prayer, intreate the Lord to turn away his displeasure: looke not upon the witch, lay not the cause where it is not, seeke not help at the hands of devils, be not a disciple of witches...'[15]

Gifford's account was theologically correct, though psychologically naïve. As Alan Macfarlane has noted, 'it was hardly likely to satisfy a man whose child was dying a lingering death; such a man would want to be shown a specific course of action against a specific evil agent.'[16] In contrast, Scot argued, the powers attributed to witches belonged to God, 'Who onelie is the Creator of all things, who onelie searcheth the heart and reines,...who onelie worketh great wonders, who onelie hath power to raise up and cast downe; who onelie maketh thunder, lightning, rain, tempests, and restraineth them at his pleasure; who onelie sendeth life and death, sicknesse & health, wealth and wo...'[17] Scot's assertion that power belonged to God alone, and was not shared with demons and witches, entailed that there was no ultimate difference between 'black' and 'white' witches. In both cases, they lacked the powers that had been attributed to them, powers which should have been limited to God.

Like Scot, most Protestant ministers saw no ultimate difference between 'black' and 'white' witches, although their reasons for so thinking were quite different to his. For William Perkins, perhaps the leading English Protestant theologian of the day, for example, witches were in league with the Devil regardless of the intent of their activities. Indeed, he saw cunning or wise folk, the 'unbinding' witches, as more abhorrent than the 'binding' ones. 'The *good witch*,' he declared, 'is he or shee that by consent in a league with the devil, doth use his helpe, for the doing of good onely. This cannot hurt, torment, curse, or kill, but onely heale and cure the hurts inflicted upon men or cattell, by bade Witches... Now howsoever both these be evil, yet of the two, the more horrible & detestable Monster is the good Witch: for look in what place soever there be any bad witches that hurt onely, there also the devil hath his good ones, who are better knowne then the bad, being commonly called *Wisemen*, or *Wisewomen*.'[18]

No doubt Perkins found the good witch more threatening because he or she was in direct competition with the clergy. As Leland Estes points out, for the Puritan clergy, in their competition for the favour of the populace, 'no weapon proved more serviceable than the charge that the opposition was in league with the Devil.'[19] They argued that those who sought help from the white witch put into jeopardy their salvation in the future life for a minor good in this one. As John Cotta put it, 'He who will be beholden unto the devil, for his life or health, then [than] choose to die in the gracious and merciful hand of the creator, can never expect to participate [in] any portion of salvation in him.'[20]

It was perhaps fortunate for the cunning folk that the English judicial system took no notice of the theological claim that they were as much in league with the Devil as their malevolent colleagues. It was the crime of *maleficium*, not the heresy of supposed Satanic leagues, that engaged the interest of the courts. Perkins started from the Devil and his human allies, the courts from the harms that witches were supposed to have done. As Estes suggests, most people probably found views like those of Perkins to be counter-intuitive if not nonsensical.

However that may be, the notion that white as well as black witches were in league with the Devil was embedded not only in Puritan theology but also in Catholic demonology. Thus, for example, the *Malleus Maleficarum* distinguished three kinds of witches, all of whom made various sacrilegious vows with the Devil: 'those who harm but are unable to heal, those who cure and do not harm as a result of a particular agreement entered into with a demon, and those who harm and heal.'[21] The claim of the *Malleus Maleficarum* that white witches were in league with the Devil was one that Scot found irrational. It is 'against the haire, and contrarie to the divels will, contrarie to the witches oth, promise, and homage, and contrarie to all reason,' he declared, 'that witches should helpe anie thing that is bewitched; but rather set forward their maisters businesse.'[22]

In *The Discoverie of Witchcraft*, Scot made the core distinction between four kinds of witches (though they were not mutually exclusive categories). The first of these was that constructed by the demonologists, both Catholic and Protestant. In the *Malleus Maleficarum*, Heinrich Kramer elaborated at length on the activities of the supreme kind of harmful witch.[23] It is a passage that Scot paraphrased as exemplary of the sorts of activities pointed to by the demonologists, among whom he named, not only the authors of the *Malleus Maleficarum* but also Johannes Nider,[24] the inquisitor Cumanus,[25] Lambertus Danaeus,[26] Andreas Hyperius,[27] Hemingius,[28] Jean Bodin, and Bartholomaeus Spineus.[29]

> And among the hurtfull witches...there is one sort more beastlie than any kind of beasts (saving woolves): for these usuallie devoure and eate yong children and infants of their owne kinde. These be they (saith he) that raise haile, tempests, and hurtfull weather; as lightning, thunder, &c. These be they that procure barrennesse in man, woman, and beast. These can throwe children into waters, as they walke with their mothers, and not be seene. These can make horses kicke, till they cast the riders. These can passe from place to place in the aire invisible. These can so alter the minds of judges, that they can have no power to hurt them. These can procure to themselves and to others, taciturnitie and insensibilitie in their torments. These can bring trembling to their hands, and strike terror into the minds of them that

apprehend them. These can manifest unto others, things hidden and lost, and foreshew things to come; and see them as though they were present. These can alter mens minds to inordinate love or hate. These can kill whom they list with lightening and thunder. These can take awaie mans courage, and the power of generation. These can make a woman miscarrie in childbirth, and destroie the child in the mothers wombe, without any sensible meanes either inwardly or outwardlie applied. These can with their looks kill either man or beast.[30]

To this list from the *Malleus Maleficarum*, Scot added a further list of such activities derived from Classical authors – Ovid, Virgil, Horace – and a range of other demonological sources.

This image of the activities of witches as derived from the demonologists and constructed by Scot was drawn almost entirely from Continental sources. In fact, there were only three English texts that have contributed to it.

The first of these was the pamphlet which is known by the title by which it was entered into the Stationer's Register on 4 May 1579: *A Brief Treatise Conteyning the Most Strange and Horrible Crueltye of Elizabeth Stile alias Bockingham & hir Confederates Executed at Abington upon Richard Galis*.[31] This work was written by Richard Galis, described elsewhere in *The Discoverie of Witchcraft* by Scot as 'a mad man' who had written a book, 'the reading wherof may satisfy a wise man, how mad all these witchmongers dealings be in this behalfe.'[32] Galis was himself the son of a victim of the witchcraft recorded in a text, also published in 1579, and known by Scot.[33] This was the second of the three English texts which contributed to his list of witches' activities. It was entitled *A Rehearsall Both Straung and True, of Hainous and Horrible Actes Committed by Elizabeth Stile, alias Rockingham, Mother Dutten, Mother Devell, Mother Margaret, Fower Notorious Witches, Apprehended at Windsor*. It was a text which recounted the story of the so-called Witches of Windsor. The third of the three English texts was the story of the witches of St. Osyth, contained in a work entitled *A True and Just Recorde, of the Information, Examination and Confession of all the Witches, taken at S.Oses in the Countie of Essex: Whereof some were Executed, and other some Entreated according to the Determination of Lawe.*

The Witches of Windsor

For Reginald Scot, men of great wisdom and authority were as likely to be the victims of cousening witchcraft as the common people. 'Were there not three images of late yeeres found in a doonghill, to the terror & astonishment of manie thousands?' he asked. Scot was in fact referring to the discovery, in London in August 1578, of wax images which the Privy Council of England believed 'verie likelie to be intended to the distruccion of her Majesties person.'[34] Prior to their discovery, on 20 August 1578, the Privy Council had written to the Lord Mayor, the Bishop of London, and other officials to encourage them to discover 'where any persons are to be found that be delighted or thought to be favourers of suche magical devices.'[35] Mendoza, the Spanish ambassador, gave further details in a dispatch to his government on 8 September. The three figures were buried in a stable, he reported: 'The centre figure had the word Elizabeth written on the forehead and the side figures were dressed like her councilors, and were covered over with a great variety of different signs, the left side of the images being transfixed with a large quantity of pig's bristles as if it were some kind of witchcraft.'[36] By 16 January of the following year, the Privy Council remained sufficiently concerned by possible threats to murder the queen by image magic to write to Sir Henry Nevell, the judge in the case, and the Dean of Windsor concerning the examination of witches taken at Windsor. The Council had heard that witches there had 'made away and brought to their deathes by certen pictures of waxe certen persons.'[37] They wished to know whether the witches of Windsor knew anything of the London images or who had made them.

The intervention of the Privy Council probably led to another examination of the witches at Windsor, or at least of Elizabeth Stile, on 28 January 1579. And the account of this examination and of her confession was given in the pamphlet *A Rehearsall Both Straung and True* mentioned above. In her confession, Elizabeth Stile admitted to having collaborated with five others – Father Rosimond and his daughter, Mother Dutten, Mother Devell, Mother Margaret – in the murder of four people by image magic. The victims were Lanckforde, a Windsor farmer, his maid, a butcher named Switcher, and Richard Galis, sometime Mayor of Windsor and the father of the author of *A Brief Treatise*, also called Richard.[38] *A Rehearsall Both Straung and True* gives us a particularly rich account of the method of murder by image magic:

> The maner of their Inchauntemente...was thus: Mother Dutten made fower pictures of Redde Wax, about a spanne long, and three or fower fingers broade for Lanckforde, for his Maide, for Maister Gallis, and for Swicher, and the saied Mother Dutten, by their counsaile and consente did sticke an Hauthorn pricke, against the left sides of the breastes of the Images, directly there where thei thought the hartes of the persones to bee sette, whom the same pictures did represente, and thereupon within shorte space, the saied fower persones, beeyng sodainely taken, died.[39]

She also confessed to the murders of a butcher by the name of Mastlyn and of a man called Saddocke, to the bewitching of a number of other people, and to the killing of a cow by witchcraft. She claimed that Mother Dutten kept a familiar spirit in the likeness of a toad which she fed with her blood, that Mother Devell fed her familiar, a black cat named Gille, and that Mother Margaret had a fiend in the form of a kitten named Ginnie. She admitted to keeping a familiar spirit in the form of a rat named Philip which she fed with blood from her right hand wrist. This keeping and nurturing of familiar spirits was a particular feature of English witchcraft. And it was the one unique English contribution to Scot's list of witches' activities. As he put it, 'Some say they can keepe divels and spirits in the likenesse of todes and cats.'[40]

Elizabeth Stile also claimed that Father Rosimond, alias Osborne, could transform himself into the shape and likeness of any beast he wished. It was a claim often made in Continental demonology about the powers of witches. 'Som saie,' declared Scot, 'they can transubstantiate themselves and others, and take the forms and shapes of asses, woolves, ferrets, cowes, apes, horsses, dogs, &c.'[41] But it was a claim rarely heard in England. Elizabeth Stile's declaration that Father Rosimond could transform himself into the form of an ape or a horse was no doubt treated sceptically by the examiners. As perhaps were her other claims about him, for he seems to have escaped from any charges that were laid. Elizabeth Stile and her colleagues – Mothers Dutten, Devell, and Margaret – were not so fortunate. They were executed on 26 February 1579.

Weaving in and out of the story told in *A Rehearsall Both Straung and True* is the other pamphlet mentioned above, that of Richard Galis in his *A Brief Treatise*. In Elizabethan witchcraft, it is a highly unusual work for it is written by a victim of witchcraft, indeed, a victim of witches from Windsor including several of those in the story told in *A Rehearsall Both Straung and True*. Scot treated the book with contempt, probably deservedly so, for even the careful modern reader, well aware of the world which Richard Galis inhabited, would question his mental well-being: 'with what impudencie he hath finished it,' declared Scot, 'with what lies and forgeries he hath furnished it, what follie and frensie he hath uttered in it; I am ashamed to report.'[42]

It provided Scot with another source for the activities of witches' familiars. For Galis was visited, or so he believed, in his bedroom at midnight by the apparition of a 'huge and mightie blacke Cat.'[43] It caused his hair to stand on end, and his heart to weaken. He became convinced that he had been bewitched by Mother Dutten.[44] Eventually he dragged her before the Magistrates, declaring that she 'for her devilish Sorceries and enchauntments cruelly practised upon divers honest men, deserveth not to live.'[45] Unimpressed, Richard Readforth the then Mayor of Windsor commanded Galis to let her go.

A friend of Galis, Richard Handley, believing himself to have lost the use of his own legs as a result of witchcraft, persuaded Galis to bring to him a witch, the sight of whom he was convinced would cure him. Galis brought four witches to him – Audrey the mistress, Elizabeth Stile, Mother Dutton, and Mother Devil,[46] all of whom declared that they neither knew the cause of his ailment, nor possessed the means to cure him. According to Galis, the four were (unreasonably) so threatened by him that they 'caused their Familiars without the which they could not doo any thing, to stirre up and against mee to incence the Maior and Burgesses of the towne of Windesor...who without any offence committed, any hurt pretended, or complaint made against mee, clapped mee up in Prison fast locked in a deep dungeon.'[47] All this suggests that he was part of a community that was unpersuaded that he was the innocent victim of witchcraft, and saw him as a trouble maker at best, seriously disturbed at worst. And it doesn't fit with his image of himself as a godly and pious hero, whose irons, like those of St Peter, were loosened by God in answer to his prayers, though as Scot wryly remarked, 'the prison doores opened not to *Richard*, as they did to Peter.'[48] Galis was released, but only on the condition that he left Windsor.

Six months later, and he was once again back in Windsor and, like the Biblical Prodigal Son, being welcomed by and reconciled to his Father. The prodigal's Father was soon after to die, unpersuaded that he was being bewitched to death, in spite of his son's convictions to the contrary. Soon, he was again making complaints to Sir Henry Nevell that he was once again the victim of witchcraft: 'mine old accustomed and raging fits began to set foote within my minde I to imagin that Sathans whelps were now setting a broch the vessel of their despite to seeke my utter spoyle and confusion.'[49] Perhaps to humour him, Nevell agreed to hear his complaints. Galis brought Audrey, Elizabeth Stile, Mother Dutton, and a Mother Nelson before him and a number of other notables.

The charges of witchcraft failed to stick though Galis was allowed to have the accused brought to the Church 'and publicly in the presence of all men to be set under the Pulpit during the time of Service.'[50] Here they were berated from the pulpit by the preacher in a ritual intended publicly to humiliate them in front of the whole community. Galis went on to report that, either stricken with guilt or with shame, Audrey and Mother Nelson died soon after, leaving the rest to determine to bring Galis to an end by vexing and troubling him every night. Informed by the cunning man Father Roseman (Rosimond)[51] that Elizabeth Stile and Mothers Dutton and Devell were responsible, he dragged Elizabeth before Nevell by a rope around her waist. Again, she was released. Undeterred, Galis beat upon the doors of Nevell and other notables every day with a cudgel.

Galis was not internally possessed by the Devil, but he was externally 'obsessed' by him. One night, around this time, while riding past the place where the witches used to gather, he did battle with Satan:

> I sudainly spied a most horrible sight and [sic] ougly feende sitting in a poore mans cart...with a payre of eies burning like the fiery flames, whose ougly shape when I behelde, falling on my knees in the middes of the dirt, I besought God to assist mee with his strength against this feende...Then rising, I went towards the place where this good fellowe was watching for his praye. At whom...I let flye with my sword, saying, avoide, Sathan, avoyde, and the name of God I charge thee to avoide, thou hast nought to do with mee...At which wordes: a great light appeared around about the carte where he sat, and therewithal

an horrible sent of brimstone was dispersed abroade,
but hee was no more seene afterwarde.'[52]

Unable to gain any satisfaction from the authorities, Galis once again left town. It was in his absence that he heard of the imprisonment, conviction, and execution of the four witches of Windsor. We do not know what it was that led the authorities finally to charge the Windsor four. We do know, from the account of Richard Galis, that the authorities were reluctant to act on the unsubstantiated accusations of such as Richard Galis. What clearly tipped the balance against them was the confession of Elizabeth Stile,[53] and perhaps the intervention of the Privy Council. For Scot, Galis' apparent 'madness' was exemplary of all claims of having been bewitched. He does not mention the reluctance of the authorities to charge the Windsor witches. This is perhaps not surprising, for the reluctance of the authorities in Windsor to accept the claims of Galis cuts against Scot's claims that, not only was the evidence of witchcraft corrigible, but also that the credulity and cruelty of the judicial authorities was central to the persecution of witches.

The Witches of St. Osyth

The dubious nature of the evidence brought against the witches of Windsor by Richard Galis was reinforced for Scot in the matter of the witches of St. Osyth. Of the witnesses in this case, he wrote, 'See whether the witnesses be not single of what credit, sex and age they are; namelie lewd, miserable, and envious poore people; most of them which speake to anie purpose being old women, & children of the age of 4. 5. 6. 7. 8. or 9. yeares.'[54] The use of children in witchcraft examinations was new, and Scot was clearly deeply troubled by it.

But it was the tactics and techniques of the Justice of the Peace, Brian Darcy, who presided over the pre-trial examinations of the witches of St. Osyth, that Scot saw as representative of the impropriety of judicial processes in the trials of witches. As we saw in chapter one, it was Darcy who adopted Continental theories of witchcraft, paraphrased Bodin in the Preface, adapted his interrogatory practices, and wove them into English judicial processes.

The story of the witches of St. Osyth is contained in a work entitled *A True and Just Recorde, of the Information, Examination and Confession of all the Witches, taken at S.Oses in the Countie of Essex: Whereof some were Executed, and other some Entreated according to the Determination of Lawe*. As I noted above, this was the third English text which contributed to Scot's list of the activities of witches in *The Discoverie of Witchcraft*. It was supposedly written by a 'W.W.', but Darcy is undoubtedly managing its production behind the scenes, and is directly contributing those parts written in the first person. It is a record of events orchestrated, managed, and even invented by Darcy. It was intended to glorify him as much as it was to detail a severe outbreak of witchcraft in St. Osyth.[55] This is reinforced by the fact that there was no recording of punishments and no indications of the trials which were to follow in the pamphlet. And although Darcy certified the documents to the Assizes held in Chelmsford on Thursday 29 March 1582,[56] there is no indication in this pamphlet that he even attended the trial. He is the centre around which revolves a text which is in consequence, as Marion Gibson remarks, 'essentially multiform, confused, and ungraspable.'[57]

The story began in early 1581. Ursley Kempe was a midwife and wet-nurse, with a side-business in 'unwitching' the bewitched. At that time, she was able to help the sick child of Grace Thurlowe.[58] Three months later, having given birth to a daughter, she and Ursley fell out when Ursley would not allow her to nurse the child. Within three months of their disagreement, the child fell out of her cradle, broke her neck, and died. Grace may have suspected that this was a witchcraft revenge. But she accepted Ursley's help when, in the middle of that year, she had 'a lamenesse in her bones, & specially in her legges.'⁵⁹ Ursley offered to help her for the sum of twelve pence. For five weeks after, Grace was well. But when Ursley asked for her payment, in cash or in kind, Grace reneged on the arrangement. Ursley said that she would get even with her. The lameness returned, to the extent that she was unable to get out of her bed or even to turn in it. On 19 February, Grace told her story to Brian Darcy.

This information was supplemented on the same day by Annis Letherdall. She gave evidence that, after a falling out between her and Ursley about four months earlier, her son had fallen ill 'with a great swelling in the bottom of the bellie, and other privie partes.'⁶⁰ On 10 February, she consulted a cunning person who informed her that Ursley had bewitched the child. When confronted by Annis, Ursley denied it. The child's condition worsened the next day, at which time Annis took him to another cunning woman, Mother Ratcliffe, to seek her help.

The next day, 20 February 1581, Ursley Kempe made her first appearance before Brian Darcy. We can assume that she denied the charges made against her by Grace and Annis, though she willingly confessed to having learnt the skills of 'unbewitching' some ten years earlier when she herself sought medical help from a cunning woman by then deceased for a 'lamenes in her bones'.⁶¹ And she went on to admit that she had used the same medicine (a mix of pig's dung and chervil) to cure several villagers from lameness caused by bewitchment. This is no doubt the source of Scot's sardonic remarks that, in contrast to the knowledge of herbs and stones in Pythagoras and Democritus, contemporary witches have 'hogs turd and chervil, as the onelie thing whereby our witches worke miracles.'⁶²

In his *Démonomanie*, Bodin had suggested that 'one must however always promise impunity, and reduce the penalty of those who will confess without torture, and who will denounce their associates.'⁶³ It would seem that Darcy, at that point in his examination, took a leaf out of Bodin's book and, taking Ursley aside privately, promised her immunity were she to confess and to name others. Only this can explain the alacrity with which he appears now able to draw out of her or (more likely) prompt her towards a richly detailed account of her activities as a malevolent witch.

Weeping and falling upon her knees, Ursley confessed to keeping four familiar spirits, two males and two females, two to punish and murder, and two to punish with illness and disease both people and animals. The two male spirits were in the likenesses of a gray cat called Tyttey and a black cat by the name of Jacke; the two females were called Pigin like a black toad, and Tyffin, like a white lamb. She admitted to sending Tyttey to punish Grace Thurlowe, and Pigin to Annis Letherdall's son. According to Darcy, she then confessed 'without any askinge of her owne free will,'[64] to killing Grace Thurlowe's daughter by sending Tyffin to tip her out of her cradle. And she went on in this confession, and in a subsequent one on the following day, 21 February, not only to implicate another woman, Ales Newman, but also to try to shift the blame from herself to Ales and the spirits. She claimed that it was Ales who had control of the spirits which she kept in a box. It was a world of bewitching and bewitched, of magic and counter magic, of corporeal imps and demons, upon which Scot poured scorn:

> And now forsooth it is brought to this point, that all divels, which were woont to be spirituall, may at their pleasure become corporall, and so shew themselves familiarlie to witches and conjurors, and to none other, and by them onlie may be made tame, and kept in a box. &c. So as a malicious old woman may command hir divell to plague hir neighbour: and he is afflicted in manner and forme as she desireth. But then commeth another witch, and she biddeth hir divell helpe, and he healeth the same partie. So as they make it a kingdome divided in it selfe, and therefore I trust it will not long endure, but will

shortlie be overthrowne, according to the words of our Savior, *Omne regnum in se divisum desolabitur*, Everie kingdome divided in it selfe shalbe desolate.[65]

Events escalated on 24 February 1581 when, in her third confession, Ursley accused a number of other women of witchcraft – Elizabeth Bennet, Ales Hunt, Annis Glascock, along with Ales Newman. A series of accusations and counter accusations ensued such that, by the end of March, fifteen people had been variously accused of witchcraft.

Bodin's tactic of offering immunity to those who confessed was used by Darcy against Elizabeth Bennet. This time he invoked the English court. 'I and other of her [the Queen's] Justices have received Commission for the apprehending of as many [witches] as are within these limites, and they which doe confesse the truth of their doeings, that shall have much favour; but the other they shall bee burnt and hanged.'[66] Darcy's threat of burning was merely that. Burning was never a punishment used in England for witchcraft in the early modern period. We do know, though, from the Preface of *A True and Just Recorde* that this is what Darcy thought they deserved. Witchcraft merited a death 'so much the more horrible,' he declared, 'by how much the honour of God is eclipsed, and the glorye due to his inviolable name most abhominably defaced...'[67] The mere threat of being either hanged and burnt or pardoned was more than enough for Elizabeth Bennet. Like Ursley Kempe, weeping and falling upon her knees, she confessed to the murder of her neighbour William Byet and his wife Joan.

As in the other two English texts upon which Scot drew for his list of the activities of witches, familiar spirits were a common and central feature of *A True and Just Recorde*. A fold out table at the end of the work gave a complete list of those accused and their crimes. But it also gave names and descriptions of the familiars together with those witches to whom they belonged. Thus, along with Ursley Kempe's four spirits, went Elizabeth Bennet's two – a black dog named Suckyn and a red lion called Lyard, Ales Hunt's two colts, Margery Sammon's two toads Tom and Robyn, Cysly Celles' two spirits variously named Sotheons Herculus, Jack or Mercury. In addition, Ales Manfield and Margaret Grevell shared four spirits, two males and two females, all black cats, and called Robin, Jack, Will, and Puppet alias Mamet, while Elizabeth Ewstace had three imps, coloured red, white, and black. Annis Herd had a veritable menagerie: 'vi. Impes or spirites like avises and black byrdes. And vi. other like Kine, of the bignes of Rats with short hornes, the Avises shee fed with wheat, barly, Otes and bread, the Kine with strew and hey.'[68]

Scot did not report on the outcomes for those whom Darcy sent to trial. It is possible, though unlikely, that he did not know. If he did know, it would not have especially suited his purposes to have reported it. In fact, only two of those accused were executed, an outcome that might have disappointed both Scot and Darcy, though for quite opposite reasons. Of the twelve women who were tried before Justices John Southcote and Thomas Gawdy in the fourth week in Lent (29 March) in 1582 at Chelmsford,[69] four were acquitted, two were discharged, four were reprieved, and only two – Ursley Kempe and Elizabeth Bennet – were hanged.[70] Brian Darcy appears to have gained little from his witch-hunting, although he did become Sheriff of Essex in 1586, perhaps as a result of the fame that accrued to him from his activities and from *A True and Just Recorde*. He died on Christmas Day, 1587, having lived long enough to see his name vilified in the pages of Scot's *The Discoverie of Witchcraft*.[71]

Scot did not deny the existence of witches, any more than he denied the existence of idolatrous images. Rather, he denied to witches the powers attributed to both witches and idols by the demonologists on the one hand, and Catholicism more generally, on the other. 'But truelie I denie not,' wrote Scot, 'that there are witches or images: but I detest the idolatrous opinions conceived of them; referring that to Gods worke and ordinance, which they impute to the power and malice of witches; and attributing that honour to God, which they ascribe to idols.'[72] Thus, Protestants who engaged in witch-hunting on the basis of the attribution of such powers to witches were no different from Catholics who attributed supernatural powers to Catholic practices. In short, for Scot, witch-hunting was nothing but a form of crypto-Catholicism:

> Trulie I for my part cannot conceive what is to go a whoring after strange gods, if this be not. He that looketh upon his neighbours wife, and lusteth after hir, hath committed adulterie. And truelie, he that in hart and by argument maintaineth the sacrifice of the masse to be propitiatorie for the quicke and the dead, is an idolater; as also he that alloweth and commendeth creeping to the crosse, and such like idolatrous actions, although he bend not his corporall knees.
>
> In like manner I say, he that attributeth to a witch, such divine power, as dulie and onelie apperteineth unto GOD (which all witch-mongers doo) is in hart a blasphemer, an idolater, and full of grosse impietie, although he neither go nor send to hir for assistance.[73]

The denial of supernatural powers to witches was in short a Protestant necessity, just as was the denial of the supernatural efficacy of Catholic practices.

Moreover, the existence of witches with the supernatural powers attributed to them by the demonologists had no Biblical precedent. As Scot pointed out, and the better part of *The Discoverie of Witchcraft* was committed to demonstrating, witches of the demonologists' sort had no role in the Bible.[74] And he went into a convoluted argument to the effect that, had witches had the powers to heal and cure diseases which are attributed to them, Christ would surely have criticised them for presuming 'to worke such miraculous and supernaturall thinges, as whereby he himselfe was speciallie knowne, believed, and published to be God.'[75]

Still, Scot was pretty astute in his recognition of the fact that to cry 'witch' was to create one. For he had no doubt that, were the number of witch-hunters to be reduced, the number of witches would soon diminish also.

Scot was concerned too to drive a wedge between the persecution of witches for those crimes which were committed by natural means, on the one hand, and those which were putatively committed by supernatural means on the other. It was a distinction that he believed Jean Bodin had obliterated. And Scot was right. Driven by a Mosaic view of the ideal state, the distinction between the secular and the religious was not one that Bodin would or even could grapple with, and the distinction between natural and supernatural crime was irrelevant. Bodin's *Démonomanie* was a work which was about the idea of justice and the implementation of it in the state through the magistracy. Thus, according to Bodin, the maintenance of the state depended upon the reward of the good and the punishment of the bad. To this end, he set out seven reasons to punish the wicked, each of which was supported by passages from the Old Testament. The first and greatest of these was to appease the divine anger (Numbers, chapter twenty-five). The second was to ensure God's blessing on the country (Deuteronomy, chapter thirteen); then to strike fear and terror into others (Deuteronomy, chapter thirteen), to preserve them from being infested and harmed by the wicked (Deuteronomy 15.19), to reduce the number of the wicked (Leviticus 12.14), to ensure that the good can live in security (Deuteronomy, chapter nineteen) and finally, to punish the wicked (Deuteronomy, chapter nineteen).[76]

The chastisement of witches with the utmost rigour, Bodin believed, was essential to ensuring all of the above. Witches committed the crime of treason against God and were, most of all, likely to incite divine wrath against the state: '[I]t is principally against those witches that one must seek vengeance with the greatest diligence and the utmost rigour, in order to bring an end to the wrath of God, and His vengeance upon us.'[77] And the fifteen crimes that he identified as those of witches were a combination of the criminal ('injuries done to men') and the heretical ('horrible blasphemies against the majesty of God').[78] Among the former he named murder (especially infanticide – 'murdering little children, then boiling them to render their humours and flesh drinkable'[79]), cannibalism, killing by poisons or spells, killing of livestock, causing famine and sterility by blighting crops, and finally (and surprisingly) 'carnal copulation with the Devil'.[80] Among the heretical crimes were the denial of God and all religion, the cursing and scorning of God, worshipping the Devil, devoting their children to Satan sometimes when still within the womb, sacrificing their children to the Devil before baptism, promising to lure others to the Devil's service, swearing oaths by the Devil, and finally (and surprisingly) incest '[f]or Satan gives them to understand that there never was a perfect sorcerer or enchanter who was not born from father and daughter, or mother and son.'[81]

Scot's strategy against Bodin was to increase Bodin's two categories of the criminal and the heretical into three, the criminal, the heretical, and the false or impossible. Among this last category he listed the following as false or impossible – sacrificing children to the Devil before baptism and burning them, devoting their children to the Devil, luring others to the service of Satan, swearing by the Devil, incest with spirits, murdering and boiling of infants, cannibalism, blighting of crops, and carnal copulation with demons.

In effect, then, Scot's aim was to eliminate the category of 'the witch', by denying the truth or possibility of those crimes adduced by Bodin which were distinctive of 'the witch'. He reduced the category of 'the witch' to that of 'the criminal' or 'the heretic'. The appropriate punishments could then be applied to those found guilty, not of witchcraft but of crime or heresy: death for murder by poisoning, trespass for killing cattle; death for the denial of God and religion, for cursing God, or for worshipping the Devil.[82]

Witches, Deluding and Deluded

As we have noted, Scot argued that the witches of the witch-hunters had no role in the Biblical text. Nevertheless, he did not deny that there were witches in the Bible. And these, he collapsed into four kinds: Pharaoh's magicians (*Praestigiatores Pharaonis* or *Hartummin*); the poisoners (*Mecasapha*); the diviners (*Kasam, Onen, Ob, Iidoni, Nahas*), and the enchanters (*Habar*). For Scot, they were all cousoners or tricksters, regardless of whether their intentions were good or bad. The category of witchcraft therefore extended well beyond the village cunning man and woman. It included within it the complete panoply of 'learned' and 'unlearned' forms of magic.

Thus, Scot was at one with his Protestant colleagues in extending the category of 'witchcraft' to cover a group of cultural practices which had been elaborated upon in the Old Testament, and particularly Deuteronomy 18.10–11: 'There shall not be found among you any one that maketh his son or his daughter to pass through the fire, or that useth divination, or an observer of times, or an enchanter or a witch, or a charmer, or a consulter with familiar spirits, or a wizard or a necromancer.'

There is little doubt that he was influenced by the theology of the Genevan reformer John Calvin. It would be going far beyond the evidence to suggest that Scot was a 'card-carrying' Calvinist. But it is not unreasonable to say, along with John L. Teall, that his theological sympathies lay in the direction of Geneva.[83] We know from *The Discoverie of Witchcraft* that Scot had read Calvin's *Institutes* and was familiar with a number of other works by him. Certainly he had read Calvin's *Commentaries on the Four Last Books of Moses*. And he cited Calvin as a supporter of his reading of deluding witches as nothing but cousenors.[84] Calvin saw the influence of Satan in all the forms of witchcraft outlined in the passage in Deuteronomy above. And he was as concerned as Scot to broaden the category of the deluding witch to astrologers, soothsayers, conjurors, pythonists, gnostics, necromancers, and so on. Witchcraft for Calvin, as for Scot, was an illusion.

Calvin, like Scot, located the ultimate source of all supernatural power in God. As we have seen, Scot denied supernatural power to any but God. For Calvin too, Satan lacked any substantial power of his own and used trickery, fraud, and illusion, though there were occasions when God allowed Satan to claim as his own supernatural works actually done by God. 'As to the actual operations of Satan,' declared Calvin,

> Whether he raises the dead, or bewitches men and beasts, or invests any substances with new forms through enchantment, we must consider that whatever miracles he appears to work are mere delusions;... Yet we have already seen how Pharaoh's magicians rivalled Moses in their miracles. Wherefore we need not wonder if, by God's permission, he should disturb the elements, or afflict the reprobate with diseases and other evils, or present phantoms to their sight.[85]

Moreover, Calvin was as sceptical as Scot in rejecting the reality of the Satanic Sabbath, though he read the fantasy of it as the consequence of Satanic bewitchment rather than *solely* the result of melancholic imaginings as proposed by Scot. Thus, he rejected the understanding of the 'charmer' of Deuteronomy 18.11 as someone who gathered snakes together by enchantment and suggested that it is evil spirits that are being alluded to. But, he continued, 'since it may be correctly translated "collecting, or gathering an assembly," I do not altogether reject the opinion of others, that it relates to those *imaginary assemblies*, to which unhappy men, whom the Devil has bewitched, *fancy themselves* to be transported to feast and dance together, and to join in wicked conspiracies, and which are commonly called "synagogues." '[86]

Thus, although Scot clearly extended any incipient doubts that Calvin held about witchcraft orthodoxy way beyond the Genevan reformer, the English sceptic nonetheless clearly stood in a Calvinist tradition. As the true enemy of Protestantism was for Calvin, not the witch of the demonologists but rather the deluding witch – the cousenor, so also was it for Scot.

In addition, as the true Protestant was, for Calvin, not King Saul who had sought help from the witch of Endor, but rather Job patiently suffering inflictions sent from God, so also was he for Scot. In 1554, Calvin had written a large series of sermons on Job.[87] We know that Scot was familiar with at least some of these. And Calvin's reflections on Job led Scot into a long ironical discursus on how an Elizabethan Job might have responded to the injuries inflicted by God on the Biblical Job:

> If anie man in these daies called *Job* should be by the appointment or hand of God thus handled as this [Biblical] *Job* was; I warrant you that all the old women in the countrie would be called *coram nobis*[88]: warrants would be sent out on everie side, publike and private inquirie made what old women latelie resorted to *Jobs* house, or to anie of those places, where these misfortunes fell. If anie poore old woman had chanced within two or three moneths to have borrowed a curtsie of seasing, or to have fetcht from thence a pot of milke, or had she required some almes, and not obteined it at *Jobs* hand; there had beene argument enough to have brought hir to confusion: and to be more certeine to have the right witch apprehended, figures must have beene cast, the sive and sheares must have beene set on worke; yea rather than the witch should escape, a conjuror must have earned a little monie, a circle must have beene made, and a divell raised to tell the truth: mother *Bungie* must have been gon unto, and after she had learned hir name, whom *Job* most suspected, she would have confirmed the suspicion with artificiall

accusations: in the end, some woman or other must have beene hanged for it.... *Job* imputed no part of his calamitie unto divels, witches, nor yet unto conjurors, or their inchantments; as we have learned now to doo. Neither sinned he, or did God any wrong, when he laid it to his charge.[89]

That witches were charlatans without any supernatural powers was taken by Scot as proven by the case of Mother Bungie of Rochester in Kent, mentioned in the passage above. Scot seems to have known all about her. But we know little of the history of Mother Bungie. In 1584, her name appeared as 'Bombus' in the 'Dictionarum Historicum & Poeticum' added to Thomas Cooper's *Thesaurus Linguae Romanae & Britannicae* with the description 'the name of a certaine devinour'.[90] If the 'M.B. of Rochester' referred to by Henry Holland in his *A Treatise Against Witchcraft* in 1590 is Mother Bungie, then she would seem to have been put on trial sometime in 1584 shortly before her death, a claim with which Scot concurs.[91] The Kentish playwright John Lyly no doubt based the character of 'Mother Bombie' in his 1594 play of that name on his knowledge of Mother Bungie. He presented her as a cunning woman: 'They say there is hard by an old cunning woman who can tell fortunes, expound dreams, tell of things that be lost, and divine of accidents to come. She is called the good woman who never did hurt.'[92] The 1595 pamphlet *A Memoriall of Certaine Most Notorious Witches* spoke of 'the cruell devises of mother *Bumby* the witch of Rochester'.[93]

According to Scot, she was a principal witch to whom came 'witchmongers from all the furthest parts of the land, she being in diverse bookes set out with authoritie, registred and chronicled by the name of the great witch of *Rochester*, and reputed among all men for the cheefe ringleader of all other witches.'[94] We can take all this as so much hyperbole on Scot's part. There is no evidence that cunning persons were ever as organised as this implies. And it goes against the core part of his argument that, in spite of the claims of the demonologists, witches formed an organised heresy with a 'cheefe ringleader'. Nevertheless, his intent is clear. For if the 'cheefe ringleader of all other witches' were a fraud, then the rest were too. And Scot claims to know, partly of his own knowledge, and partly from her husband and others, of her voluntary death bed confession of her fraudulent behaviour:

> '[H]ir cunning consisted onelie in deluding and deceiving the people: saving that she had (towards the maintenance of hir credit in that cousening trade) some sight in physicke and surgerie...and also that she never had indeed anie materiall spirit or divell (as the voice went) nor yet knew how to worke anie supernaturall matter, as she in hir life time made men believe she had and could doo.'[95]

Scot was, then, as opposed to the cunning man or woman as any of his Protestant contemporaries, although for quite different reasons – they, because they believed that the cunning person, whether acting with good or ill intent, was in league with the Devil; he, because he believed that they were all alike charlatans. In contrast to his peers who demonised witches, Scot disempowered them.

But Scot recognised too that the power of witchcraft was as dependent upon its customers as its suppliers. He was as ready to blame those who sought the services of witches as those who provided them. And he thought of those who believed in its power as children, fools, melancholics, or papists. Credulous individuals he may have held them to have been, but he did provide a cultural explanation of the hold of witchcraft upon the 'common people'. They have been infatuated, he believed, by poets, liars, and couseners, bewitched by tales told by old, doting women, their mothers' maids, and morrow masse preests,[96] and have so unthinkingly and uncritically accepted all of it over such a long period of time, 'that they thinke it heresie to doubt in anie part of the matter.'[97] His greatest adversaries were, as he put it, 'yoong ignorance and old custome.'[98] It was, in short, a foundational mode of thinking about the everyday, one sustained by suppliers and consumers of magic and witchcraft.

It was Scot's aim to radically rethink the everyday, to perceive illusion and sophistry where once had been seen supernatural power and demonic intervention. His primary strategy to do so was to drive a wedge between religion and magic, between the sovereignty of God and the sovereignty of the Devil and his minions. According to him, in the case of individual misfortune, the appropriate religious response was, like that of Job, to engage in scrutiny of the self and spiritual amendment.[99] There were few in his time, Scot believed, who would with patience endure the hand and correction of God. Indeed, to see the cause of misfortunes in wrongs done to the self by others and to seek remedies for misfortune by recourse to magic was to deny the providence of God in human affairs. As Scot put it,

> [I]f it be true, which they [the witchmongers] affirme, that our life or death lieth in the hand of a witch; then is it false, that God maketh us live or die, or that by him we have our being, our terme of life appointed, and our daies numbred…. And if there be no affliction nor calamitie, but is brought to passe by him, then let us defie the divell, renounce all his works, and not so much as once thinke or dreame upon this supernatural power of witches. Neither let us prosecute them with such despight, whome our fansie condemneth, and our reason acquiteth: our evidence against them consisting in impossibilities, our proofes in unwritten verities, and our whole proceedings in doubts and difficulties.[100]

To assert supernatural power to be the sole prerogative of God, to deny it to the Devil and witches, and to explain it all as nothing but cousening was one thing. And the elaborate explanations of the cousening arts in *The Discoverie of Witchcraft* were intended to substantiate this account of 'magical' artifice. Witches, at least many of them, *were* deluders. But that they were frauds and charlatans failed effectively to explain the outcomes of apparent *maleficia*, the witchcraft accusations that arose as a consequence, the elaborate legal procedures which followed, and *most crucially* the confessions by those accused that ensued, not only to acts of *maleficia*, but also to deals done with the Devil. This pointed not so much to a witch deluding others as to their powers, but to a witch who deluded herself into believing that she had them.

To explain all this, Scot constructed another radically different narrative of witchcraft and *maleficium*, one which had at its core not a deluding and cousening magician but a deluded innocent who had mistakenly come to believe in the supernatural powers attributed to her by others and who wrongly accepted the truth of the accusations made against her by those who were 'of the basest, the unwisest, & most faithles kind of people.'[101] The accused were, as a result, he declared, 'abused, and not abusors.'[102]

This narrative of deluded, rather than deluding, witches was one that he constructed from the English stories with which, as we have seen above, he was most familiar – that of the witches of Windsor in *A Rehearsall Both Straung and True* in 1579 and Richard Galis's *A Brief Treatise* in the same year, and that of the witches of St. Osyth in Brian Darcy's *A True and Just Recorde* in 1582. Scot's narrative appeared twice in *The Discoverie of Witchcraft*, in a condensed form in his prefatory letter to Sir Thomas Scot, and in chapter three of Book one. This is the briefer version of the story that is told by the accusers, one which Scot believed consisted of guesses, presumptions, and impossibilities, 'contrarie to reason, scripture, and nature.'[103] It was one grounded in neighbourly conflict as a consequence of demands for charity, refusal, neighbourly conflict and guilt, revenge, inexplicable misfortunes, suspicion and formal accusation.

> She was at my house of late, she would have had
> a pot of milke, she departed in a chafe because she
> had it not, she railed, she curssed, she mumbled and

whispered, and finallie she said she would be even with me: and soone after my child, my cow, or my pullet died, or was strangelie taken. Naie (if it please your Worship) I have further proofe: I was with a wise woman, and she told me I had an ill neighbour, & that she would come to my house yer it were long, and so did she; and that she had a marke above hir waste, & so had she: and God forgive me, my stomach hath gone against hir a great while. Hir mother before hir was counted a witch, she hath beene beaten and scratched by the face till bloud was drawne upon hir, bicause she hath beene suspected, & afterwards some of those persons were said to amend.[104]

The narrative created by Scot has some twentieth-century analogues. Thus, for example, in his monumental work *Religion and the Decline of Magic,* Keith Thomas identified the form of narrative outlined here by Scot as the dominant pattern in sixteenth and seventeenth-century witchcraft stories. As he puts it, 'the most common situation of all was that in which the victim (or, if he were an infant, the victim's parents) had been guilty of a breach of charity or neighbourliness, by turning away an old woman who had come to the door to beg or borrow some food or drink, or the loan of some household utensil…. The witch is sent away empty-handed, perhaps mumbling a valediction; and in due course something goes wrong with the household, for which she is immediately held responsible.'[105] Alan Macfarlane has analysed the same stories as the consequence of population growth, a corresponding increase in poverty, and strains on the informal institutions that had traditionally dealt with the old and the poor – Church relief, the manorial organisation, and ties between families and neighbours.[106]

It would be quite anachronistic to suggest that Scot's intent, like that of Thomas and Macfarlane, was to provide a functionalist explanation of sixteenth-century witchcraft. And it is of course difficult to discern what 'real events' lay behind the stories, the narrative form of which Scot parodies in his witchcraft narrative.[107]

What we can say is that Scot's intent was to 'demythologise' the narratives which he drew upon, in order to create a 'naturalistic' account of how witchcraft accusations arose. And he did so, by imbedding them in social conflict and denying them any supernatural or magical resonances.

Similarly, with regard to his image of the witch, we do not know if Scot was drawing upon a popular English non-literary stereotype of the witch, though it is a reasonable assumption that he was. But there is little doubt that he was crucial in inventing a literary stereotype. Indeed, his 'demythologised' narrative was dependent upon creating a *persona* for the witch as someone outside of the bounds of normalcy – physically, mentally, and morally and religiously, sufficient to inspire fear, loathing, and horror, persuading both themselves and others of their supernatural powers. 'One sort of such as are said to bee witches,' wrote Scot,

> [A]re women which be commonly old, lame, bleare-eied, pale, fowle, and full of wrinkles; poore, sullen, superstitious, and papists; or such as knowe no religion: in whose drousie minds the divell hath gotten a fine seat; so as, what mischeefe, mischance, calamitie, or slaughter is brought to passe, they are easily persuaded the same is doone by themselves; imprinting in their minds an earnest and constant imagination hereof. They are leane and deformed, shewing melancholie in their faces, to the horror of all that see them. They are doting, scolds, mad, divelish; and not much differing from them that are thought to be possessed with spirits.[108]

We can hear rhetorical echoes of Scot's description in a number of later caricatures of the witch. In 1646, the minister John Gaule was critical of those who saw a witch 'in every old woman with a wrinkled face, a furr'd brow, a hairy lip, a gobber tooth, a squint eye, a squeaking voice, or a scolding tongue.'[109] A popular fable of 1655 described a Kentish witch as 'long nos'd, blear eyed, crooked-neckt, wry-mouth'd, crump-shoulder'd, beetle-brow'd, thin-bellied, bow-legg'd, and splay-footed.'[110] For Scot, as for others, witchcraft and a vicious tongue went together, or so it was believed. Some Essex church wardens noted that it was only hearsay that a woman accused as a witch was so, 'but she ys develishe of her tonge.'[111] More generally, witches and scolding housewives coalesced.

For Scot, then, women were witches, and the male witch an exception. There is one case of the initiation of a male witch into a Satanic cult in Scot.[112] But when witches are spoken of generically in *The Discoverie of Witchcraft*, almost without exception, Scot used the feminine pronoun. That women were more prone to become witches was a demonological commonplace. It was a tradition that went back to the *Formicarius* (Anthill) of the Dominican theologian Johannes Nider (c. AD 1380–1438) and was consequently and subsequently imbedded in the *Malleus Maleficarum*. Nider and Kramer linked witchcraft to feminine spiritual weakness and carnal susceptibility to the demonic.[113]

It was as uncontroversial within English discussions of witchcraft as it was within Continental accounts. Thus, for example, Alexander Roberts, in his *A Treatise of Witchcraft* in 1616, listed those attributes of women which made them prone to witchcraft. They outnumbered males by one hundred to one, he declared, because they were more credulous, desired to know improper things, were more open to receive the impressions offered by the Devil, talked too much, were more prone to sin, and were generally thoroughly nasty pieces of work when crossed:

> This sex, when it conceiveth wrath or hatred against any, is unplacable, possessed with unsatiable desire of revenge... and when their power herein answereth not their will... the Divell taketh the occasion, who knoweth in what manner to content exulcerated mindes, windeth himselfe into their hearts, offereth to teach them the means by which they may bring

to passe that rancor which was nourished in their breasts, and offereth his helpe and furtherance herein.[114]

And it was a theological commonplace that the evidence for the weakness of women, and their capacity to be seduced – literally for some, metaphorically for most – by Satan was grounded in the story of Eve in the Garden of Eden. The most commonly adduced reason for Satan approaching Eve in the Garden when she was alone was her status, as 1 Peter 3.7 put it, as 'the weaker vessel.' Henry Holland spoke for most when he declared that 'Sathan begins his battery where the wall is weakest, he knew that even then the woman was the weaker vessel.'[115] Thomas Browne made the same point more elegantly: 'the Serpent was cunning enough,' he wrote, 'to begin the deceit in the weaker; and the weaker of strength, sufficient to consummate the fraud in the stronger.'[116] That, like Eve, women were more prone to the temptations of Satan made them more likely to be witches. John Stearne, for example, in 1648 explained witchcraft as a female phenomenon, since women were more easily displeased with and vengeful to men because of Satan's 'prevailing with *Eve*.'[117]

Although Scot accepted that women were more likely to be deluded into thinking that they had witchcraft powers, Scot was unable to endorse such explanations. In part, this was the consequence of his reluctance to adopt such a literal reading of Scripture. But more importantly, this account assumed that the *real* temptation of Eve by Satan prefigured the contemporary *real* temptations by the Devil of women to become his minions, and it assumed the reality of the powers which they gained as a consequence.

Scot needed an account which denied supernatural powers to such women. And he needed one which, at the same time, provided an explanation, not of why more women were in league with the Devil than men, but of why women were more likely to come *deludedly to believe* that they had made a compact with Satan and had supernatural powers. For this he turned to the concept of melancholy. This was a notion that enabled him to render them powerless by declaring them mad.

Mad and Melancholic Imaginings

There was nothing particularly original about Scot's account of melancholy. He was clearly reliant upon the standard early modern humoural account of melancholy, derived from Classical sources, and especially from the Greek physician Galen (second century AD). According to this, the ideal healthy person would have the four humours in the body in an exact proportion: blood would be the most abundant humour, then phlegm, followed by melancholy and choler. In reality, persons differ in the proportions of the humours in their bodies, their complexions or temperaments being designated according to the dominance of the one or the other as sanguine, choleric, phlegmatic, or melancholy, with the first the most desirable, and the last the least. It was little distinguished from madness, though on occasion, melancholy would be viewed as a flaw in the imagination, madness as a flaw in the reason.[118] Scot was at one with his contemporaries in seeing it as a form of madness due to the dominance of 'black bile' ($μέλαινα$ $χολή$) in the body unaccompanied by either fever or frenzy, more prevalent in the old than the young, and involving the impairment of the imagination.[119] It was usually accompanied by hallucinations, and fear and sorrow with no apparent cause.

It was upon the hallucinatory aspects, rather than its 'depressive' aspects that Scot focused. 'You shall understand,' he wrote, 'that the force which melancholie hath, and the effects that it worketh in the bodie of a man, or rather of a woman, are almost incredible.'[120] And he went on to list a number of delusions of melancholics: that they were monarchs or princes, animals, urinals, or earthen pots; one that thought he was Atlas bearing the heavens upon his shoulders; and another that thought that his nose was as big as a house, so that 'no freend nor physician could deliver him from this conceipt, nor yet either ease his greife, or satisfie his fansie in that behalfe.'[121] It is somewhat odd that all of the specific examples which Scot gave of melancholics concerned men rather than women, for examples of the latter would better have suited his cause. Still, he was drawing his examples from Johann Weyer's *De Praestigiis Daemonum*. And of the twelve particular cases of melancholy discussed by Weyer in Book three, chapter seven of that work, only one of these concerned a woman. Be that as it may, Scot's intention was clear, namely, to align the delusions of melancholics (regardless of gender) with those of witches. This enabled him to suggest that if the fantasies of melancholics were as false and impossible as those of witches, then the latter were to be classified with the former, especially since witches were old, female and, like many melancholic women, post-menstrual.

Scot looked to Weyer for more than merely examples of melancholics. For Weyer, like Scot, also looked to melancholy to explain the delusions of female witches. Weyer argued that women were more susceptible to the blandishments of the Devil, not only because they were inconstant, credulous, wicked, and uncontrolled in spirit, but also because they were melancholic. Thus, 'stupid, worn out, unstable old women' were particularly open to seduction by him.[122] He gave the standard Galenic explanation that, in the case of melancholy, 'the senses are corrupted in various ways by this one humour or by the sooty vapour of black bile which infects the abode of the mind, and from which proceed (as we know) all those phantastical monstrosities.'[123] But he went further than this. For in the case of Weyer, in contrast to Scot, while the explanation of melancholy followed the Galenic model, a demonological account was superimposed upon this medical one. In effect, melancholy was the effect of a demonic cause.

The attribution of the cause of melancholy to demons or evil spirits, or to preternatural or supernatural factors more generally, was not unusual in early modern Europe. The imagination, the seat of melancholy, was often conceived as interacting both with the physical and the supernatural realms, and as the link between the two. Thus, for demonologists, the Devil was able to 'enter' the body via the imagination and create or at least worsen melancholy. The Barbarite friar Francesco Maria Guazzo, for example, in his *Compendium Maleficarum* in 1608 saw the Devil as the external cause of melancholy, epilepsy, paralysis, blindness, deafness, and other diseases. For him, a natural and a demonological explanation of disease were not incompatible. 'Is it not possible,' he inquired, 'for sicknesses to spring from natural causes, and at the same time possible for demons to be the instigators of such sicknesses?'[124] In the case of melancholy, he wrote, the Devil 'induces the melancholy sickness, by first disturbing the black bile in the body, and so dispersing a black humour throughout the brain and the inner cells of the body: and this black bile he increases by superinducing other irritations and by preventing the purging of the humour.'[125]

Like Guazzo, Weyer saw the Devil as the ultimate cause of melancholy. But unlike Guazzo, Weyer emphasised the connection between melancholy and delusions. And this enabled him to argue that the Devil was responsible for making melancholic women susceptible to his illusions. The Devil can do this more easily, declared Weyer,

> [I]n instruments suited to his subterfuges – such as women or persons afflicted with a disease of the spirit.... And just as the use of reason is impaired in persons who are drunk, or delirious, or melancholic (because of their humors and vapors), the Devil (with God's permission) is no less able, being a spirit, to stir up such humors and make them receptive to his illusions, and corrupt the reason so that forms of non-existent things are apprehended as real objects.[126]

An apologist for Weyer like Gregory Zilboorg, determined to read him as the founder of modern psychiatry, attempted to read Weyer's references to the Devil and demons as metaphors for mental states, and went as far as to suggest that it was doubtful if Weyer even believed in the Devil.[127] This is a matter of somewhat anachronistic wishful thinking on Zilboorg's part. It is difficult to read the above passage from Weyer along these lines. For Weyer, witches were the passive deluded victims of demonic machinations, and consequently should not be punished as if they were active collaborators with the powers of evil.

There is no such ambivalence in Scot. For him the medical explanation excluded any supernatural one. If melancholics can believe false and impossible things, asked Scot,

> Why should an old witch be thought free from such fantasies, who (as the learned philosophers and physicians saie) upon the stopping of their monethlie melancholicke flux or issue of bloud, in their age must needs increase therein, as (through their weaknesse both of bodie and braine), the aptest persons to meete with such melancholicke imaginations: with whome their imaginations remaine, even when their senses are gone. Which *Bodin* laboureth to disproove, therein shewing himselfe as good a physician, as else-where a divine.[128]

This ironically intended reference to Bodin deserves a comment. At the end of his *Démonomanie*, Bodin included a refutation of Weyer. Bodin refused to recognise any connection between melancholy and witchcraft for the simple reason that, citing both Hippocrates and Galen, women do not suffer from melancholy. And the reason for this, and the reason why women were healthier than men, is that menstruation, by purifying the body, preserved women from disease. Bodin failed to give any account of what happened to women who failed or ceased to menstruate. And, in arguing that women were immune to melancholy, Bodin was out of tune with many of his contemporaries who were not uncritical of Galen, who accepted the reality of melancholic women, and on humoural grounds. Like Weyer and Scot, many believed that the interruption in younger women or the cessation of menstruation among older was a cause of melancholic delusions. The non-menstrual woman was, in effect, 'a putrefying sink of ill humours.'[129] Thus, for example, Sir William Monson's wife who in 1597 consulted Simon Forman, the London astrologer and practitioner of physic, was described as 'much subject to melancholy and full of fancies... She hath not her course and the menstrual blood runneth to her head... And she thinks that the devil doth tempt her to do evil to herself.'[130]

Of course, the counterargument to both Weyer and Scot was not to deny melancholy in women as Bodin did, but to argue that female witches were manifestly not necessarily melancholic. This was the strategy adopted by King James in his response to Weyer and Scot in the *Daemonologie*. And his response was a clearly neo-Galenic one, intended *medically* to refute the readings of both Weyer and Scot on the melancholic origins of witchcraft delusions. The humour in the melancholic, declared the King, is black, heavy, and earthy, and the corresponding symptoms in those who suffered from melancholy were leanness, paleness, and desire of solitude. But many of those who confessed to, or were convicted of, witchcraft were the exact opposite: 'some of them rich and worldly-wise, some of them fatte or corpulent in their bodies, and most part of them altogether given over to the pleasures of the flesh, continuall haunting of companie, and all kind of merrines... which are thinges directly contrary to the symptoms of Melancholie.'[131]

Scot drew most of his information about melancholy from Weyer although, as we have seen, he did not accept Weyer's mix of medical and demonological explanations. The marginal notes in *The Discoverie of Witchcraft* also make it clear that he drew upon the work of the Italian philosopher and physician Girolamo Cardano (1501–76) and, in particular, upon his 1557 work, *De rerum varietate* (On the Variety of Things). Cardano, like Scot, gave an explanation of witchcraft which denied demonic interventions.

Witches were mostly lonely old women who, as a consequence of poor nutrition, became melancholic and delusional.

But to counter Bodin's critique of Weyer, and specifically his denial of the possibility of melancholic women, it was to the Swiss physician and Zwinglian theologian Thomas Erastus (1524–1583) that Scot turned.[132] And he quoted Erastus to the effect that 'These witches, through their corrupt phantasie abounding with melancholike humours, by reason of their old age doo dreame and imagine they hurt those things which they neither could nor doo hurt; and so thinke they knowe an art, which they neither have learned nor yet understand.'[133]

Thomas Erastus was both a supporter and a critic of Weyer. He had written his first response to Weyer's *De Praestigiis Daemonum* in 1570 under the title 'Disputatio de lamiis', subsequently published as a chapter in his 1571 anti-Paracelsian work entitled *De medicina nova Philippi Paracelsi* (On the New Medicine of Philipp Paracelsis). The debate continued after the publication, in 1577, of a new edition of *De Praestigiis Daemonum* that included a new chapter entitled 'A refutation of certain objections which have been raised against the preceding chapter' (Book six, chapter 24) which directly addressed Erastus's concerns. This, in its turn, provoked Erastus to write his *Repetitio disputationis de lamiis seu strigibus* (1578).[134]

The choice of Erastus by Scot to support his naturalistic account of witches' delusions was, on the face of it, a strange one. Erastus, like Weyer and Scot, denied to witches the power to do harm. But nonetheless, unlike Weyer and Scot, he advocated the death penalty to those found guilty of witchcraft. This was primarily because he believed that witches, seeking supernatural powers, had entered into a pact with the Devil. Thus, while they could not be found guilty of the crime of *maleficia* they were guilty of apostasy, idolatry, heresy, and bestiality (with the Devil) and should be punished accordingly. Thus, whereas Weyer saw witches as victims of the Devil's illusions, and hence legally innocent, Erastus saw them as active participants in their alliance with the Devil, and therefore legally culpable.

Scot himself was perhaps not quite clear on Erastus's position. For elsewhere he remarked (though perhaps ironically) that Erastus was 'a principall writer in the behalfe of witches omnipotencie' though recognizing their 'powers' to be nothing but illusions. And Scot went on wrongly to claim that, in spite of this, 'yet defendeth he [Erastus] their flieng in the aire, their transferring of corne or grasse from one feeld to another, &c.'[135] For Erastus *did*, pace Scot, rule out the powers of witches in themselves to do anything beyond that which other humans could do. 'For beyond the desertion of God and the divine cult, and the flight into the camp of the devil,' he wrote, 'nearly everything [that they claim to accomplish] are fabrications and fictions or positively uncertain and inconstant, slippery and changeable.'[136]

The analysis of melancholic witches and their demonic delusions had, as Weyer, Erastus, and Scot realised, clear legal implications. In the case of Scot, it enabled a persuasive explanation of confessions to witchcraft which were made voluntarily. For Scot, confessions to witchcraft made as a result of the torturing of the supposed witch could be safely ignored, or at least treated briefly. It seemed to him a matter self evident that such confessions were corrigible and untrustworthy. Similarly, confessions made as a consequence of 'faire words and allurements' were not to be regarded.[137] Scot's presumption was that the mere enumeration of the presumptions, interrogatories, and cautions used by the inquisitors was sufficient to demonstrate their absurdity. So he could easily explain confessions falsely made in the hope of pardon promised or punishments lessened. And he was personally aware of at least one case of a person who attempted suicide when their confession to witchcraft was rejected by the courts: 'I my selfe have knowne, that where such an one could not prevaile, to be accepted as a sufficient witnesse against himselfe, he presentlie went and threwe himselfe into a pond of water, where he was drowned.'[138] But his diagnosis of melancholy provided an explanation of the false confessions made by those who truly believed in the melancholic delusions that they were indeed witches. And it demonstrated the injustice of their convictions. This melancholic humour, he declared, 'is the cause of all their strange confessions: which are so fond [silly], that I woonder how anie man can be abused thereby.'[139]

For an instance of a melancholy-induced case of false confession, Scot looked to the story of Ade Davie, wife of Simon Davie, a woman from the town of Selling in Kent. We owe our knowledge of the case to Scot. It was a case of which he himself had personal knowledge, having spoken to Ade's husband after the event. Ade Davies' melancholy had come upon her suddenly. She grew to be, wrote Scot, 'somewhat pensive and more sad than in times past'. Her husband was reluctant to make her troubles widely known, lest he be suspected of ill treating her. She became unable to sleep 'through sighing and secret lamentation'. She was 'troubled and disquieted with despaire.' When he demanded to know the cause of her 'extraordinarie moorning', she fell down before him begging his forgiveness for having grievously offended both God and him. She went on to confess that she had 'bargained and given hir soule to the divell, to be delivered unto him within short space,' and that she had bewitched her husband and her children. So persuaded was she that she was a witch, 'that she judged hir selfe worthie of death; insomuch as being reteined in hir chamber, she sawe not anie one carrieng a faggot to the fier, but she would saie it was to make a fier to burne hir for witcherie.'[140]

In response to her confessions, her husband comforted her as best he could with a theological declaration of the Devil's powerlessness over her. In effect, Simon Davie was expressing the so-called Ransom theory of the atonement, the predominant view of the Church for its first thousand years, according to which Christ offered his life as a ransom paid to the Devil for our salvation.

'Wife, be of good cheere,' he said. 'this thy bargaine is void and of none effect: for thou hast sold that which is none of thine to sell; sith it belongeth to Christ, who hath bought it and deerelie paid for it, even with his bloud, which he shed upon the crosse; so as the divell hath no interest in thee.'[141] 'Be content,' he continued, 'by the grace of God, Jesus Christ shall unwitch us: for none evill can happen to them that feare God.'[142]

When the time arrived for the Devil to come and take possession of the woman, Simon watched and prayed earnestly, while Ade read psalms and prayed to God for mercy. The Devil was defeated, for 'suddenlie about midnight, there was a great rumbling beelowe under his chamber windowe, which amazed them exceedinglie. For they conceived that the divell was beelowe, though he had no power to come up, because of their fervent praiers.'[143] Of this apparently demonic rumbling, as reported by Simon, Scot needed to provide a natural explanation: 'as for the rumbling, it was by occasion of a sheepe, which was flawed, and hoong by the wals, so as a dog came and devoured it; whereby grew the noise which before I mentioned.'[144] Scot did not, *in principle* could not, believe that the Devil had been deterred by their prayers. He did claim that she recovered from her melancholy and became a 'right honest woman', somewhat ashamed of her imaginings, 'which she perceiveth to have growne through melancholie.'[145]

Scot may well have believed that Ade Davie was delivered from melancholy by God in answer to the fervent prayers of her husband and herself. This would be in keeping with his doctrine of the sovereignty of God. But the overall intention of the story was to suggest that, although she was quite deluded in believing so, her voluntary confessions of having made a deal with the Devil and of having bewitched her husband and her children would have been sufficient to convict her in a court of law: 'any judge in the world, if she had beene examined; and have confessed no lesse' would have cried 'Guiltie; & would hasten execution upon her,' even though God knew 'she had bewitched none, neither insued there anie hurt unto anie, by hir imagination, but unto hir selfe.'[146]

For Scot, the falsity of voluntarily made confessions arising from melancholy was reinforced, not only by the natural impossibility of those things which witches claimed to do, but by the improbability of their having done so. Witches confessed to things done which were so against their self interest that it was impossible to believe that any sane person would have thus acted. Thus, confessions to have acted so arose from madness: 'what creature being sound in state of mind,' asked Scot, 'would (without compulsion), make such manner of confessions as they do; or would for a trifle or nothing, make a perfect bargaine with the divell for hir soule, to be yielded up unto his tortures and everlasting flames, and that within a verie short time?'[147] Moreover, Scot argued, if the confessions of witches were true, natural, social, and political chaos would be the consequence. 'One old witch might overthrowe an armie roiall: and then what needed we any guns, or wild fire, or any other instruments of warre.'[148]

At the end of the day, however, Scot was aware that the falsity of confessions voluntarily made was a consequence, not only of melancholy, but also of the ideological edifice which they apparently supported, namely, demonology. And the falsity of witchcraft confessions therefore was crucially dependent on demonstrating the feeble foundations upon which demonology was constructed.

CHAPTER THREE

Demonology

Demonological Foundations

By the time of the publication of *The Discoverie of Witchcraft* in 1584, the Continental image of witchcraft as a combination of *maleficia* and heresy (the witch being a member of an alternative religion) had been in existence for some two hundred years.[1] Pope Eugenius IV put it succinctly in 1437. In a letter to inquisitors, he bemoaned the loss of Christians to the faith who 'sacrifice to demons, adore them, seek and accept responses from them, pay homage to them, give written compacts through which by a single word, touch or sign they can perform or take away whatever *maleficia* they choose, cure diseases, regulate the weather, provoke tempests, and sign pacts as to other unspeakable things.'[2]

Scot was the first Englishman to introduce European demonology as it had developed in Europe to English readers. Until the time of Scot, witchcraft trials in England had been trials for the committing of *maleficia*. The notion that witches were members of an heretical sect was not extant within the English tradition. Moreover, in spite of Scot's presentation of the key features of European demonology and his debunking of the Continental construction of witchcraft as a heresy, and King James VI's promulgation of Continental demonology in his *Daemonologie* in 1597, the primary focus of witchcraft persecution in England remained crimes and not heresy.[3] Neither Scot's critique nor

James' support appear to have made any notable difference to this.

Be that as it may, the aim of Scot's critique of the crimes of witchcraft was to demonstrate that all its evidences were corrigible in practice and impossible in principle. So too with the evidences that suggested to the demonologists the existence of an heretical religion, with its devotees committed to the worship and service of Satan, Scot's critique was directed at the incredibility of the apparent evidences and the impossibility, in principle, of a religion based on a pact sealed with the Devil, the devotees of which worshipped Satan and practised malevolent and benevolent magic. In *The Discoverie of Witchcraft*, and particularly in Books three, four, and five, Scot expounded in a fairly systematic way the key features of European demonology – the pact with the Devil, the Sabbath and magical transportation to it, transformation into the form of animals, and sex with the Devil.

The development of these key elements of demonology in Europe was in itself intellectually dependent upon three foundational ideas within the history of European witchcraft. First, there was the notion that witches were not merely individuals with supernatural powers derived from the Devil but were members of a vast Satanic cult, an inverted form of the Christian faith. Second, there was the development of a complex demonology arising from the growth of angelology more generally. And third, there was the critical assumption that the world of demons could corporeally interact with the human realm.

Scot himself traced the origins of the notion of witches in league with the Devil to the initiation of a young man, together with his wife, into a Satanic sect. It is a story that, as Scot points out,[4] was originally told by the Dominican theologian Johannes Nider (*c.* AD 1380–1438). Although Scot does not tell us so, it occurs in the fifth book of Nider's work the *Formicarius* (the *Anthill*), which was devoted to 'witches and their deceptions'. The *Formicarius* was the most important of early works on witchcraft. Written in 1437 and

1438, it went through seven printed editions between 1475 and 1692, and was a major source for the *Malleus Maleficarum* of 1486. Thus, for example, all of the three accounts of the witches' Sabbath included in the *Formicarius*, one of which is that of the young man mentioned above, are included in the *Malleus Maleficarum*.[5]

We do not know whether Scot had read the *Formicarius*. Nor do we know whether he had read Nider's other work which treats of witchcraft, the *Preceptorium divine legis*, to which Scot also referred in a marginal note. What we do know is that all Scot's references to Nider can be found in the *Malleus Maleficarum* and the likelihood is therefore high that his knowledge of Nider's works is drawn from there, including the story of the young man's initiation into a Satanic cult.[6]

According to Heinrich Kramer, in the *Malleus Maleficarum*, a young man in Berne, together with his wife, had been arrested and imprisoned separately from her. In the hope, and the promise, that repentance and a full confession would secure his forgiveness after death, and accepting the inevitability of his execution for his crimes, he gave a full account of his initiation:

> "The procedure," he said, "by which I was led astray is this. It is first necessary that on Sunday, before the Holy Water is consecrated, the prospective disciple should enter a church with the masters[7] [that is, already initiated witches] and in their presence renounce Christ, the Faith in Him, Baptism and the whole Church, and then do homage to the masterling [the demon].... By this method," he said, "was I led astray. So was my wife, whom I believe to be so obstinate that she would rather endure the flames than be willing to confess to the smallest truth. But, alas, we are both guilty." The truth was found to be exactly as the young man said. After confessing in advance, he was seen to die in great contrition. His wife, on the other hand, though convicted by witnesses, was unwilling to confess to any of the truth, either under

torture or in death. Instead, when the fire had been prepared by the executioner, she cursed him with the vilest words and was in this way burned to ashes.[8]

With this notion in place of a cult of witches, both male and female, the decisive step towards the development of the witches' Sabbath had been taken.

The development of European witchcraft was also intellectually dependent upon the development of a complex demonology. And this was the unhappy side, as it were, of the development of European angelology. As David Keck has demonstrated, the systematization of angelology in the Western intellectual tradition from the middle of the twelfth century to the end of the fourteenth century was the consequence of three fundamental changes in modes of theological thinking in the thirteenth-century University. Firstly, the introduction of new logical techniques and methods, such as the *quaestio*, deriving from Aristotle, formalised the means of asking and answering theological questions. Secondly, again under Aristotelian influence, there was an increasing interest in the use of philosophical and metaphysical categories to explore the nature of creatures. And finally, and most importantly, with the development of formal theological textbooks, particularly the *Four Books of the Sentences* of Peter Lombard (*c.* AD 1100–1160) with its discussion of angels in Book two, angelology became a formal part of theological training.[9] Thus, at the highly competitive University of Paris in particular,

> That prospective masters of theology had to deliver commentaries on the *Sentences* meant that theologians would have a professional incentive to explore in greater and greater depth the questions raised by the Master's text. An ambitious theologian could not simply repeat what Lombard had stated, rather he had to delve deeper, probe more tenaciously, and reason more accurately than not only Lombard but also other commentators if he were to establish

himself as a leading theologian. Lombard's text thus provided the scholastics with a formal occasion for angelology by presenting a coherent structure for discussing the nature of the angels that was open to new categories and concepts.[10]

Lombard devoted the second Book of his *Sentences* to discussion of the creation and formation of corporeal and spiritual things. And 'Distinctions' two to eleven within this Book dealt with angelogy and its sub-discipline, demonology. According to Lombard, all spiritual and corporeal beings were made in the beginning at the same time together with the world. Before the ruin of certain of them, all the angels were located in Heaven (the *Empyrean*). They were created as discrete, indivisible, and immaterial beings, with intelligence, memory, and will, including the freedom to do good or evil. Following the *Celestial Hierarchy* of Pseudo-Dionysius (*c*. AD 500), the first treatise devoted completely to the issue of angels, Lombard accepted that there was an angelic hierarchy at the time of their creation, 'according to which some were constituted superiors, others inferiors, according to the Wisdom of God.'[11] Thus, while the angels were equally spiritual, indissoluble, and immortal, they were different in the subtlety of their essence, their wisdom, and their free will.

At the time of their creation, all were by nature good, though their free will entailed the freedom to choose between good and evil. Shortly after, as a consequence of the misuse of their free will, certain angels fell from the good, and were cast down from Heaven into 'this gloomy [caliginosum] air of ours,'[12] chief amongst whom was Lucifer. From this time, though angelic freedom of will remained, the character of the angels, both fallen and unfallen, was fixed, the good being confirmed in grace freely chose to do only good, the evil angels so confirmed in malice that the willing of the good was impossible. In short, the division of the angelic and demonic hierarchies was fixed from shortly after the creation and, one might add, the rest of history was played out in the resulting conflict between the hierarchies of good and evil (albeit, at least theoretically, under the overarching divine providence), with both angels and demons deputed to guard and to tempt human persons.

It was in the *Sentences* of Peter Lombard too that the third foundational idea underlying European witchcraft was brought into the discussion. This was the issue of the corporeal nature of angelic beings both good and evil. It was an issue that Lombard left open, ensuring that debate on it would become part of the theological curriculum. 'Wherefore some think,' declared Lombard,

> Who supporting (themselves) on the words of (St.) Augustine, seem to say, that all the Angels before (their) confirmation and/or lapse had bodies of air formed from a purer and superior part of the air...for the good angels, who persisted (in the Truth), such bodies were conserved, so that in them they may be able to work and not to suffer, which (bodies) are of so great a refinement, that they do not prevail to be seen by mortals unless they have been clothed over by some grosser form...but to the evil angels (their) bodies were changed in (their) downfall, into the worse quality of the thicker air. For just [as] they were cast down from a more worthy place into an inferior place, that is into the shadowy air, so those tenuous bodies (of theirs) were transformed into worse and thicker bodies.[13]

As Lombard intimated, Augustine's position (albeit ambivalent) was that demons (or *daemones*) had spiritual or aerial bodies, assumed from the air into which they had fallen from Heaven. 'Now it may well be,' wrote Augustine, 'that demons have a kind of body of their own, as learned men have thought, composed of the thick moist air of this atmosphere whose pressure we feel when the wind is blowing.'[14] This neo-Platonic account of the nature of demonic bodies was influential in Renaissance Platonism.[15] But European witchcraft was more directly influenced by the account of the corporeal nature of demons offered by Thomas Aquinas.

His position has been aptly described by Walter Stephens as the view that angels and demons have bodies that are both real and not real, that is, 'virtual bodies'.[16]

In contrast to Augustine's apparent support of the Platonic account, Aquinas believed that Augustine merely stated the Platonists' position without endorsing it personally. Aquinas himself supported Aristotle's denial of the Platonists' account of demons united to aereal bodies: 'The angels have not bodies naturally united to them,' he declared.[17] In spite of his philosophical commitment to the incorporeal nature of angels and demons, Aquinas was of course aware of Scriptural accounts of angels appearing in bodily forms simultaneously to more than one person, and incapable, therefore, of being dismissed as an (internal) delusion. 'From all this,' he concluded, 'it is clearly shown that such apparitions were beheld by bodily vision, whereby the object seen exists outside the person beholding it, and can accordingly be seen by all. Now by such a vision only a body can be beheld. Consequently, since the angels are not bodies, nor have they bodies naturally united with them…, it follows that they sometimes assume bodies.'[18] Thus did the notion of angelic (and demonic) virtual bodies synchronise reason and revelation.

The bodies assumed by spiritual beings were, according to Aquinas, made of air, appropriately condensed, shaped, and coloured by the Divine power as the need arose. Such beings appeared in their assumed bodies to be living men, though they could not exercise those functions that are special to living subjects. Thus they only appeared to perceive, talk, and eat. And most crucially for later witchcraft, they could not procreate, though they could be involved in apparent sexual activity, semen stealing, and gender changing as incubi and succubi:

> Still if some are occasionally begotten from demons it is not from the seed of such demons, nor from their assumed bodies, but from the seed of men taken for the purpose; as when the demon assumes first the

form of a woman, and afterwards of a man; just as they take the seed of other things for other generating purposes ... , so that the person born is not the child of a demon, but of a man.[19]

Thus, virtual (if not real) sex with demonic entities was placed, as a consequence, on the European witchcraft agenda.

The Demonic Pact

In his work *Demon Lovers*, Walter Stephens cogently suggests that witchcraft theorists were driven by resistance to scepticism. The attitude of the demonologists towards their theories, he argues, occupied an uncomfortable space between belief and scepticism: 'The luxuriant proofs [of witchcraft] of the 1400s and 1500s display neither belief nor rationalistic scepticism. Instead, they are saturated with an attitude best expressed as "these things cannot *not* be happening in the way in which I propose".'[20] In contrast to the late antique and early medieval attitude of 'this cannot be false,' and the modern rationalist's stance of 'this cannot be true,' the demonologists' position was 'this cannot *not* be true'.

This is a valuable insight. And it enables us more precisely to delineate the intellectual space that Reginald Scot's *The Discoverie of Witchcraft* occupied, both in its critique of witchcraft generally and of European demonology in particular. It would do an injustice to Scot to view him as a modern rationalist who had adopted the position 'this cannot be true.' For in contrast to the modernist intellectual dismissal of witchcraft theory, Scot, like the demonologists, sees the need to develop particular explanations of apparent witchcraft evidences, and an overarching theory to account in principle for their impossibility. Thus, Scot, like the demonologists rhetorically positioned himself in the space between belief and scepticism. But in contrast to the demonologists' 'this cannot *not* be true,' the strategic intention of *The Discoverie of Witchcraft* was to demonstrate the truth of the proposition 'this cannot *not* be false.' In contrast to the witchcraft theorists who were driven by the will to believe in witchcraft, Scot was driven by a will to unbelieve; and, in contrast to their resistance to scepticism, his scepticism was driven by a resistance to belief.

The pact between the witches and the Devil was a particular form of the demonic pact which was perceived as a precondition of all magical powers. Following Augustine, superstitious practices in general, and witchcraft and sorcery in particular, were viewed as originating in a compact between men and demons.[21] The practice of magic generally was seen as the consequence of a pact with the Devil, either explicit or tacit. Thus, according to Aquinas, a pact was explicit when the sorcerer invoked demonic assistance, and tacit when, without acts of conjuration, a person performed an act with the aim of effecting something which either does not naturally follow, or which is not expected as the result of the direct intervention of God.[22] This was a distinction that blurred the boundaries between popular superstitions on the one hand, and sorcery and witchcraft on the other, and it negated the difference between benevolent and malevolent magic. And thus it led to the demonization of the domains of popular magic and superstition. As John Gaule put it in 1646,

> The Fathers, and Schoolmen therefore are not much amisse in defining witchcraft by superstition: making this to be the Genus, and gathering the other in all the species under it, so that no kind of Witch-craft may be named which is not found upon superstition, and works not by it. Because in this main act, superstition and Witch-craft both agree; to apply the Creature as means unto those ends and uses; unto which it is neither apt by its own nature, nor thereunto ordained by divine Institution.[23]

The distinction between the explicit and the tacit pact is one with which, interestingly, Scot does not seem to have been familiar. This is probably the result of his drawing primarily on the *Malleus Maleficarum* for his discussion of the pact. For the *Malleus*

Maleficarum was less interested in magic in general (the domain of the tacit pact), and interested especially in witchcraft defined as an express pact with the Devil, the consequent participation of a witch in acts of *maleficium*, and the actual harm caused as a result. By virtue of the pact made with the Devil, declared Heinrich Kramer,

> The sorceress has offered and bound her entire self to the Devil – really and truly and not merely in the fantasy and imagination. Thus, it is in fact appropriate that she should really and bodily work with the Devil. For this is the purpose of all the works of sorcerers, in which it is always by his working that they carry out acts of sorcery through touch or vision or speech or some other device of sorcery.[24]

Scot, like the *Malleus Maleficarum*, was only concerned with the explicit pact. He divided it into two kinds, the one solemn and public, the other secret and private.[25] And, again like the *Malleus Maleficarum*, he had little to say about the private league beyond paraphrasing the *Malleus Maleficarum* to the effect that the Devil, visibly or invisibly, speaks privately with a person promising to make them prosperous on condition of their obedience to him.[26] No doubt, he believed that accounts of such private leagues could be explained as the result of melancholy.

But for his account of the demonologists' public pact he drew directly, not only on the *Malleus Maleficarum*,[27] but also particularly on the Dominican Bartolomeo della Spina's 1523 *Quaestio de Strigibus* (An Investigation of Witches), Bodin's *Démonomanie*, and the 1575 English translation of Lambert Daneau's *Dialogus de veneficiis*. According to Scot, and paraphrasing the *Malleus Maleficarum*, witches came together at certain assemblies at fixed times where they not only saw the Devil but held familiar conversations with him. In these, the Devil exhorted them to remain faithful to him, promising them prosperity and long life in return. The witches thus assembled commended a new disciple (whom they call a novice) to him. If the Devil found the young witch ready to renounce the Christian faith, despise the sacraments, spit at the time of the elevation of the Host, and ignore fasting, he joined his hand with hers, and she promised to observe and keep all the Devil's commandments.[28] The Devil also demanded that she worship him, and that she grant him both her body and soul to be tormented in everlasting fire, an offer which, as Scot will argue elsewhere, is, at the end of the day (or the world), not really much of a bargain.[29] The Devil also charged her to bring as many people as possible to join their society. He taught the witches how to make ointments out of the bowels and other parts of unbaptised children to fulfil all their desires.

In the *Malleus Maleficarum*, Kramer elaborated demonic infanticide with a story from Nider's *Formicarius*. According to Kramer, when asked about the method by which infants were captured, a certain captured sorceress replied,

> We prey on babies, especially those not yet baptized but also those baptized.... with our ceremonies we kill them in their cribs or while they lie beside their parents, and while they are thought to have been squashed or to have died of something else, we steal them secretly from the tomb and boil them in a cauldron until all the flesh is made almost drinkable, the bones having been pulled out. From the more solid matter we make a paste suitable for our desires and arts and movements by flight, and from the more runny liquid we fill a container... Whoever drinks from this container is immediately rendered knowledgeable when a few ceremonies are added, and becomes the master of our sect.[30]

Scot incorporated the basic details of this account into his summary of the Sabbath, together with a remark from Bartolomeo della Spina to the effect that witches had the duty of killing one child every fortnight, or at least one per month.[31] From Spina too, Scot drew the story of the resurrected ox, according to which witches in Italy would enter the palaces of nobles, and eat and drink what was available which would be fully replenished by the lady Minerva, Sibylla, or Diana. They would also kill and eat an ox which was also resurrected to its former state and condition by 'the ladie of the fairies'.[32]

The bargain with the Devil was sealed, according to Scot, by a verbal oath or in writing, sealed with wax, and often signed in blood, 'sometimes by kissing the divels bare buttocks; as did a Doctor called *Edlin*, who (as *Bodin* says) was burned for witchcraft.'[33] And he again paraphrased Bodin in his telling of the dancing that was always included in the Sabbath and the witches singing 'Har, Har, divell, divell, danse here, danse here, plaie here, plaie here, *Sabbath, sabbath*. And whiles they sing and danse, everie one hath a broome in hir hand and holdeth it up aloft. Item he [Bodin] saith that these night-walking or rather night-dansing witches, brought out of *Italie* into *France*, that danse, which is called *La volta*.'[34] Scot did not report Bodin's claim that it made men homicidally frenzied and caused women to abort. But Scot's contemporaries would have been familiar with its erotic postures, and court circles would have known that Elizabeth I danced it with the Earl of Leicester around 1580.

Scot could have derived any amount of further information on the Sabbath from Bodin, Spina, or the *Malleus Maleficarum*. But he chose to supplement Bodin's account of demonic dancing with more detail derived from Daneau's *Dialogus de veneficiis*.[35] Although he nowhere said so, it did at least provide him with an opportunity to demonstrate that Protestant demonologists like Daneau could be as credulous as their Catholic counterparts. Little fresh was added to the sum of information provided to his readers by his abbreviated account of Daneau. But he did reiterate the erotic nature of the meetings with their dancing and singing of bawdy songs and their kissing of the Devil's bare buttocks, and he emphasised Daneau's claim that witches 'really' travelled to the Sabbath on staffs provided by the Devil. In addition, he recognised the strong emphasis in Daneau on witches as poisoners, and repeated Daneau's claim that witches had to offer the Devil dogs, cats, hens, or their own blood every day afterwards.

Perhaps most importantly, he did remind his readers of Daneau's belief that the pact with the Devil was sealed by the Devil marking the witch 'either with his teeth or his claws'.[36] It was a mark, declared Daneau, which the witch

> [A]lwayes beareth about him, some under the eye liddes, others betwene their buttocks, some in the roofe of their mouthe, and in other places where it may be hid & concealed from us...yet may I say thus more certenly and truly, that there is none of them upon whom he hath not set some note or token of his power & prerogative over them: which to thintent [sic] the judges and such as are set in aucthoritie of life and death...let them specially provide, that when any of these shalbe convented before them, to poulie [polle] and shave them where occasion shall serve, al the body over, least haply the marke may lurke under the heare in any place.[37]

Daneau's commitment to the idea that the pact with the Devil was sealed with the Devil's mark played little role in the writings of the early demonologists. The *Malleus Maleficarum*, for example, makes no reference to it. It was on other occasions referred to, if only to refute it.[38] Still within Protestant Geneva from 1537 onwards, the Devil's mark became part of every witchcraft confession, and by 1548 those suspected of witchcraft were being routinely and systematically searched for it.[39] So Daneau would no doubt have been familiar with the practice of searching for the Devil's mark from his time in Protestant Geneva from 1560 to 1562, and again from 1572 to 1581.[40]

John Knox had learnt not only his theology but also his demonology from Calvinist Geneva. So it is not surprising that the Devil's mark, as evidence of the demonic pact, often accompanied by the 'pricking' of the witch in search of a mark insensible to pain which did not bleed, was a common feature of witchcraft in Reformation Scotland (as it was in parts of Protestant Europe) from the late sixteenth to the early eighteenth century.[41]

In spite of its prevalence in Scotland, Daneau's endorsement of the Devil's mark as evidence of the Devil having sealed the bargain with biting or scratching of the witch, and Scot's notice of it, it was not a sign of witchcraft that became widespread in England. In England, where *maleficium* was more the focus of persecution than heresy, the notion of the demonic pact was less marked and consequently the belief in the demonic mark as key evidence of it was marginalised. Rather, the mark subtly changed in England as a result of that distinctive feature of English witchcraft, the keeping of familiar spirits.

The keeping and nurturing of familiars in animal or human form became in England one of the decisive features of witchcraft. As Michael Dalton put it in his *The Countrey Justice* in 1618, witches ordinarily have a familiar or spirit 'which appears to them, sometimes in one shape, sometimes in another; as in the shape of a man, woman, boy, dog, cat, foal, hare, rat, toad, &c. And to these their spirits they give names.'[42] Witches paid a price for their familiars. They had to be fed bread, milk, animals – the witch's own blood. Thus the European Devil's mark was supplemented in England by the witch's mark – a super-numinary nipple or teat by which the English witch fed her familiars. Where European witches were demonic lovers, English witches were demonic mothers. Or perhaps rather, in the English context, the sexual, the maternal, and the demonic were complexly interwoven.[43] Thus, the European search for the sign of the demonic pact was transformed in England into the search for the place from which the familiar was nurtured by the witch's blood, and the meaning of the marks became fluid and ambiguous.

It is rather surprising that Scot, although being fully aware of these marks, made little of them. For quite detailed accounts of

Demonology

them were present in English texts from 1566. Thus, in that year, in the trial of Mother Agnes Waterhouse, the marks of the accused were examined at the request of the Queen's Attorney:

> Agnes Waterhouse when dyd thye Cat suck of thy bloud never saide she, no saide hee, let me se, and then the jayler lifted up her kercher on her heade and there was diverse spottes in her face & one on her nose, then sayde the quenes attorney, in good faith Agnes when dydde he sucke of thy bloud laste, by my faith my lorde sayde she, not this fortnyght.[44]

As we have seen already, Scot certainly knew that witches said that they kept 'divels and spirits in the likenesse of todes and cats.'[45] And the presence of familiars was a notable feature of the cases outlined in *A Rehearsall Both Straung and True* in 1579 and in the story of the witches of St. Osyth contained in *A True and Just Recorde, of the Information, Examination and Confession of all the Witches, taken at S.Oses* in 1582, with both of which texts, as we saw in the last chapter, he was familiar. Moreover, in several places the latter text refers to 'sucked spots'.[46] But neither Scot nor anyone else at this time had put together the European Devil's mark, insensitive to pain and incapable of bleeding, with the English witch's marks caused by her feeding of familiars.

Indeed, interestingly enough, the two ideas continued to run parallel for another hundred years. Thus, for example, in the 1697 edition of Michael Dalton's *The Countrey Justice*, judges were encouraged to look for both nipples and marks, the former evidence of their having familiar spirits, the latter of their having made a bargain with the Devil. The witch, he declared,

> [H]ath some big or little Teat upon their Body, and in some secret place, where he sucketh them. And besides their sucking, the Devil leaveth other marks upon their body, sometimes like a blew spot or red spot, like a flea-biting... And these the Devils marks be insensible and being pricked will not bleed, and

be often in their secretest parts, and therefore require careful and diligent search.[47]

Dalton's source for the passage above was Richard Bernard's 1627 *A Guide to Grand-Jury Men*. And Bernard, like Dalton, supported two different marks as evidence of witchcraft, one by 'sucking, or otherwise by the Devils touching,' though it was for him (in contrast to the European tradition), the sucking of blood by the Devil that sealed the Satanic pact, and (like Dalton) both kinds of marks were insensible to pain and did not bleed.[48]

Still, as early as 1612, in *The Witches of Northamptonshire*, the two marks had become one in an expansion of a passage from the *Daemonologie* of King James. In his work, James had remarked that there were two ways to assist in the trial of witches: the one was 'their fleeting [floating] on the water,' the other 'the finding of their mark, and the trying the insensibleness thereof.'[49] This was quite in keeping with the European tradition of the witch's mark, as we might expect from a Scottish king. But in *The Witches of Northamptonshire*, we read that there are two signs or tokens by which to detect and find witches, again 'their fleeting on the water', but this time 'the marke *where the Spirits sucke*, and by the trying of the insensibleness thereof.'[50]

This was a peculiarly English hybrid of the Devil's mark – both maternal and erotic. It was undoubtedly the consequence of the introduction of the European Devil's mark into England by a Scottish king, who as both James VI of Scotland and James I of England was something of a hybrid himself. But it was Reginald Scot who, some twelve years before the publication of the *Daemonologie*, told of the European Devil's mark to an English reading public, and he therefore holds the somewhat dubious honour of having been the first Englishman to do so.

As we would expect, Scot was having none of all this. The impossibility of it went to the core of Scot's argument, namely, that the bargain of the sort described by the demonologists

Demonology

assumed that which was impossible, that is, the corporeality of the Devil: 'That the joining of hands with the divell, the kissing of his bare buttocks, and his scratching and biting of them, are absurd lies; everie one having the gift of reason may plainlie perceive: in so much as it is manifest unto us by the word of God, that a spirit hath no flesh, bones, nor sinewes, whereof hands, buttocks, claws, teeth, and lips doo consist.'[51] But he also put forward a number of other arguments, all of which went to demonstrating that the Satanic pact could not but be false: there was no evidence for it in the Scriptures, the age of miracles was over, no reasons can count as good reasons for that which is beyond reason, the visible covenant with God made in the sacrament of baptism should be of more force than the invisible covenant with the Devil, and there was sheer folly in exchanging paltry profits on this side of the grave for eternal punishments in the fires of hell on the other.

Moreover, their confessions were not to be given credence. Their confessions were, after all, to impossible crimes. They were made by persons 'diseased both in bodie and mind, wilfullie made or injuriouslie constrained,'[52] and where made voluntarily, sometimes by those in search of their own destruction: 'so doo they also (I saie) confesse voluntarilie, that which no man could proove, and that which no man would ghesse, nor yet beleeve, except he were as mad as they; so as they bring death wilfullie upon themselves: which argueth an unsound mind.'[53]

Scot was aware too of accounts of the compact with the Devil and of the Sabbath by 'third parties'. And he recognised that these required an additional explanation. These accounts seemed less corrigible than those made by witches themselves, and they appeared on the face of it to be good evidence of the truth of the Satanic cult since they came from those of 'sound mind'. Discounting such as these was the purpose of the long account of the noble Gentlewoman of Lyons and the report of her adulterous lover that Scot drew from Bodin's *Démonomanie*, dramatised, and placed immediately before his disproof of the bargain and the Sabbath.

In Bodin, it served as one of three examples of 'magical' transportation to the Sabbath of the husbands or lovers of committed witches. The 'form' of the tale was the same in each case. The innocent partner of a witch was transported to the Sabbath after greasing his body with the witch's ointment and witnessed the Sabbath activities of witches and demons. During the course of the festivities the witch's husband or lover mentioned the word 'God', at which point all the company disappeared, and he was left naked and alone. After having found his way back home, each denounced his wife to the authorities who confessed to her crime.

In Bodin, it was to be found within the context of stories about whether witches (and their husbands or lovers) were *really* bodily transported to the Sabbath and not merely *apparently* so only in their imaginations. Scot's intention was to damage the credibility of such third person accounts. And to do so, he chose the only one of the three stories from Bodin that had an adulterous lover rather than a virtuous and pious husband. He did so in order to be able to critique the lover's credibility by virtue of his lack of virtue as the noblewoman's adulterous lover. 'There was,' wrote Scot,

> [A] noble Gentlewoman at *Lions*, that being in bed with a lover of hirs, suddenlie in the night arose up, and lighted a candle: which when she had done, she tooke a box of ointment, wherewith she anointed her bodie; and after a few words spoken, she was carried awaie. Hir bedfellow seeing the order hereof, lept out of his bed, tooke the candle in his hande, and sought for the ladie round about the chamber, and in everie corner thereof. But though he could not find hir, yet did he find hir box of ointment: and being desirous to know the vertue thereof, besmeared himselfe therewith, even as he perceived

hir to have done before. And although he were not so superstitious, as to use anie words to helpe him forwarde in his busines, yet by the virtue of that ointment (saith *Bodin*) he was immediatlie conveied to *Lorreine*, into the assemblie of witches. Which when he sawe, he was abashed, and said; In the name of God, what make I heere? And upon those words the whole assemblie vanished awaie, and left him there alone starke naked; and so was he faine to return to *Lions*.... But he had so good a conscience...that he accused his true lover for a witch, and caused hir to be burned. But as for his adulterie, neither *M .Mal* nor *Bodin* doo once so much as speake in the dispraise thereof.[54]

On Sabbatical Travels

Scot was never averse to turning Catholicism against itself and seeking justification for his arguments in Catholic sources. Thus, for example, in his first marginal note to Book three, chapter sixteen, in which he cited 'Authorities condemning the fantasticall confessions of witches', we can find him drawing our attention to an intellectual tradition of debate about the corporeal transportation of witches to the Sabbath that goes back to the twelfth-century *Liber de spiritu et anima* of pseudo-Augustine, Gratian's *Decretum* (*c.* AD 1140), and the tenth-century canon *Episcopi*, wrongly attributed to the Council of Ancyra held in 314.[55]

The canon *Episcopi* is the oldest source for the Western notion that witches 'flew' and that they gathered together by night to attend meetings. Its authority derived from its having been included in the mid-twelfth century in what was to become the most important collection of ecclesiastical law, namely Gratian's *Decretum*. And it appealed to Scot because, in contrast to the European notion of the witch that developed after AD 1400, it declared that the nocturnal travelling of women to the Sabbath was nothing but a dream or an illusion, and that the gatherings that followed were similarly imaginary. According to the canon *Episcopi*,

> It is also not to be omitted that some wicked women perverted by the devil, seduced by illusions and phantasms of demons, believe and profess themselves, in the hours of night, to ride upon certain beasts with Diana, the goddess of pagans, [or else with Herodias] and an innumerable multitude of women, and in the silence of the dead of night to traverse great spaces of earth, and to obey her commands as of their mistress, and to be summoned to her service on certain nights…. Wherefore the priests throughout their churches should preach with all insistence to the people that they may know this to be in every way false…. Whoever therefore believes that anything can be made, or that any creature can be changed to better or to worse or be transformed into another species or similitude, except by the Creator himself who made everything and through whom all things were made, is beyond doubt an infidel [and worse than a pagan].[56]

The above passage from the canon *Episcopi* is an abbreviated form of it. In this form, it mirrors Scot's version of it in Book three, chapter sixteen of *The Discoverie of Witchcraft* (which he drew from Gratian's *Decretum*). Scot omitted some sections of the canon *Episcopi* for reasons we will shortly see. Regardless of that, the passage in its original was to be a central problem for later demonologists who needed to justify the reality of the night flight (and the reality of the Sabbath) when canon law incorporating the canon viewed such nocturnal travel as illusory.

For this reason, in the form given by Scot, it certainly served his purposes well. For, on the one hand, it suggested that 'night riding' was illusory (and therefore false); and, on the other, it found the belief that certain beasts could be transformed by Diana to enable them to carry wicked women vast distances at high speeds, in breaching the doctrine of creation, was a form of idolatry. And Scot's argument was reinforced by the suggestion in the canon *Episcopi* that illusory dreams and visions could occur which have no supernatural cause at all.

In fact, in his rendering of the canon *Episcopi*, Scot omitted a passage which suggested that there could be experiences 'in the spirit' which were true because caused by God (such as the visions of Ezekiel). This did not serve his purposes at all. For, as we will see, with some notable exceptions, for Scot most experiences 'in the spirit' were not real. He had no place for 'true' visions. And he was even less well served by the reason given by the canon *Episcopi* for experiences 'in the spirit' that were false, namely, that they were caused by Satan. Thus, he omitted from his translation a long passage in the canon *Episcopi* which informs us that Satan himself 'when he has captured the mind of a miserable woman and has subjugated her to himself by infidelity and incredulity, immediately transforms himself into the species and similitudes of various personages and deluding the mind which he holds captive and exhibiting things, joyful or mournful, and persons, known or unknown, leads it through devious ways.'[57]

Be that as it may, Scot, like the Catholic demonologists, saw the clear implications of the canon *Episcopi*, namely, that if it were correct then *all their talk of assemblies and bargains was incredible*. It was a problem that the demonologists had exegetically to get around. Thus, Bartolomeo della Spina, for example, not only suggested that the Council of Ancyra was not authoritative but that, even if it were, the witches of his time differed so much from those described in the canon *Episcopi* that its description of flying women was not relevant to contemporary circumstances.[58] Scot was outraged describing him as a 'yoong beetle-head' who has 'made a new leaden beetle, to beate downe the councell, and to kill these old women.'[59]

The opinion of the canon *Episcopi*, that night flying was nothing but dreams and illusions, had been reinforced by a story from the *Vita Sancti Germani* (Life of St. Germain). Written by Constantius of Lyon sometime before AD 494, it was well known in the later medieval period as a consequence of its incorporation into one of the most popular works of the later medieval period, namely the *Golden Legend* of Jacobus de Voragine (*c*. AD 1228-1298). Among demonologists, it was known as a result of its inclusion in Johannes Nider's *Formicarius*, together with a condensed version of the canon *Episcopi* account, and the story of a woman who claimed to fly by night with Diana and other women but was decisively shown by a Dominican monk never to have left her bed.[60]

According to the *Golden Legend*, St. Germain, while visiting a house, is surprised to see the table being laid again. On asking why this was done, he was told that the table was prepared for certain good women who journeyed through the night. Germain stayed up to see who would turn up for the evening meal. He saw a troop of spirits enter in the form of men and women and inquired of his hosts if they knew these persons. They were identified as the neighbours (in Nider, the *female* neighbours) of the host. Germain forbade the spirits to leave, and made inquiries in the homes of the neighbours, all of whom were found sleeping in their beds. He then called upon the spirits to tell the truth, and they declared that they were demons who in this way sought to deceive men.[61]

There was another possibility raised by the *Malleus Maleficarum*, in response to the story from the *Life of St. Germain*: 'it was clearly possible for the demons to set themselves alongside their husbands as they slept, as if the women were sleeping with their husbands, during the intervening period of time when the search for the wives was being conducted.'[62] It was a possibility raised in another anecdote given in the *Malleus Maleficarum* concerning a woman from the village of Bühl, in the diocese of Basel, who had been arrested and burnt to ashes. For six years, we are told, she had an incubus demon impersonating her beside

Demonology

her husband as he slept. This occurred three times a week and on other holy nights while she was paying homage to the Devil.[63]

It is illuminating to see the way in which the *Malleus Maleficarum* dealt with the nest of issues surrounding these Sabbatical travels: the travel of witches to these Sabbaths in their physical bodies; the apparent travel of witches in visions, dreams, or imaginations; the capacity of demons to impersonate at feasts the innocent who were lying by night asleep in their beds; and, the capacity of demons to impersonate the witches at their feasts by replacing them in their beds at night.

The *Malleus Maleficarum*, in spite of the canon *Episcopi*, was strongly committed to the physical transportation of witches. It did so by melding together infanticide and Sabbatical travels. Witches made a paste from the limbs of children, especially those killed by them before baptism. Following the demon's instructions, they smeared it on a seat or a piece of wood. When this had been done, 'they are immediately carried into the air, whether by day or night, and visibly or (if they wish) invisibly.'[64] In some cases, rather than using ointments, the witch was transported by means of demons in the form of animals, at other times merely by the demon's invisible power.

But how was the *Malleus Maleficarum* to square this with the claim of the canon *Episcopi* that the women who believed that they physically flew by night were deluded by the Devil? It did so, like Bartolomeo della Spina, by distinguishing between the women described in the canon *Episcopi*, and real witches who committed crimes and had made a bargain with the Devil, and by claiming that the delusions of the former did not also apply to the latter: 'it is a false interpretation of the Canon when they wish to ascribe such imaginary transportations of bodies to the entire category of superstition and to all its varieties, so that *all sorceresses are transported only in the imagination* in the way that those women are.'[65]

Still, while the *Malleus Maleficarum* wanted to argue for the truth of the physical transportation of witches, and for the falsity of the imaginations of the women in the canon *Episcopi*, it wanted also to argue for the *truth* of the 'imaginary' mode of transformation in the case of witches. That is to say, like the canon *Episcopi* itself, it recognised the possibility of both true and false 'visions', of true and false experiences in the imagination. Thus, witches had 'true' experiences in their imaginations. 'The sorceresses,' it declared, 'are transported *both in body and in fantasy*'.[66] And it was motivated to do so by the confessions of witches. One of these witches, we read,

> was in the town of Breisach, and when asked whether they are able to be transported in fantasy and imagination or in body, she answered that they can in both ways. For if by chance they did not wish to be transported bodily but still wished to know everything that was being done by their associates at that gathering, then the method followed by them was that in the name of all the devils she would place herself on her left side propped up by her elbow, then there would come forth from her mouth something like a kind of grey steam, which would allow her to observe clearly the individual activities going on there.[67]

What is clear is that the relationship between the *Malleus Maleficarum* and the canon *Episcopi* is a complex one. On the one hand, we can discern a continuity between the flying women of the tenth-century canon and the Sabbatical travels of the witches of the fifteenth century. The *Malleus Maleficarum* combined the dreaming old women of the canon *Episcopi* with the Devil who caused their dreams to create witches committed to him. On the other hand, the discontinuities are just as striking, even more so. For the women of the canon served Diana rather than the Devil. They were the innocent victims of demonic machinations rather than active and voluntary participants in a Satanic cult. Most importantly, what the canon *Episcopi* held to be illusory, the *Malleus Maleficarum* took

Demonology

to be completely true. Indeed, as the *Malleus Maleficarum* saw it, there was nothing in common between the two groups of women. Only thus was it able to sustain the authority of canon law and its own commitment to the reality of Sabbatical travelling. The *Malleus Maleficarum* was, in short, committed to both the continuity and the discontinuity between itself and the canon *Episcopi*.

That the witches *truly* travelled to the Sabbath in their imaginations also enabled the *Malleus Maleficarum* to dispense with the problem discerned by St. Germain: that is, the apparent presence of witches in their beds while putatively elsewhere. And, in a piece of more than obscure casuistry, the *Malleus Maleficarum* also claimed that the possibility that demons impersonated women at the Sabbatical feasts, as St. Germain had supposed, was mentioned only so that no one would believe the impossibility of demons impersonating women in their beds.[68]

Perhaps not surprisingly, and probably wisely, Scot failed also to offer a systematic critique of the position of the *Malleus Maleficarum*. But we can nevertheless piece together the elements of his argument. First, Scot completely rejected the possibility of physical travel to the Sabbath. And he did so by invoking the authority of the Neapolitan natural magician Johannes Baptista Neapolitanus, more commonly known to us as Giambattista Della Porta (1535–1615). He was a physician and sceptic to whom Scot, as a supporter of natural magic, would have been attracted. For in his *Magiae Naturalis* (Of natural Magic) in 1558, he had denied the demonic origin of magic and presented it as the consummation of natural philosophy. In Book two, chapter twenty-six of this work, in a section entitled 'Lamiarum Unguenta' ('unguents of witches'), Della Porta reported on his experiment to test the belief that witches flew by covering themselves with an ointment.

Scot was no doubt influenced to seek out Della Porta's *Magiae Naturalis* from his reading of Johann Weyer's *De Praestigiis Daemonum*. For there, under the title of 'Ointments of the Lamiae and certain sleep-producing plants which greatly disturb the mind,' Weyer had given an account of Della Porta's experiment.⁶⁹ And he wouldn't have been discouraged by Bodin's description of Della Porta as a venomous magician.

Scot was no doubt delighted by Della Porta's experiment, and he translated it closely. After detailing Della Porta's two recipes for transportation, the one based on the fat of young children, the other on the blood of a flitter mouse, he gives us Della Porta's account of his experiment:

> Now (saith he) when I considered throughlie hereof, remaining doubtfull of the matter, there fell into my hands a witch, who of hir owne accord did promise me to fetch an errand out of hand from farre countries, and willed all them, whome I had brought to witnesse the matter, to depart out of the chamber. And when she had undressed hir selfe, and froted [rubbed] hir bodie with certeine ointments (which action we beheld through a chinke or little hole of the doore) she fell downe thorough the force of those soporiferous or sleepie ointments into a most sound and heavie sleepe: so as we did breake open the doore, and did beate hir exceedinglie; but the force of hir sleepe was suche, as it tooke awaie from hir the sense of feeling: and we departed for a time. Now when hir strength and powers were wearie and decaied, shee awooke of hir owne accord, and began to speake manie vaine and doting words, affirming that she had passed over both seas and mountains; delivering to us manie untrue and false reports; we earnestlie denied them, she impudentlie affirmed them.⁷⁰

Through Della Porta, Scot was able effectively to tie the use of ointments to journeys of the imagination rather than the body. And Della Porta was of help too in Scot's theory of the melancholic origins of Sabbatical travelling. He was able to suggest that, according to Della Porta, such imaginary journeys were false rather than

Demonology

true: 'This (saith he [Della Porta]) will not so come to passe with everie one, but onlie with old women that are melancholike, whose nature is extreame cold, and their evaporation small.'[71]

Thus, for Scot, Della Porta's account took care of both physical and imaginary Sabbatical travels. As for the story from the *Life of St. Germain* of demons impersonating women at Satanic feasts, Scot turned the argument of the *Malleus Maleficarum* on its head. In the *Malleus Maleficarum*, the story was introduced so that, granting it was possible for demons to impersonate women at Satanic feasts, no one would believe the impossibility of demons impersonating women in their beds. In *The Discoverie of Witchcraft*, although Scot declares it to be false, he argues that if it could be true that demons impersonated women at such feasts, it would make false all talk of Sabbaths and any forms of travel to them.

Scot was of course aware that the capacity of the Devil to transport persons to other physical locations had some important Biblical precedents, notably, in the Devil's carrying Jesus to the top of a high mountain or the pinnacle of the temple in order to tempt him (Mt. 4.5, 8; Lk. 4.5, 9).[72] And he was no doubt aware that Weyer had dealt with the issue in Book three, chapter twelve of his *De Praestigiis Daemonum*. On this issue, little help for Scot was to be found in Weyer. For Weyer himself had no problem with the notion that the Devil and his angels were not only able to transport men in their imaginations to far off places 'but also truly snatches up bodies and carries them through the air.'[73] And consequently, Weyer was able to affirm that Christ was physically transported by Satan. A virtuous God, declared Weyer, only permits Satan to do those things which he has decreed, in order to recall the virtuous or punish the impious. And allowing demons to transport witches to their assemblies was neither of these.

Scot tried his usual *reductio ad absurdum*. Surely, he asked, those demonologists who were supporting the physical transportation of witches on the grounds of that of Jesus were not suggesting 'that Christ had made anie ointments, or entred into anie league with the divell.'[74] More substantially, he turned to Calvin and his *A Harmony of the Gospels Matthew, Mark and Luke*. First published in 1555, it was translated into English in 1584 by the radical Puritan 'lame' Eusebius Paget (as he habitually called himself). This is no doubt the version that Scot used.

In his commentary on the temptations of Christ by the Devil, Calvin took up the issue of whether Christ was really lifted up to a pinnacle or whether this was done in a vision. Scot was right to seek support in Calvin, for the overall tenor of Calvin's position was that the lifting up of Christ by the Devil to the pinnacle of the temple, and more particularly, his showing of all the kingdoms of the earth to him, were more visionary than real. It should be noted though that Scot made more use of Calvin than he was strictly entitled to. For while Scot's declaration that 'So farre are the verie words of *Calvine*' was true,[75] he stopped his paraphrase of Calvin just short of Calvin's assertion that the matter was uncertain and that he would rather 'suspend my judgement, then geve the contentious occasion of quarelling.'[76] Neither here nor anywhere else does Calvin give us his opinion on Sabbatical travels. But it could be claimed on the basis of the above that he would have viewed them as imaginary, though whether truly, like the *Malleus Maleficarum*, or falsely so (like Scot) cannot be determined.

Night travelling was never a part of English witchcraft beliefs before Scot's *The Discoverie of Witchcraft*. In this case he was preaching to the unconverted. It never did become so, not I suspect as a consequence of anything Scot had written. Rather, even when elements of Continental witchcraft became part of English witchcraft in the seventeenth century, I am not aware of any case where Sabbatical travelling was part of the evidence entered or any confessions made. No doubt this was a consequence of the fact that King James in his *Daemonologie*, having one of his more complicated sceptical moments, maintained that the Devil created such dreams in the minds of witches, while simultaneously deluding others to believe that they have met them, and even committing the harm to men and beasts which these witches in their imaginative state believed that they had done.⁷⁷

Animal Transformations

As I have noted above, the canon *Episcopi* attests to the popular belief, in the tenth century, that there was a nocturnal society of women devoted to the goddess Diana who travelled great distances riding on the backs of beasts on certain nights to render her service on particular nights on her command. It was a belief that the canon rejected as illusory. But it was one that was demonologically transformed after AD 1400 to become the flying of witches to their meetings to worship the Devil.

The same can be said of the transformation of men into animals. The popular Classical and medieval belief that a person can transform himself or be transformed by another into an animal, often a wolf (lycanthropy), was demonologised into the capacity of the Devil to adopt an animal form, of witches to change themselves into animals empowered by the Devil, and of witches to turn people into animals. It was a belief that Scot described as 'this impossible, incredible, and supernaturall, or rather unnatural doctrine of transubstantiation.'⁷⁸ As in the case of Sabbatical travelling, he brought the authority of the canon *Episcopi* to bear upon it.⁷⁹ It was particularly Jean Bodin whom Scot had in his sights. And Scot began his discussion of such transformations in the first chapter of Book five with a number of stories drawn from the *Démonomanie* of Bodin: of werewolves eating people; of a werewolf who, having had his wolf's feet cut off, became a man without hands or feet; and, of witches who transformed themselves into wolves to devour men, women, and cattle, or into cats who both committed and received much hurt.

But for his exemplary story of the transformation of a man into an ass by a witch, Scot drew upon the *Malleus Maleficarum*. It was a story that enabled him not only to ridicule the demonological tradition of transformations, but also to question that most famous of transformations found in *The Golden Ass* of Apuleius (late second century AD).

According to the account in the *Malleus Maleficarum*, a ship disembarked travellers in the city of Famagusta in the Kingdom of Cyprus. One of these, a young man,[80] went to a woman's house to see if she had any eggs for sale. Believing that he would not be missed, she gave him the eggs, and told him to return were he to miss his ship. Before embarking, he ate the eggs and shortly thereafter became mute and virtually senseless. When he tried to board his ship, he was beaten off with sticks by people shouting, 'look, look, what's up with the donkey?' He began to think that he had been bewitched for, although he could not speak, he could understand others. He returned to the house of the woman, and served at her beck and call for more than three years, where he was thought of by all except the witch and her colleagues to be an animal.

One day, in his fourth year, he entered the city before noon, and passed a church in which Divine Service was being held. Not daring to go in, at the point in the Mass when the Sacrament was elevated, he placed his rear knees and lower legs on the ground and joining his front feet together, raised them up. When certain merchants from Genoa saw this, in astonishment they followed the donkey. Shortly afterwards, they saw it being beaten by the witch. Suspecting sorcery, they had her and the donkey taken into custody. After being questioned under torture, she confessed the crime and promised that she would restore the youth to his true form. After she had done so, however, she was again arrested, and punished for the crimes she had committed.[81]

Scot failed here to make any distinction between the relative positions of Bodin and the *Malleus Maleficarum* on this matter. Indeed he went as far as to suggest that Bodin and the *Malleus Maleficarum* agree on physical transformation. In fact, while Bodin strongly argues for the reality of the transformation of humans into animals, the *Malleus Maleficarum* argues only for the demonically created illusion of it.[82] In the *Malleus Maleficarum*, in the case of the young traveller, those around him were tricked by Satan into seeing him as an animal. He too seemed, to himself, to be an animal, at least in his 'imagination and faculty of estimation, which are attached to bodily organs, and not in his reason, which was not hobbled by God so that he would not understand he was a human.'[83] Scot, not unexpectedly, opposed both the arguments of Bodin and the *Malleus Maleficarum*; but, in order to do so effectively, he needed to get around the authority of Augustine.

In *The City of God,* Augustine told a number of stories about the transformation of humans into animals. Among these was one that Augustine had heard in Italy of landladies who were in the habit of giving drugs in cheese to travellers by which means they were turned into pack animals on the spot. They were used to carry commodities of all kinds, until such time as having finished their labours, they were returned to their usual form. Like Apuleius in *The Golden Ass*, Augustine informs us, though they were in the bodily form of animals, their minds remained human and rational throughout.

Augustine was heir to a Classical tradition in which the boundaries between species were permeable and fluid. But he was also heir to a Christian tradition that believed in the separation of species as ordained by God and the qualitative uniqueness of the human, made as it was in the image of God. As Ambrose put it in the fourth century, 'those made after the likeness and image of God cannot be changed into the form of beasts.'[84]

Augustine believed that these stories of transformation of humans into animals were either untrue or so extraordinary that belief in them should be withheld, although he recognised that it was within the power of God to effect such changes if he wished. Beyond that, however, Augustine would not go. Thus, he rejected the possibility of demons transforming human beings into animals. If they do perform any such feats, he wrote, 'it is merely in respect of appearance that they transform beings created by the true God, to make them seem to be what they are not.'[85] What people experienced, therefore, was either an illusion produced by demons in the imagination, or a phantom double of the imagination made by them and corporeally presented to others. Augustine's remained the dominant view. It was reinforced and refined by Aquinas,[86] whence into the *Malleus Maleficarum*, the position of which was essentially that of Augustine. Most demonologists were not inclined to disagree.[87]

It was not a solution that Scot was willing to endorse. For Scot believed that Augustine gave these stories more credence than he should have, even going so far as to suggest that they may be interpolations by 'some fond papist or witchmonger.'[88] And, on the principle of 'set a witchmonger to catch a witchmonger', he cited the French Calvinist demonologist, Lambert Daneau, as a denier of that which 'S. *Augustine* and *Apuleus* doe credibly wryte,' namely 'that Sorcerers can chaunge men into other formes & shapes, ye is to wit, into wolves, Beares, & Asses.'[89] In fact, Scot was very selectively referencing Daneau on this issue, for Daneau was a firm supporter of the Augustinian position and it is clear that Scot had read the relevant section of Daneau.[90] Still, although Scot cannot bring himself to accept Augustine's account, he did recognise that it counted against Bodin's theory of physical transformation.

Against the possibility of the transformation of humans into animals, Scot mounted several theological arguments. The first of these went to the fixity of species after the day of creation. Quite simply, 'God hath endued everie man and everie thing with his proper nature, substance, forme, qualities and gifts, and directeth their waies…. And therefore it is absolutelie against the ordinance of God (who hath made me a man) that I should flie like a bird, or swim like a fish, or creepe like a worme, or become an asse in shape.'[91] And he had no sympathy for views that, drawing on the Aristotelian distinction between substance and accidents, and the doctrine of transubstantiation, made distinctions between the transformation of the accidents of the human

Demonology

into the animal and the preservation of the substance of the individual – the ratio or reason. Not surprisingly he was as critical of the Catholic doctrine of the transubstantiation of bread and wine into body and blood in the Mass as he was the transformation of men into animals.

His assertion of the doctrine of the fixity of species was reinforced too by that of the qualitative uniqueness of the human, both in body and soul. 'What a beastlie assertion is it, that a man, whom GOD hath made according to his owne similitude and likeness, should be by a witch turned into a beast? What an impietie is it to affirme, that an asses bodie is the temple of the Holy-ghost? Or an asse to be the childe of God, and God to be his father; as it is said of man.'[92] And he strongly hinted at that somewhat anthropological reading of the nature of man, developed by Aristotle, expressed by Ovid in his *Metamorphoses*, and affirmed by both Augustine and Aquinas, that saw man's upright stature in contrast to the beasts as indicative, not only of his qualitative distinction from the animals, but also of his capacity to look upwards to the divine original, in whose image he was made.[93]

Scot's arguments were buttressed by any number of Biblical quotations. But Bodin, too, had a Biblical precedent for his account of real and not just illusory transformations. This was the story in the Old Testament book of *Daniel* of King Nebuchadnezzar's apparent transformation into a beast.[94] According to this, for his pride, Nebuchadnezzar was driven from the company of humans, and dwelt among the beasts of the field where he ate grass like an ox. The audience at Shakespeare's *All's Well That Ends Well* would have picked up the Biblical allusion in 'I am no great Nebuchadnezzar, sir, I have not much skill in eating grass' (4.5, 20-1). In the history of the interpretation of this verse, Nebuchadnezzar was the type of the descent into madness.[95] Still, for those few demonologists who argued for the real physical transformation of humans into animals, and Scot's nemesis Bodin was one, Nebuchadnezzar was the Biblical archetype.

103

Scot read *Daniel* as quite simply declaring that Nebuchadnezzar merely lived as if he were a beast, rather than having been transformed into one. And, as all appeared to agree, it had nothing to do with the actions of demons or witches. This reading was of a piece with Scot's tendency to find metaphor in the Bible where the literal was impossible. Scot does not appear to accept the reading of Nebuchadnezzar as a mad man. Nevertheless, as for those who did think themselves to be wolves or other animals, Scot was again able to provide a unified account by looking to melancholy as the cause of their delusions. And it was in Weyer that he found his explanation. 'For *Lycanthropia*, he wrote, 'is of the ancient physicians called *Lupina melancholia*, or *Lupina insania*. J.Wierus declareth verie learnedlie the cause, the circumstance, and the cure of this disease.'[96] This was one of those few points on which Weyer, Scot, and King James were agreed. James took it to have been produced by 'a naturall super-abundance of Melancholie, which as wee reade, hath made some thinke themselves Pitchers, and some horses, and some one kind of beast or other.'[97] And like Weyer, but unlike Scot, he saw Nebuchadnezzar as a madman.[98]

Sex and the Devil

At the end of Book three of *The Discoverie of Witchcraft*, somewhat in the manner of a modern television network warning its viewers of 'adults only' material coming up, Scot advised those of his readers 'whose chaste eares cannot well endure to heare of such abhominable lecheries as are gathered out of the bookes of those witchmongers' to pass over the first eight chapters of the following Book.[99] For it is in these eight chapters that Scot ridiculed the demonologists' accounts of sex with the Devil, of impotence caused by witches, of penis stealing, and told his stories of bawdy priests and lecherous monks.

The *Malleus Maleficarum* was Scot's key source for his account of sex with the Devil and demonic impotence, and the first four

Demonology

chapters of Book four in *The Discoverie of Witchcraft* summarised the relevant parts of this work.[100] Or at least it should be said, Scot paraphrased the more salacious parts, ignoring for the most part the extensive metaphysical discussions of the *Malleus Maleficarum* in which the teachings of Aquinas on demonic reality were adapted and refined. Scot's strategic intention is reasonably clear. For the recitation of the details without the metaphysics drives the reader towards the inevitable conclusion that this could not not be false.

Having informed his readers of the claim of the *Malleus Maleficarum* that demons assume 'virtual' bodies in all their interactions with humans, Scot began his account of 'bawdie Incubus and Succubus' by distinguishing the activities of incubi before AD 1400 when they ravished women against their will and after AD 1400 when witches consented willingly to their desires. It is a distinction that he attributed in a marginal note to Johannes Nider in his *Formicarius* and to the thirteenth century Dominican theologian Thomas of Brabant (Thomas of Cantimpré) and his *Bonum universale de apibus* (The Universal Good of Bees). In fact, it is a distinction that he drew straight from the *Malleus Maleficarum*,[101] and one which was there proved by the confessions of witches themselves that they were not innocent victims, but willing collaborators with the Devil in sexual activities.

Scot himself made nothing of this distinction. But he did recognize that, according to the *Malleus Maleficarum*, witchcraft originated in demonic sex. The *Malleus Maleficarum* affirms, he wrote,

> [T]hat All witches take their beginning from such filthie actions, wherein the divell, in likenes of a prettie wench, lieth prostitute as *Succubus* to the man, and reteining his nature and seede, conveieth it unto the witch, to whome he delivereth it as *Incubus*... M. Mal saith, There can be rendred no infallible rule, though a probable distinction may be set downe, whether *Incubus* in the act of venerie doo alwaies powre

[pour] seed out of his assumed bodie. And this is the distinction; Either she is old and barren or yoong and [capable of being] pregnant. If she be barren, then dooth *Incubus* use hir without decision of seed; bicause such seed should serve for no purpose. And the divell avoideth superfluitie as much as he may; and yet for hir pleasure and condemnation togither, he goeth to worke with hir.[102]

And Scot went on to summarise the claim of the *Malleus Maleficarum* that semen is not gathered from that which is shed in dreams since its procreative power is less than that gathered during the carnal act itself. He repeated the remark that older witches were sworn to procure as many young virgins for incubus as possible.

To a significant extent, Scot was content to let the *Malleus Maleficarum* speak for itself with little commentary. Omitting a rather 'dull' section from the *Malleus Maleficarum* on the times and places which the Devil preferred for his carnal acts, Scot returned to it with a discussion of the visibility of the demon during demonic sex to the witch and his invisibility to the onlooker, except on occasions to a cuckolded husband. The proof of this, at least for the authors of the *Malleus Maleficarum*, wrote Scot, was that:

> Manie times witches are seene in the fields, and woods, prostituting themselves uncovered and naked up to the navill, wagging and mooving their members in everie part, according to the disposition of one being about that act of concupiscence, and yet nothing seene of the beholders upon hir; saving that after such a convenient time as is required about such a peece of worke, a blacke vapor of the length and bignesse of a man, hath beene seene as it were to depart from hir, and to ascend from that place.[103]

The pleasure and delight gained from sex with the Devil was, according to Scot, greater than that with any mortal man (though the *Malleus Maleficarum* makes it only, all other things being equal, no less so).

Scot's selectivity with respect to the *Malleus Maleficarum* is most clearly in evidence in his discussion of the methods by which witches impeded the force of procreation. He showed no interest in the stories in the *Malleus Maleficarum* that dealt with the use of sorcery to inflict barrenness on the inhabitants of a certain house, nor with its use to bring about miscarriages. Rather, he gave an outline of one story from the *Malleus Maleficarum* concerning the inability of a young man so afflicted by sorcery that he was unable to have sex with more than one woman. Scot turned this into a story about the licentiousness of the clergy by turning the young man into 'a young Priest'.[104] His remaining three stories from the *Malleus Maleficarum* focused on penis stealing and retrieval through the power of witchcraft.

In the first of these, a young man in Ravensburg who had had sex with a woman in the town lost his 'instruments of venerie' as a result of witchcraft such that 'in that place nothing could be seene or felt but his plaine bodie.' He was sent by another witch to the one he suspected of bewitching him to persuade her to restore his penis. When she refused, he began to strangle her with a towel saying, 'Restore me my toole, or thou shalt die for it.' Swollen and black in the face, she agreed. While he was loosening the towel, she put her hand into his codpiece and touched the place saying 'Now hast thou thy desire,' and he felt himself at that moment restored.

The second story is not dissimilar. A friar from Speyer reported that a young man had confessed to him the loss of his penis. The incredulous priest made the young man undress and saw the complaint to be true. He advised the young man to go to the witch whom he suspected and to entreat her to restore his penis to him. The witch did so, and the young man returned to the priest to show his gratitude. Making him pull down his breeches, the priest verified the truth of this visually.

The original of the third of these stories is clearly a medieval joke about the lasciviousness of priests, though it is not a joke that the *Malleus Maleficarum* gets. Scot thought such stories were laughable, although these were for him no jests. For they were written by judges who made decisions for life or death on them. According to Scot's version, a young man whose penis had been stolen,

> Went to a witch for the restitution thereof, who brought him to a tree, where she shewed him a nest, and bade him clime up and take it. And being in the top of the tree, he tooke out a mightie great one, and shewed the same to hir, asking hir if he might not have the same. Naie (quoth she) that is our parish preests toole, but take anie other which thou wilt.[105]

These stories, as they are presented in the *Malleus Maleficarum* and in Scot, clearly relate to acts of *maleficium* by witches without any obvious involvement of the Devil. And all three of them suggest that the penises had been physically removed. But it is clear from the *Malleus Maleficarum* that Kramer read them as involving both witches and demons. The compact of witches and demons was always the focus of the *Malleus Maleficarum*'s interests. It is clear too that the *Malleus Maleficarum*, and Scot was aware of it, did not believe that penises were literally stolen by witches. Rather, the first two of the above stories demonstrate that they were merely concealed by an act of conjuring carried out by demons. '[I]t should in no way be believed,' declared the *Malleus Maleficarum*, 'that such members are torn out of or separated from the body. Instead, they are hidden by the demon through the art of conjuring, so that they can be neither seen nor touched.'[106] Thus was the Devil able to make that which was really there appear to be invisible. The position of the *Malleus Maleficarum* here is consistent with its position on transformation of humans into animals. In that case too, the Devil was able to make things appear other than what they truly were. Invisibility is the limiting case of this.

Demonology

Can the Devil make that which was not really there appear to be visible? The story of the nest penises demonstrated just this: 'The pronouncement is that all this clearly happened through an illusion of conjuring carried out by demons in the ways mentioned above, the demons throwing the organs of sight into confusion by shifting pictures of perception to the faculty of the imagination.'[107]

These are demonological subtleties in which Scot was not particularly interested. He was more interested in his having caught out the *Malleus Maleficarum* in what he thought was a contradiction, namely, that the authors believed that penis stealing was both illusory *and* real. 'If a witch deprive one of his privities, it is done onlie by prestigious meanes, so as the senses are but illuded. Marie [marry] by the divell, it is reallie taken awaie, and in like restored.'[108] No doubt Scot has discerned one of the more puzzling aspects of the *Malleus Maleficarum*'s account of penis stealing. The position of the *Malleus Maleficarum* on penis stealing when both demons and sorceresses were involved is consistent: It is a demonically created illusion. But the *Malleus Maleficarum* concluded its discussion of this topic by asking if there was any difference in the removal in the case where the demon had taken away the male member by himself, without the cooperation of a sorceress. The answer given by the *Malleus Maleficarum*, which Scot has clearly picked up on, was as follows: 'in a situation where he has taken away a member by himself, he would really and truly take it away and would really and truly restore it whenever he has to restore it.'[109] The *Malleus Maleficarum* went on to make it perfectly clear that, unless forced to by a good angel, there were no circumstances in which the Devil would prefer to work alone rather than through sorceresses. But the question remains why the author of the *Malleus Maleficarum* felt the need to argue for the Devil's power *really* to do so.

The answer to this goes to the distinction that the *Malleus Maleficarum* makes between the different modes in which demons interact with humans. In the case of demonically created illusions, demons can enter our bodies and work on our imaginations:

> For instance, from the memory which is in the back part of the head, a demon brings forth a picture of a horse by moving in location an image of the fantasy up to the middle part of the head, where the compartment for the force of the imagination is, and then in sequence up to the common sense of perception, whose seat is in the front part of the head. They can so suddenly change everything and throw it into confusion, that such forms are necessarily considered in the estimation to be the same as if they were being shown to the external vision.[110]

Thus, in the case of the nest of penises, it would be a mistake to claim that 'in members assumed in this way there are demons showing themselves, in the way that in assumed bodies made from air they regularly appear to sorceresses and sometimes to other humans, and interact with them.'[111] And, by the same token, it would also be a mistake to claim that, when witches thought that the demons were present in assumed bodies, they were really only dealing with illusions of the imagination. And the text went on to explain why it was necessary for the Devil, on occasion, to do more than create illusions and to appear in an assumed body. '[I]t should be said,' we read,

> [T]hat if the demon wished to show nothing grander than the mere presence of a human effigy, then there would certainly be no need for him to appear in an assumed body, since he could achieve this well enough through the change mentioned above [of images in the head]. As it is, because he has grander activities to carry out (for example, speaking, eating, and also engaging in filthy acts), it is necessary that he should in fact be present, actually offering himself to the vision from the outside in an assumed body.[112]

In short, the *Malleus Maleficarum* strategically located itself in the space between demonically created illusions and the real activities of demons in their assumed bodies, the mode of the activity of the demons being context dependent.

In this space, the reality of the spirit world and its interactions with the human could never have come into doubt. And the issue of such interactions being *solely* the products of the imagination could not have arisen. But for Scot, for whom there is no possibility of corporeal interactions between spirits and persons of any sort, they can only be illusory – the result, not of demonic activity, but of disease:

> But in truth, this *Incubus* is a bodilie disease... although it extend unto the trouble of the mind: which of some is called The mare, oppressing manie in their sleepe so sore, as they are not able to call for helpe, or stir themselves under the burthen of that heavie humor, which is ingendred of a thicke vapor proceeding from the cruditie and rawnesse in the stomach: which ascending up into the head oppresseth the braine, in so much as manie are much infeebled thereby, as being nightlie haunted therewith.[113]

Here, Scot was drawing on another parallel tradition of the incubus or *mara* in early modern thought, one which went back to Galen. According to this, the experience of being spiritually attacked was a nightmare caused by an imbalance in the humours. As the Swiss minister, Ludwig Lavater, succinctly put it, '*Incubi & Succubi*, (which we call Maares), are night spirits or rather Divels, which leape upon men in their sleepe. The Physicians do affirme, that these are nothing else but a disease.' It is a disease of the stomach, he later wrote, in which sufferers 'imagine that a man of monstrous stature sitteth on them, which with his hands violently stoppeth their mouth, that they can by no meanes cry out, and they strive with their hands and armes to drive him awaie, but all in vain.'[114]

For his exemplary medical diagnosis, Scot related a story told in the *De Cerebri Morbis* (1549) of Jason Pratensis which he had, in fact, derived from Weyer's *De Praestigiis Daemonum*.[115] According to this, a priest came to Jason complaining vehemently of his ill health, as evidenced by his being reduced to 'a verie ghost consisting of skinne and bone. &c.' Almost every night, he continued, there came to him an unknown woman, who lay so heavily upon his breast that he couldn't catch his breath, nor could he cry out, nor throw her off him. Jason told him that he was vexed with a disease called incubus or the mare, and the rest was fantasy and imagination. The priest, unconvinced by this diagnosis, told Jason that he had sought help from a friar, but that his remedy of prayer was of no use. Then, advised by a cunning woman that he was being molested by a witch, he followed her suggestion that he 'should pisse, and immediately should cover the pispot...and before night the witch should come to visit me.' Soon after, a witch came to his house, but he was unable to persuade her to cease molesting him at night. Eventually, after three or four meetings, Jason was able to persuade the priest of his disease and eventually recovered.[116]

Even Scot appeared unconvinced by this account. As Scot knew, 'the mare' was about suffocation and paralysis. The medical reading did little to explain the sexuality inherent in the demonological narratives of incubi and succubi. Thus he had to weave into his account another explanation.

This went to the invention of incubi and succubi by the clergy to excuse their lechery. It was illuminated by a story about St. Sylvanus, Bishop of Nazareth, which Scot had found in the *Malleus Maleficarum*.[117] There, it occurred in a section devoted to the discussion of how demons can injure reputations. According to this, the Devil began to woo a noblewoman in bed at night and to entice her verbally to debauchery, before sexually assaulting her. When she shouted out, the Devil hid under her bed in the guise of Bishop Sylvanus. When he was discovered there, he lied that he was Bishop Sylvanus. The next morning, after the Devil had disappeared, 'the holy man suffered a very serious loss to his reputation.' His disgrace was only cleared up when the Devil, in a demoniac's body, confessed to his impersonation at the tomb of St. Jerome.[118] Scot inverted the story. The demon pretending to be St. Sylvanus was, in reality, the Bishop pretending to be the Devil. 'Oh excellent peece of witchcraft or cousening wrought by Sylvanus,' he declared.[119]

Scot had also read in the Flemish Protestant theologian Andreas Hyperius that Merlin the magician was begotten without carnal copulation. His source was Hyperius' 1563 *Methodi Theologiae* (Methods of Theology).[120] Such stories, he believed, were mere inventions to excuse the lechery of idle priests and bawdy monks and 'to cover the shame of their lovers and concubines.'[121] But he knew too that such stories had a Biblical source in Genesis 6.4: 'There were giants on the earth in those days; for after the sons of God [filii dei] came in unto the daughters of men, and they bare children to them; these are the mighty men which were of old, men of renown.'

The division in the history of the interpretation of this verse depended on the reading of 'sons of God' as angels (or demons) or humans ('the sons of Seth').[122] Augustine, in *The City of God*, had favoured the latter reading.[123] In spite of the dominance of the Augustinian reading within the history of the Christian interpretation of this verse, there was a flirtation with a demonological reading. Aquinas had accepted the Augustinian reading of 'the sons of God' as referring to humans. But his account of demonic gender switching and semen stealing opened up the possibility of a demonic role in the production of Biblical giants, regardless of the human nature of the 'sons of God.' On the basis of the capacity of demons to know the virtues of the semen of the donor male and of the recipient of it, and in the light of the giants of Genesis 6.4, Aquinas argued that it was possible that children born as a consequence of demonic intervention might be more powerful or larger (*maioris virtutis*) than other men.[124]

These were arguments seized upon by the *Malleus Maleficarum* to reassert the authority of Genesis 6.4 in the case for reading procreation with the assistance of 'incubi'. And to these arguments, the *Malleus Maleficarum* added, not only the authority of Aristotle's claim that that which seems true to many cannot be false, but also 'the deeds and words of sorceresses who really and truly carry out such acts.'[125] Kramer repeated Aquinas's claim that, on the basis of Genesis 6. 4 and the 'know how' of the Devil, those begotten in this way are strong and large in body, and he added that in such sexual acts was the origin of witches.[126]

Scot stood in the tradition of reading 'the sons of God' as a reference solely to humans. He poked fun at both Aquinas and the *Malleus Maleficarum* for their demonological account of giants.[127] Among the early Fathers he looked for support to John Chrysostom, who read 'the sons of God' as 'the sons of Seth' and rejected the reading of 'angels'.[128] But it was to his contemporary, the Protestant Andreas Hyperius, that he turned to conclude that there was no scriptural evidence to support the intervention of incubi or succubi in the account in Genesis 6.4.[129]

Witchcraft, as constructed by the demonologists, was ultimately dependent on the establishment of the corporeality of demons and the possibility of their corporeal interaction with humans. Sex with the Devil was the ultimate form of such interaction. And it was here that Scot's key argument against the demonology of sex was to be found. Scot opposed demonology with physiology. Sex was only possible among beings essentially corporeal. Spirits were, by nature, incorporeal and, therefore, incapable of the desires of the flesh: 'Item, where the genitall members want, there can be no lust of the flesh: neither dooth nature give anie desire of generation, where there is no propagation or succession required. And as spirits cannot be greeved with hunger, so can they not be inflamed with lusts.'[130]

Scot paid no attention to the complex arguments by which the *Malleus Maleficarum* attempted to explain how demons can, in their assumed bodies, be said to speak to, see, hear, eat with, and have sex with sorceresses.[131] Its claim that while angels in assumed bodies could both chew and swallow food they were unable to digest and expel it, but possessed 'a power by which food is immediately broken up into the previously existing matter' must have stretched the credulity of even the most sympathetic reader.[132] Scot was certainly not one of these. We may nonetheless discern a critical echo of the *Malleus Maleficarum* in Scot's declaration that a spirit 'neither dooth eate nor drinke.'[133] For him, spirits that ate and drank were the stuff of outdated superstition and fairy tales. And he was covinced that, in times to come, the belief in witches and walking spirits would be as derided and condemned as was that in Robin Good-fellow and Hob goblin in his:[134]

> In deede your grandams maides were woont to set a boll of milke before him [incubus] and his cousine Robin good-fellow, for grinding of malt or mustard, and sweeping the house at midnight: and you have also heard that he would chafe exceedingly, if the maid or good-wife of the house, having compassion of his nakednes, laid anie clothes for him, beside his messe of white bread and milke, which was his standing fee. For in that case he saith; What have we here? Hemton hamten, here I never more will tread nor stampen.[135]

Although aware of the demonological account of semen stealing and gender switching, at this point in his argument Scot ignored it. Rather, his rhetorical strategy was to restrict all talk of generation and conception to physiological processes in real and not assumed bodies. Thus, within his critique of the capacity of incubi to procreate, there lay a Galenic account of conception. According to this, blood flows from the liver into the heart where it is highly energised by vital spirits produced by the heart from air in the lungs. This highly energised blood is transformed into semen when it reaches the testicles. Without blood, heart, and spirits, conception is impossible. Thus Scot: 'But the power of generation consisteth not onlie in members [externa organa], but chieflie of vitall spirits, and of the hart: which spirits are never in such a bodie as *Incubus* hath, being but a bodie assumed, as they themselves saie.'[136]

At the end of the day, of course, Scot rejected all talk of assumed bodies, and thus all possibility of demonic interaction with humans. The essential incorporeality of spirits entailed the impossibility in principle of their interaction with humans. And with that, the whole edifice of witchcraft and demonology – the pact with the Devil, the Sabbath and magical transportation to it, transformation into the form of animals, and sex with the Devil – collapsed.

CHAPTER FOUR

Magic

Poisons and Potions

'CHASAPH, being an Hebrue word, is Latined *Veneficium*, and is in English, poisoning, or witchcraft.'[1]

Scot was writing for a Protestant audience, one for whom the doctrine of *Sola Scriptura* was a key one. Thus, a core strategy of *The Discoverie of Witchcraft* was to demonstrate that the witchcraft constructed by the demonologists had no Biblical authority. In the broadest terms, therefore, Scot was intent on showing that such witchcraft as was mentioned in the biblical texts had no connection with the Devil or demons. For him, it could be explained completely without invoking the realm of spirits, the result of 'this-worldly' activities alone. So Scot's aim was to demonstrate that those terms in the Hebrew Bible that could be read as referring to witchcraft had to be read as solely to do either with poisoning, conjuring, or cousening and not as invoking the spiritual realm.

Thus, in Books six to sixteen of *The Discoverie of Witchcraft*, Scot read all magic and witchcraft in terms of four broad Biblical categories: magicians, poisoners, diviners, and enchanters. As I noted in chapter one, this analysis was derived from Weyer, although Scot collapsed Weyer's nine categories into four:

> The first were *Praestigiatores Pharaonis*, which (as all divines, both Hebrues and others conclude) were

but cousenors and jugglers, deceiving the kings eies with illusions and sleights; and making false things to appear as true: which nevertheles our witches cannot doo. The second is *Mecasapha*, which is she that destroieth with poison. The third are such as use sundrie kinds of divinations, and hereunto perteine these words, *Kasam, Onen, Ob, Idoni*. The fourth is *Habar*, to wit: when magicians, or rather such, as would be reputed cunning therein, mumble certeine secret words, wherin is thought to be great efficacie.[2]

Scot devoted Book six to an exposition of poisoning witches under the heading of 'Chasaph'. He did not deny that there were in ancient Israel such witches 'which did much hurt among the children of Israel.'[3] But he nonetheless collapsed the category of *veneficia* (poisoners) into that of the deluding or cousening witch. Thus, he wrote, 'I will not denie that there remaine such until this daie, bewitching men, and making them beleeve, that by virtue of words, and certain ceremonies, they bring to pass such mischeefes, and intoxications, as they indeed accomplish by poisons.'[4]

But, if the *veneficiae* were nothing but a form of the deluding or cousening witch, why were they so singled out by Scot? The answer lies in his discussion of Exodus 22.18. This was the key Biblical text to justify capital punishment for the crime of witchcraft. Almost all of the English versions of the Bible prior to *The Discoverie* had translated this verse: 'Thou shalt not suffer a witch to live'. So Scot was (almost) correct in his claim that 'in all our English translations, *Chasaph* is translated, witchcraft.'[5] But he argued that the more appropriate translation from the Hebrew was not 'witch' but rather 'poisoner'. It was a reading that he derived from the Greek translation of the Old Testament, the Septuagint.[6] And he looked for support to the following passage of *The Antiquities of the Jews* by Josephus (*c.* AD 37–*c.* 100): 'Let no one of the Israelites keep any poison that may cause death, or any other harm; but if he be caught with it, let him be put to death, and suffer the very same mischief that he would have brought upon them for whom the poison was prepared.'[7]

Poisoners they may have been, but he also accepted that they often tricked others into thinking that they achieved their results by their supernatural powers rather than by poison.[8] Thus, they were doubly guilty, not only for committing the crime of murder, but for blasphemy: 'they make men beleeve they do them [miracles], and thereby cousen the people, and take upon them the office of God, and therewithal also blaspheme his holie name, and take it in vaine.'[9] As both murderers and blasphemers, Scot had little mercy for the poisoners and was not opposed to the death sentence for them: '[U]nder this one sentence (Thou shalt not suffer a poisoner or a witch to live),' he concluded, 'is forbidden both murther and witchcraft; the murther consisting in poison; the witchcraft in cousenage or blasphemie.'[10] As for the other key Biblical passage which seemed to recognise the existence of witches who dealt with demons (diviners, observers of times, enchanters, witches, necromancers, charmers, consulters with familiar spirits, wizards), namely Deuteronomy 18.10-11, 'these were all couseners, everie one abusing the people in his severall kind; and are accurssed of God.'[11]

The principal form of poisoning, though presumably accidental, consisted for Scot in 'love cups', potions intended to procure love, but more often, he claimed, leading to insanity and death. This was not surprising considering the ingredients in the long list that Scot gives. These consisted of the tail and penis of a wolf, brains of cats and lizards, the bones of a frog devoured in an antheap, the garments of the dead, candles burnt before a corpse, needles used to sew the dead in their winding sheets, and so on.[12] It was all lies and old wives' tales, he declared.

Be that as it may, Scot was in no doubt that poisoning, accompanied by cousening or not, was a most heinous crime, more wicked, more dangerous, and more vile than any other. For it was a crime that turned the social and, more particularly, the domestic order upside down:

> [T]he strong cannot avoid the weake, the wise cannot prevent the foolish, the godlie cannot be preserved from the hands of the wicked; children maie hereby kill their parents, the servant the master, the wife hir husband, so privilie, so inevitablie, and so incurablie, that of all other it hath beene thought the most odious kind of murther.[13]

Scot illuminated the category of 'poisoners' with stories that he drew from Weyer. Only one of these concerned a male poisoner, a butcher from Wittenberg, whose main trade was retrieving the carcases of dead animals that had starved to death. He accelerated his supply lines by poisoning the animals and had grown rich as a result. Eventually arrested, he confessed to his crimes and was put to death with hot tongs by which the flesh was torn from his bones. In keeping with his sympathy for the underclasses, Scot remarked that 'We for our parts would have killed five poore women, before we would suspect one rich butcher.'[14]

And yet, in spite of his criticism of English justice and his sympathy for poor women, Scot selected from Weyer one story which dealt with one hundred and seventy women in Rome executed for murder by poison. And he changed Weyer's story of forty men and women executed for plague-spreading to forty women ('"Veneficiae" or witches').[15] Scot certainly gives the appearance that the vast majority of poisoners were female. He was no doubt gilding the lily in order to reinforce his stated conviction that poisoners were predominantly women, indeed the inventors of the art: 'it appeareth that they have been the first inventers, and the greatest practisers of poisoning, and more naturallie addicted and given thereunto than men.'[16] There is nothing particularly noteworthy in this claim. For the propensity of women to poisoning was an early modern stereotype that went to the close connections of women to food, to medicine – and to witchcraft.[17]

Magic

Pythonists and Ventriloquists

'This word *Ob*, is translated *Pytho*, or *Pythonicus spiritus* ... *Pythonists* spake hollowe; as in the bottom of their bellies, whereby they are aptly in Latin called *Ventriloqui*.'[18]

Scot had any number of contemporary instances in his native Kent of seers, prophetesses, oracles, ecstatics, and demoniacs, indeed any who claimed to speak in the tongues of angels or demons, which he included in his category of Pythonists. Scot classified them as Pythonists and viewed them all as fakes and frauds. Elizabeth Barton, the so-called 'Holy Maid of Kent', was one of them. Scot no doubt knew of her from her inclusion in William Lambarde's *A Perambulation of Kent*, first published in 1570. But he had a more direct connection with her, too. For she was the servant of the father or grandfather of Scot's first wife, Jane Cobbe. The mention of her name by Scot would have no doubt been sufficient for his readers to have recalled one of the most famous nuns of the reign of Henry VIII. For Lambarde, she was a follower of the Devil, along with other 'Monkes, Friars, Priestes, Nonnes, and the whole rablement of his religious armie.'[19] Lambarde, for his part, relied for his account on a no longer extant pamphlet written during Elizabeth's lifetime by an Edward Thwaites and entitled *A marveilous woorke of late done at Court of Streete in Kent*.

In 1525, at around the age of nineteen, Elizabeth Barton was afflicted with a painful illness for a period of seven months or more, 'a great infirmitie in her bodie, which did ascende at divers times up into her throte, and swelled greatly.'[20] She began to demonstrate prophetic abilities, predicting the death of a child lying in a bed near her. In the period that followed, sinking into deep trances as if she were dead, she spoke of things done elsewhere as if she could see them clearly. She spoke also

> [O]f heaven, hell, and purgatory, and of the joies and sorrowes that sundry departed soules had and suffered there: Shee preached frankly against the

corruption of maners and evill life: She exhorted repaire to the Church, hearing of Masse, confession to Priestes, praier to our Lady and Saincts, and (to be short) made in al points, confession and confirmation of the Popish Creede and Catechisme...[21]

During a later trance in 1533, it was reported that she would lie upon the ground, her eyes bulging out, her tongue protruding, her lower jaw sometimes hanging low down or moving from side to side while her arms and legs flailed about.[22] Scot would have been pleased to have known of Archbishop Thomas Cranmer's report of that trance in a letter of 20 December 1533 that it lasted for three hours, 'a voice within her belly, as if it had been in a tun, the which voice when it told anything of the joys of heaven, it spake so sweetly and heavenly, every man was ravished in the hearing thereof, and contrary, when it told anything of hell, it spake so horribly and terribly that it put the hearers in a great fear.'[23]

In 1526 she entered the Benedictine priory of St. Sepulchre in Canterbury where she continued to enter into ecstatic states, to visit her favoured pilgrimage site, our Lady of Court-of-Strete, and there to work miracles – 'lighting candels without fire, moistning womens breastes that before were drie and wanted milke, restoring all sortes of sicke to perfect health, reducing the deade to life againe, and finally doing al good, to all such as were measured and vowed (as the popish maner was) unto her at Court of Strete.'[24] Her fame was sufficient for her to have been granted audiences with the King, Cardinal Wolsey, Sir Thomas More, and Archbishop of Canterbury William Warham.

But it was her intervention into the matter of the divorce of Henry VIII from Katherine of Aragon in order to marry Anne Boleyn that was to bring about her downfall. For she claimed to have received a revelation from God 'that if the King proceeded to the divorce of Queene Catherine, he shoulde not bee King of this Realme one moneth after.'[25] It was an intrusion into the world of politics that Elizabeth was not to live long to regret. In March 1534,

Magic

she and a number of others were indicted for high treason. Found guilty, she was hanged and beheaded on 20 April 1534 at Tyburn with five others and her head impaled on London Bridge. A sermon preached on 23 November 1533 claimed that she had confessed that she 'had never in her whole life any revelation from God but that they were of her own feigning, wherein she used much craft to make and devise them consonant and agreeable to the minds of them who were resorting unto her.'[26] That she was a fake was to become the dominant English Protestant reading of her revelations, and the one which Scot was reflecting in his classification of her as a Pythonist or Ventriloquist.[27]

Scot was aware too of several notable cases of those possessed by demons. Thus, he gives us the title of a pamphlet no longer extant of a twenty-three-year-old Dutchman possessed by ten devils in 1572 who was later found to have been a fraud.[28] And he was familiar with the story from London in 1574 of two possessed girls, Agnes Briggs and Rachel Pinder, probably from his having read the pamphlet entitled *The disclosing of a late counterfeyted possession by the devyl in two maydens within the citie of London* (1574). Both Agnes and Rachel exhibited many of the symptoms of demonic possession – the ability to enter into trances, to speak from the stomach in the voice of the Devil, to vomit assortments of strange objects, to have visions of the Devil in human and animal form, and to disfigure their faces severely. And both, at the end of the day, confessed to having faked their possessions.[29]

For his exemplary tale of fraudulent possession, however, Scot looked to that of Mildred Norrington from Westwell in Kent, only some six miles from Scot's village of Smeeth. Her story was contained in a pamphlet no longer extant, though published (probably in full) by Scot in *The Discoverie of Witchcraft*.[30] According to this, Mildred, the seventeen-year-old 'base' daughter of Alice Norrington, became possessed by Satan on 13 October 1574. The text consists, in the main, of a conversation between a number of local worthies and the demon which had possessed

Mildred. The voice of the demon, we read, was quite different from Mildred's.

The demon eventually identified himself as 'Sathan' and admitted to having been sent into Mildred by old Alice in Westwell Street. He claimed that he had been with her for twenty years, kept in two bottles, one hidden under the wall behind her house in Westwell, the other buried in Kennington. He also admitted to having another spirit as an accomplice, 'little divell'. A year before, he had been sent in the likeness of two birds to kill Mildred. Sathan and 'little divell' had also killed three other people at her request, a gentleman Richard Ager and his son of Dig, and Wolton of Westwell's wife. They also stole meat, drink, and corn from the villagers for her. The Devil was then commanded, in the name of Jesus Christ, to leave the girl and never to trouble her or anyone else again. Eventually he was expelled from Mildred in the presence of nine persons, including the vicar of Westwell, Roger Newman, and the vicar of Kenington John Brainford: 'And then we kneeled downe, and gave God thanks with the maiden; praieng that God would keepe hir from sathans power, and assist hir with his grace.'[31] We do not know what happened to old Alice. There is a strong hint in Scot that she was executed as a result. 'How could mother *Alice* escape condemnation and hanging, being arraigned upon this evidence?' Scot asked.[32] But it seems more probable that this is but a rhetorical move on Scot's part, that old Alice was not arrested nor hanged for bewitching people to death, but that Mildred was exposed as a fraud and confessed to being so before any action was taken against old Alice. For Scot concluded his account by remarking:

> But to make short worke with the confutation of this bastardlie queanes enterprise, & cousenage [ie. Mildred Norrington's]; you shall understand, that upon the brute of hir divinitie and miraculous transes, she was converted before M. *Thomas Wotton* of *Bocton Malherbe*, a man of great worship

Magic

> and wisedome... through whose discreet handling of the matter, with the assistance and aid of M. *George Darrell* esquire... the fraud was found, the coosenage confessed, and she received condigne punishment... after due triall she shewed hir feats, illusions, and transes, with the residue of all hir miraculous works, in the presence of divers gentlemen, and gentlewomen of great worship and credit, at *Bocton Malherbe*, in the house of the aforesaid M. *Wotton*.[33]

Scot cast his net of cousenage far from contemporary Kent to ancient Greece and the Oracle of Apollo at Delphi. The Delphic Oracle was called *Pytho*, Scot informs us, because Apollo slew there a serpent so called.[34] But the link between the Delphic pythonists and Scot's *Ventriloqui* is more opaque. It becomes clear when we recall Scot's reliance on Weyer. For in his *De Praestigiis Daemonum*, Weyer dealt with the Delphic Oracle under a section entitled 'Concerning Pythonic Diviners and *gastrimanteia or belly-divining*.' Weyer made the link between Pythonists and Ventriloquists clear. The Pythian women at Delphi spoke through their stomachs and were called 'belly-talkers' (*Ventriloqui*). And he quoted St. John Chrysostom (*c.* AD 347–407) in support:

> This Pythia is said to have been a woman who was seated upon a tripod with her legs spread apart and who then received the wicked spirit sent from below, who entered stealthily into her genital parts, thence to speak out. She was thereupon filled with frenzy; frothing at the mouth, with her hair in disarray, she began to act wildly – like a Bacchant – and spew forth mad oracles.[35]

Scot saw the Delphic oracles as credible only by virtue of their ambiguity, the cunning of the priests involved in them, and the credulity of those who consulted them. It was a credulity that extended beyond pagans to Christian Saints. And Scot took

St. Gregory Neocaesariensis (*c.* AD 213–*c.* 270), more commonly known as Gregory Thaumaturgus, as the very model of Christian gullibility. For his account of St. Gregory's encounter with the Delphic Oracle, puzzingly, Scot refers us to the *Ecclesiastical History* of Eusebius (*c.* AD 260–*c.* 340). No such account appears in this work. But we do know of it from the *Life of Gregory the Wonder Worker* by Gregory of Nyssa (*c.* AD 330–*c.* 395).

Scot rephrased and paraphrased the story as one about the temple of Apollo. But in Gregory of Nyssa's account, it is merely a temple notable for its priests being possessed by demons while delivering their oracles. According to this tale, while on his way to Neocaesarea, Gregory Thaumaturgus sought shelter in this temple. On entering, he terrified the demons by invoking the name of Christ and purifying the air with the sign of the cross. When, at dawn, the temple custodian presented his customary service to the demons, they told him that the temple was barred to them because of Gregory. Despite his best efforts, the custodian was unable to bring the demons back into the temple. Furious with Gregory, he threatened to haul him off to the authorities to denounce him for his presence as a Christian and an enemy of the gods in the temple and for destroying the powers inherent in it. Gregory responded by telling the custodian that he had the power to drive the demons away and make them settle where he wished. The custodian asked him to demonstrate this power by returning the demons to his temple, whereupon Gregory wrote on a piece of 'paper' 'Gregory to Satan: Enter!' and gave it to the custodian. The custodian placed the letter on the altar and the demons were able to return to their former duties.[36] Scot was seriously unimpressed: 'For if *Gregorie* had beene an honest man, he would never have willinglie permitted, that the people should have beene further cousened with such a lieng spirit: or if he had beene halfe so holie as *Eusebius* maketh him, he would not have consented or yeelded to so lewd a request of the priest, nor have written such an impious letter.'[37]

Scot found a contemporary analogue to the oracle at Delphi in the so-called 'Rood of Grace' and the picture in stone of St. Rumwald or, more popularly, St. Grumbald (whom Scot facetiously called Rumball) at Boxley Abbey in Kent.[38] This rood or crucifix was able to respond to its supplicants, according to *The Perambulation of Kent*, by bowing down and lifting itself up, shaking its hands and feet, nodding its head, rolling its eyes, and smiling or frowning, while the picture of Saint Rumwald was so heavy that it could not be lifted unless, in response to offerings of penitential money, the mechanism behind it were activated. The Rood of Grace was publicly exposed as a puppet in Kent and later in London at St. Paul's Cathedral in 1538 in a sermon by Bishop Hilsey of Rochester, during which he demonstrated all its movements, and after which he broke it into pieces. Subsequently, Bishop Hugh Latimer took the small statue of St. Rumwald to the door of the Cathedral 'and threw [it] out of the Church, though the inhabitants of the country whence it came, constantly affirmed that eight oxen would be unable to remove it from its place.'[39] And, as with the Delphic Oracle, Scot saw the knavery of priests at the source of the fraud.

The Pythonist of Endor

'The woman of *Endor* is comprised under this word *Ob*: for she is called *Pythonissa*.'[40]

The Biblical so-called witch of Endor was, of all 'ventriloquists', the most famous. After the death of the prophet Samuel, Saul was once again confronted by an army of the Philistines. Deeply afraid, he sought divine guidance but, having offended God through his disobedience, no help was forthcoming from the usual ways of seeking advice – dreams, oracles, or prophets. Thus Saul sought guidance from 'a woman that hath a familiar spirit.'[41] Saul went at night and asked the woman to divine Samuel for him by a spirit. When Samuel appeared, only she could see him. After she described him, Saul perceived him as Samuel. He prophesied to Saul that, for his disobedience to God, 'the Lord will also deliver Israel with thee into the hands of the Philistines: and tomorrow shalt thou and thy sons be with me. The Lord also shall deliver the host of Israel into the hand of the Philistines.'[42] The key issue for interpreters of this verse before Scot was the nature of that which the woman and then Saul had actually seen. Was it Samuel himself, or his soul or spirit, or some illusory likeness of him conjured up by God or the Devil?[43] It was a problem that had not been solved in Patristic, medieval, nor in Scot's time. Scot's position, a virtually unique one, was clear.[44] It was neither Samuel himself nor a demonic illusion of him. Rather, it was cousening on the part of the witch of Endor.[45] And his overall strategy was to use the arguments for each side against the other, leaving his own position the only one left standing.

Jean Bodin supported the view that it was Samuel himself or at least an 'effigy' of him (*l'image*) that had been raised up.[46] And he claimed support not only from Justin Martyr but also from the Rabbinic interpreters.[47] Scot had clearly read the two key sources that supported the position that Samuel was merely an illusion and criticised the view that it was 'really' Samuel, namely Ludwig Lavater's *Of Ghostes and Spirits* (1572) and Peter Martyr's *Loci Communes* (1576), translated into English in 1583 as *The Common Places*.[48] In response to the position represented by Bodin, Scot mounted the usual arguments: that the souls of the righteous were in God's hands awaiting judgement and could not be removed from there; that, since God would not answer Saul by living Samuel, he was unlikely to by dead Samuel; that neither witches nor the Devil had the power to call up the dead; and that the passage in Ecclesiasticus 46.20 which referred to Samuel 'prophesying after his death' was not decisive. And Scot was content to follow Peter Martyr and Lavater in their argument that the weight of Augustine's argument was against its being Samuel himself who was raised, though Scot studiously ignored Augustine's judgement, which was also that of Martyr, Lavater, and Johannes Weyer, that the Samuel conjured up was a demonic illusion.[49]

The view that Samuel was an illusion of Satan was the dominant one in Scot's time, especially among Protestant writers. It was an opinion difficult for English Protestants to avoid after 1560, when it received the support of the Geneva Bible in its marginal gloss: Saul's recognition that it was Samuel was 'to his imaginacion, albeit it was Satan, who to blinde his eyes toke upon him the forme of Samuel, as he can do of an Angel of light.'[50] The opinion that it was really Saul was not the majority opinion among Catholic commentators. Certainly it was far too redolent of the doctrine of Purgatory for the comfort of Protestant commentators.

That Samuel was a demonic illusion was a majority opinion of which Scot was aware. But Scot did not attempt a detailed refutation of it. He was more determined to place the witch of Endor in the context of contemporary frauds like Alice Norrington. 'I perceive the woman of *Endors* spirit was a counterfeit,' he wrote, 'and kept belike in hir closet, or in the bottle, with mother *Alices* divell at *Westwell*, and are now bewraied and fled togither to *Limbo patrum, &c.*'[51] And he drew to the attention of his readers a Mr. Feates of whose fraudulent activities he had personal knowledge. According to Scot, (Bomelio) Feates, a conjurer, otherwise known as Hilles, had sold to Dr Burcot, sometime physician to Queen Elizabeth when she was suffering from smallpox,[52] a familiar spirit by means of which he had hoped to work miracles or make money. Feates was also known for a dog that could do tricks, and for magical effects that Scot knew required the help of a confederate.[53]

Be that as it may, Scot retold at length the story in the first Book of Samuel in order to demonstrate that the whole encounter could be better explained by cousenage than by either the real appearance of Samuel or a demonic illusion of him. Thus, he claimed, it was either the witch herself or she and a confederate who fooled Saul into believing that he was seeing and hearing Samuel: 'When *Saule* told hir, that he would have *Samuel* brought up to him, she departed from his presence into hir closet, where doubtles she had hir familiar; to wit some lewd craftie preest, and made *Saule* stand at the doore like a foole... to heare the cousening answers, but not to see the cousening handling thereof, and the couterfetting [sic] of the matter.'[54]

Scot's preferred explanation was that, in his conversation with Samuel, Saul was seeing and hearing the witch's confederate disguised as Samuel. But he was not averse to an explanation that Saul had not seen Samuel at all. Rather, Saul was dealing with the ventriloquising witch alone, and that she 'Speaking as it were from the bottome of hir bellie, did caste hir selfe into a transe... answering to *Saule* in *Samuels* name, in hir counterfeit hollow voice: as the wench of *Westwell* spake... and this is right *Ventriloquie*.'[55]

Miracles, Oracles, and Apparitions

Scot's suggestion that the witch acted alone by ventriloquy would have allowed him neatly to round off Book seven. But the story of the witch of Endor had raised issues not only about witchcraft but of apparitions, of miracles, and of oracles and prophecies. Scot did not wish his denial of the veracity of the Biblical story of Saul and Samuel to be taken as his considered opinion on the veracity of the supernatural in the Biblical records. As a Protestant, Scot would not have wanted to have subverted the authority of the Bible by a denial of all Biblical miracles, oracles, and prophecies. Rather, he developed an argument that allowed him both to accept the miracles and prophecies of the Bible and yet to deny the veracity of any contemporary claims of such. Thus, he argued that, while miracles, oracles, and prophecies occurred in Biblical times, they were no longer theologically necessary since the coming of Christ and his apostles. And consequently, whatever may have been the case before the time of Christ, apparent miracles, prophecies, apparitions, divinations, and so on since then could not but be false and fraudulent. This was a declaration that enabled Scot to extend his critique well beyond the borders of witchcraft to the domains of Catholicism itself.

For Scot, as for others, this doctrine of the cessation of miracles was a key element in Protestant propaganda against Catholicism. It was a Protestant assertion of the redundancy of the Catholic paraphernalia of faith in the light of the authority of the Word of God preached to men. Before now, declared Scot,

> God did send his visible angels to men: but now we heare not of such apparitions, neither are they necessarie. Indeed it pleased god heretofore, by the hand of *Moses* and his prophets, and speciallie by his sonne Christ and his apostles, to worke great miracles, for the establishing of the faith: but now whatsoever is necessarie for our salvation, is conteined in the word of God: our faith is alredie confirmed, and our church established by miracles; so as now to seeke for them, is a point of infidelitie.[56]

The doctrine of the cessation of miracles was not unique to Scot. Rather, by his time it had become something of a Protestant commonplace. Miracles were viewed as a distraction from the Word of God, and apparent miracles were more likely the work of the Devil than of God. In 1550, Bishop John Hooper had included the cessation of miracles as fifty-seventh among his one hundred articles of faith. 'I believe,' he wrote,

> [T]hat this holy doctrine of the gospel in the very time by God appointed was confirmed & approved by heavenly miracles, as well by Jesus Christ himself, the prophets and apostles, as by other good and faithful ministers of the same Gospel; and that after such a sort, that for the confirming thereof, there is now no more need of new miracles; but rather we must content ourselves with that is done, and simply and plainly believe only the holy scripture without seeking any further to be taught; watching and still

> taking heed to ourselves that we be not beguiled and deceived with the false miracles of Anti Christ, wherewith the world at this day is stuffed; which miracles are wrought by the working of Satan, to confirm all kinds of idolatry, errors, abuses, and iniquities.[57]

What Scot and his contemporaries, both Protestant and Catholic, might have included within the domain of the miraculous is anything but clear. What we can say is that they were heirs to the distinction between natural, preternatural, and supernatural causation formulated by Aquinas. As Lorraine Daston and Katherine Park have pointed out, Aquinas in his *Summa Contra Gentiles* distinguished between three kinds of physical occurrences. The first were natural – that which *is* always or *is* for the most part. This natural order can be violated in either of two ways. It can be disrupted by miracles – acts performed directly by God without the mobilisation of secondary causes (the supernatural). Or it can be interrupted by unusual events that depend on secondary causes alone and require no suspension of God's ordinary providence (the preternatural).[58] The last two categories of event are also distinguished from the first by the fact that they cause wonder – to all in the case of the supernatural, to the uninstructed in the case of the preternatural. In practice, the boundary between the supernatural and the preternatural was opaque and, therefore, contestable, as was that between the preternatural and the natural. But, in principle, while supernatural events could only be caused by God, preternatural events could be caused either by the operations of nature by itself or through the activities of created spirits such as angels, demons, or other spirits.

If Scot's world was one in which the domain of the supernatural had decreased as a result of the doctrine of the cessation of miracles, it was nevertheless one that was permeated by the preternatural. Indeed, the early modern period had seen an upsurge

Magic

of interest in the realm between the natural and the supernatural. As Lorraine Daston remarks:

> Marsilio Ficino's revival of magic, both natural and demonic, imbued scholarly Neoplatonism with a strong affinity for the occult; the new printing centers north and south of the Alps spewed out edition after edition of books of secrets retailing household recipes, virtues of herbs and stones, tricks of the trade and 'natural magic'; the witchcraft trials concentrated theological and legal attention on the precise nature of demonic meddling in human affairs; the voyages of exploration brought back tales and trophies of creature and landscapes more marvelous than anything in Pliny or Mandeville; the religious and political upheavals set in motion by the Reformation also triggered an avalanche of crude broadsides and learned Latin treatises that anxiously interpreted comets, monstrous births, rains of blood, and any number of other strange phenomena as portents.[59]

We do not know if Scot was aware of the Thomistic distinction of the natural, preternatural, and supernatural. But what we can say is that his denial of miracles since the time of Christ encompassed not only the supernatural but the preternatural as well; or perhaps more accurately, that the denial of miracles embraced not only the interventions of God in the world, but the possibility of any interventions in the world by spirits of any sort, including those of the dead, angels, demons, astral spirits, and so on. Thus, not only are the Devil and his minions no longer engaged in human affairs, but any form of spiritual occultism is ruled out of court. The only form of the preternatural that remained conceptually viable for Scot was that form of natural magic which did not invoke spirits of any sort. In this, he was no doubt influenced by his reading of Giambattista Della Porta's *Magiae Naturalis* (1558). For there, Della Porta made the exact distinction between two kinds of magic that informed Scot's rejection of spiritual magic and his support for natural magic:

> There are two sorts of magick: the one is infamous, and unhappie, because it has to do with foul spirits, and consists of Inchantments and wicked Curiosity; and this is called Sorcery; an art which all learned and good men detest; neither is it able to yeeld any truth of Reason or Nature, but stands meerly upon fancies and imaginations, such as vanish presently away, and leave nothing behinde them; as *Jamblichus* writes in his book concerning the mysteries of the *Aegyptians*. The other Magick is natural; which all excellent wise men do admit and embrace, and worship with great applause, neither is there anything more highly esteemed, or better thought of by men of learning... that Magick is nothing else but the survey of the whole course of Nature. For, whilst we consider the Heavens, the Stars, the Elements, how they are moved, and how they are changed, by this means we find out the hidden secrecies of living creatures, of plants, of metals, and of their generation and corruption; so that this whole Science seems meerly to depend upon the view of nature.[60]

Natural magic for Della Porta, as for Scot, was not so much a branch of the preternatural but of the natural, and its investigation a part of the natural sciences, indeed the consummation of natural philosophy (*naturalis philosophiae consummatio*).[61]

But Scot did not only extend downwards (as it were) the domain of the miraculous to include spiritual forms of the preternatural and thus to argue for their demise, he also extended the doctrine of the cessation of miracles outwards to embrace the prophetic and the oracular. Neither the capacity to predict the future, nor even the ability to tell where lost things were to be found (as Samuel did), had survived Biblical times. 'Thus', he concluded, 'that gift of prophesie, wherewith God in times past endued his

Magic

people, is also ceased, and counterfeits and couseners are come in their places... And thinke not that so notable a gift should be taken from the beloved and elect people of God, and committed to mother *Bungie*, and such like of hir profession.'[62]

For reasons that we have already noted, Scot believed that oracles, both ancient like those of Apollo or modern like the Rood of Grace, were devices to defraud the people for the profit of priests. Yet, even if it were the case, he admitted, that before the time of Christ there were authentic oracles, they have ceased. And Scot alluded to the so-called Ransom theory of the atonement, according to which Christ offered his life as a ransom paid to the Devil for our salvation. Oracles, he wrote, along with witchcraft, conjurations, and so on were 'knocked on the head, and nailed on the crosse with Christ, who hath broken the power of divels, and satisfied Gods justice, who also hath troden them under his feete, & subdued them, &c.'[63] In spite of the ransom paid by Christ, fraudulent oracles were transferred from Delphi to Rome. They continued within the Catholic Church, partly for profit, partly to gain admiration from the simple. Only in the reigns of Henry VIII and Queen Elizabeth had oracles ceased in England where 'at this hour they are not onlie all gone, but forgotten here in this English nation, where they swarmed as thicke as they did in *Boeotia*.'[64]

Scot's argument in Book eight that miracles, prophecies, and oracles had existed prior to the time of Christ but had ceased since then, demonstrated his adherence, as a Protestant, to the authority of Scripture. But at this point in *The Discoverie of Witchcraft*, it played a much more important role for his overall case. For it provided the theoretical foundations for his critique of the better part of the rest of the Book – that in an age where miracles, prophecies, and oracles were no more, contemporary forms of the preternatural, popular and elite, had no credibility. Scot's scepticism was directed, therefore, not only at witches and demonologists, but also at astrologers, dream-readers, nativity-casters, augurers, Cabalists, figure-casters, enchanters, alchemists, and spiritual magicians. And where both the supernatural and the preternatural realm of spirits were no more, only a natural reading of the world remained.

Reading the Stars

'The Hebrew word Kasam expounded, and how farre a Christian may conjecture of things to come.'[65]

In the light of Scot's claims that all oracles and prophecies have ceased, we might have expected him to have ruled out the divinatory arts on principle. Yet he began his discussions on the specifics of divination by distinguishing divinations that were commendable from those that were condemnable. In fact, Scot was beginning his account of divination with that most contentious of early modern subjects, namely, astrology. He, like many of his contemporaries, wanted to draw the line between legitimate and illegitimate forms of astrology, between its learned and godly practitioners, and, lurking in the corners of the same profession, 'a great number of counterfets and couseners.'[66] So, for him, it was desirable to find a middle way between those so condemnatory of divination that they denied 'those things that in nature have manifest causes, and are so framed, as they foreshew things... by the order, lawe, and course of nature proposed unto us by God' and those on the other side 'so bewitched with follie' that they believed 'that the publike and private destinies of all humane matters, and whatsoever a man would knowe of things come or gone, is manifested to us in the heavens: so as by the starres and planets all things might be knowne... that nothing should be taken in hand or gone about, without the favourable aspect of the planets.'[67]

Scot was here inchoately drawing upon the early modern and medieval commonplace that there was a broad distinction between 'natural astrology' and 'judicial astrology'.[68] Generally, the former could be defined as focused on the relationship between the movements of the stars and the planets and natural phenomena – the

Magic

weather, agriculture – and large scale human events – mortality, epidemics, politics, and war. Judicial astrology, on the other hand, focused on the relationship between astral events and predictions or prophecies relevant to particular individuals. These, in turn, could be broadly divided into three kinds: 'nativities', based on maps made at the moment of a person's birth or at a later time based on information about the time of birth; 'elections' which had to do with choosing the right moment for a particular course of action such as marriage or travel according to the disposition of the heavens; and practical, more personal, and more urgent 'horary questions'.[69]

From the beginning of the sixteenth century, as Patrick Curry points out, astrology had come under new intellectual and moral pressure. This was partly the result of Renaissance humanism's attempt to save the freedom of the will from the inexorability of astral influences. It was the result, too, of the Reformation's determination only to recognise a direct and unmediated relationship between God and man, and thus to view astrology as a form of idolatry. Consequently, as Curry puts it, 'the line supposedly dividing natural from judicial astrology became heavily policed.'[70] It was a line, therefore, that Scot, like many others, was keen to draw. And the line for Scot was in effect drawn in terms of his distinction between the natural and the preternatural.

Scot's critique of astrology was a determinedly Protestant one. He was familiar with Calvin's objections to astrology, and had probably read Calvin's criticism of it in his 1549 treatise against astrology. This was published in English in 1561 under the title *An Admonicion Against Astrology Judiciall*. As we have seen, Scot often paraphrased his sources closely. But I can find no close citations of Calvin's *Admonicion*, and few indirect allusions to Calvin, in Scot's admittedly brief discussion of astrology. Nevertheless, Scot's position on astrology was essentially that of Calvin, although Scot himself may have read Calvin's criticism of astrology as a more stringent one than Calvin intended.

In the *Admonicion*, Calvin distinguished between true (or natural) and judicial astrology. The former is 'the knowledge of the natural order and disposition that God hath set in the starres & and [sic] planets to judge of their office propertie and vertue & to bring all to their end and use.'[71] The latter, 'this bastardly Astrologye,'[72] consisted for Calvin of nativities, elections, and horary questions generally.[73] Unlike many natural astrologers, however, Calvin restricted natural astrology to 'natural' events and denied the possibility of astral influence on any human affairs at all. Thus, the dispositions of the stars and the planets were not relevant to the fortunes of kingdoms.[74] Nor were they relevant to wars, pestilences, and famines. These were rather to be read as God's judgements upon human sins.[75] So too for Scot, natural astrology was limited to the connection of astral events to weather and agriculture: 'Surelie it is most necessarie for us to know and observe diverse rules astrologicall; otherwise we could not with oportunitie [sic] dispatch our ordinarie affaires.'[76] And he put forward a catena of Biblical verses to justify it.

Moreover, like Scot who declared his acceptance of 'the conjectures or forewarnings of physicians',[77] Calvin accepted medical astrology as a legitimate form of natural astrology. Although in the practice of medical astrology the boundaries between natural and judicial magic were particularly fluid, that it *could* be conceived as a part of natural and not judicial astrology, was in part because the astrological practitioner construed his astrology in terms of the dominant Galenic humoural physiology. But it was also because the relationship between the stars and disease was configured, not in terms of any individual's particular disposition, but by the relation between a particular celestial pattern, a distinctive set of symptoms, and particular forms of treatment.[78] As Calvin summarised it, 'Likewise the phisicians doe drawe out of the true Astrologye all the judgment ỹ they have to ordeyne bloode lettings or drinks or pills & other things in due time. Therefore we must needes confesse that there is a certain

Magic

convenience betywxte the starres or planets and the disposition of a mans body.'[79]

It was this principle of the connection between heavenly bodies and human disposition that left Calvin ambivalent about the casting of nativities. He admitted that there was some connection between individual humoural temperament ('complexions' and 'affections')[80] and the stars but did not view it as a decisive one: 'For at the moste the starres may emprinte certaine qualities in the persones but they can not cause that this thing or ye shuld fall upon them aftrwarde of other occasions.'[81] And he was equally dismissive of any other forms of astrological soothsaying.[82] Scot was similarly uncertain about the relation of stars to temperament.[83] And he was just as scornful as Calvin of prognostications on the future based on such 'nativities', and as equally derisive of any forms of fortune telling.

Divining and Dreaming

'The interpretation of this Hebrue word Onen, of the vanitie of dreames and divinations thereupon.'[84]

Scot was on firm Protestant ground in his support for the doctrine of the cessation of miracles. The ground under his feet was less solid in his extension of this to the claim that prophecies, too, had ceased. As Keith Thomas remarks, while some orthodox members of the Church of England thought that Christians had all the revelation they needed, others felt that the possibility of further messages from God could not be ruled out.[85] And it was in dreams that many thought prophecies were still imbedded and that the future could still be discerned.

This explains Scot's declaration that the prophecies of Biblical times were delivered (with the exception of Moses) through dreams. For the merging of the two enabled him to say of dreams that which he had said of prophecies: 'We that are christians must not now slumber and dreame, but watch and praie, and meditate upon our salvation in Christ both daie and night. And if we expect revelations in our dreames, now, when Christ is come, we shall deceive our selves: for in him are fulfilled all dreames and prophesies.'[86]

Scot had read the two most important works on the interpretation of dreams in the sixteenth century. The first of these was Thomas Hill's *The Moste Pleasaunte Arte of the Interpretation of Dreames* (1576). This defined true dreams as those which were 'signifiers of matters to come' from a cause outside of the body, while false dreams signified only 'present affections and desires of the body.'[87] This was a distinction similar to that made by the Greek physician Artemidorus of Ephesus in the most popular of sixteenth-century dream manuals, *The Interpretation of Dreams*, a work which went through twenty four English editions after its first translation in 1518. Artemidorus drew a distinction between two types of dreams, the *enhypnia*, those which indicated only a present state of affairs, and the *oneiroi*, those which predicted the future either directly (*theorematikoi*) or allusively (*allegorikoi*).[88]

These were distinctions that Scot rejected. Unlike Hill and Artemidorus, he argued that no dreams were relevant to the future, that all dreams were natural, and that their causes were to be found not outside of but within man: 'For they are the inward actions of the mind in the spirits of the braine, whilest the bodie is occupied with sleepe.'[89] Thus, all dreams were merely the result of the events of the day stored up in the mind and mixed together in sleep when the mind could not discriminate or analyse them. Nightmares which appeared to be the result of magic or demons arose 'from the heavie and black humor of melancholy',[90] while pleasant dreams occurred when the 'grosse humors' were spent.[91]

Scot was familiar with a number of Classical dream theories, those of Plato and Macrobius, Aristotle, Avicenna, Averroës, and Cicero. But it was Cicero, in particular, who 'confuteth the vanitie and follie of them that give credit to dreames.'[92] And he quoted a quatrain translated by Abraham Fleming from the second book of the most popular medieval school book for teaching

Latin, the *Disticha Catonis*. It was a verse with which all those who learnt Latin in England in the sixteenth century would have been familiar:

> Regard no dreames, for why the mind
> Of that in sleepe a view dooth take,
> Which it dooth wish and hope to find,
> At such time it is awake.[93]

So, with the interpreters of dreams, Scot really had no patience. Only *after* any event could they credibly apply the dream to that which had subsequently occurred. Any credit given to dreams, he declared, 'Proceedeth of follie: and they are fooles that trust in them, for whie they have deceived manie... And therefore those witches, that make men beleeve they can prophesie upon dreames, as knowing the interpretation of them, and either for monie or glorie abuse men & women therby, are meere couseners, and worthie of great punishment.'[94] As for those who believed that witches had the power to put dreams into men's minds, or that dreams could show where to dig or search for money, he was contemptuous.

Guessing Upon Uncertain Toys

'Nahas, is To observe the flieng of birds, & comprehendeth all such other observations where men do ghesse upon uncerteine toies.'[95]

Scot was aware that augury, in its strictest sense, is divination by reference to the flight of birds. But, with two exceptions, he used the term to include all forms of fortune telling. The two exceptions were physiognomy and palmistry, the former the art of predicting the future from the features of the face, the latter from the features of the hand. He omitted these, he claimed, for their 'tediousnes and follie'.[96] But he was no doubt aware that fortune tellers had been denounced in sixteenth-century statutes for 'feigning themselves to have foreknowledge in Physiognomy, Palmistry, or other abused sciences, whereby they bear the people in hand they can tell their destinies, deaths and fortunes, and other such like fantastical imaginations.'[97] It was a law that was probably more honoured in the breach than the observance. Scot was keenly aware that then, as now, people desired to know what the future held. And he knew that fortune tellers had a good market for their apparent skills: 'But men in all ages have beene so desirous to know the effect of their purposes, the sequele of thinges to come, and to see the end of their feare, and hope; that a seelie witch, which had learned anie thing in the art of cousenage, may make a great manie jollie fooles.'[98]

As with his discussion of dreams, Scot had mined his Classical and theological sources – the Hermetic writings, the neo-Platonists Plotinus, Iamblichus and Porphyry, Plato and Aristotle, Augustine and Aquinas. From these generally, he drew a distinction between divine, natural, and casual auguries. With the first two of these categories, Scot had no criticisms. Divine auguries were, in Christian terms, forewarnings of God's blessing or wrath and had Biblical precedents. Natural auguries were concurrences of events noticed in the past, the occurrence of one of which was a sign of the imminence of the other as 'if one heare the cocke crow manie times together, a man may ghesse that raine will follow shortly.'[99] And consequently, casual auguries appear to be those where, in the absence of consistent evidence from the past, the happening of one event in the present has no predictive value for future fortune or misfortune. Into this last category, Scot placed all popular superstitions. 'Amongst us,' he wrote,

> [T]here be manie women, and effeminat men (marie papists alwaies, as by their superstition may appeere) that make great divinations upon the shedding of salt, wine, &c: and for the observation of daies, and houres use as great withcraft [sic] as in anie thing. For if one chance to take a fall from a horsse, either in a slipperie or stumbling waie, he will note the daie and houre, and count that time unluckch [sic] for a journie. Otherwise, he that receiveth a mischance, wil

Magic

consider whether he met not a cat, or a hare, when he first went out of hfr [sic] doores in the morning; or stumbled not at the threshhold at his going out; or put not on his shirt the wrong side outwards; or his left shoo on his right foote.'[100]

Among the casual auguries, Scot also placed the sacrifice of animals for divinatory purposes. This enabled him to make the claim that all pagan religions arose as a perversion of the original Hebrew sacrifices ordained by God. It was an easy segue to a criticism of Catholicism as an instance of pagan sacrifice and idolatry. The Pope was said to follow their example, 'in prophaning of Christs sacraments, disguising them with his devises and superstitious ceremonies; contriving and comprehending therein the follie of all nations.'[101] And Scot did not miss the opportunity to suggest that the daily sacrifice of Christ in the mass was cannibalistic: 'in the end of their sacrifice...they eate him up rawe, and swallow downe into their guts everie member and parcell of him.'[102] Of the religions, then, only Protestantism was left standing.

Scot left us few clues to the sixteenth-century works which he may have read on divination. Surprisingly, he didn't refer to any of the many prognosticatory almanacs available at the time, such as *the Kalendar of Shepherdes* (1506), *Godfridus* (1554), or *Erra Pater* (1582). But he may have been familiar with the *Arcandum*, translated from the French by William Warde and published in 1562, and again in 1564 and 1578. For in his discussion of *Sortilegium*, or casting of lots (in the broadest sense), he referred to the '*Pythagoras* lot'. He went on to give a brief description of the way the future was predicted by a complex arithmetical calculation based on the ascription of numerical values to a person's name. It was the method given in rich detail in the *Arcandum*, and intended to 'finde the fatall destiny, constellation, complexion, & natural inclination of every man and childe by his birth.'[103]

The correspondence between numbers and letters in the '*Pythagoras* lot' did however provide Scot with an opportunity to deal with the Jewish Cabala, or at least with the Cabala as constructed by the mainly Christian thinkers of the Renaissance. Scot was dependent for his account of the Cabala on Cornelius Agrippa's *De Incertitudine et Vanitate Scientiarum et Artium* (*On the Uncertainty and Vanity of the Arts and Sciences*), first published in 1530. The Agrippa of this work was, at least on the face of it, a much more sceptical one than the *Magus* of his *On Occult Philosophy* who had provided the model for Christopher Marlowe's *Doctor Faustus*.[104] At the end of the first book of *On Occult Philosophy*, Agrippa was endorsing the use of Hebrew letters in magical activities:

> Now if there be any originall [language], whose words have a naturall signification, it is manifest that this is the Hebrew.... There are therefore two and twenty Letters, which are the foundation of the world, and of creatures that are, and are named in it, and every saying, and every creature are of them, and by their revolutions receive their Name, Being, and Vertue... For hence voices, and words have efficacy in Magicall works: because that in which nature first exerciseth Magicall efficacy, is the voice of God.[105]

In contrast to this, the Agrippa of *On the Uncertainty and Vanity of the Arts and Sciences* was persuaded that there 'can chaunce to the life and salvation of our Soules, nothing more hurtfull and pestilente, than these Artes and Sciences'.[106] Scot had read Agrippa's *On Occult Philosophy*. But it was chapter forty-seven of *De Incertitudine et Vanitate Scientiarum et Artium*, entitled 'Of the Cabalists', that Scot mined for Agrippa's critique of the Cabala as 'nothing but superstition and follie'.[107] As Agrippa had concluded,

> Therfore this Jewishe *Cabala* is nothing else but a certaine most pestilent superstition, wherewith at their will they do gather, devide, and transpose the woordes, names, and letters dispersed in the Scripture,... applie to them the woordes of God, defaming the Scriptures, and saying that their fained

matters be forged out of them, they doe maliciously invey against the Lawe of God, and assaie to bring in violent and blasphemouse proufes of their traitorous dealing, thorow reckenings of words, sillables, letters, and numbers impudently wrested.[108]

Thus, Cabalists, like all other diviners, were nothing but couseners. Whereas in other men, declared Scot, the discernment of the telling of one lie is sufficient to render suspect the telling of any future truth, among diviners, one truth accidently spoken is sufficient to render credible whatever they say, however incredible or impossible it be.[109] Uninspired guesswork was at the core of their enterprise, or predictions sufficiently broad to fit any possible outcomes. And the credulous played into their hands. The less likely a thing was to be true, the more inclined we were to believe it. As Scot perceived, it was the combination of cunning and fraud with good psychology on the part of the diviners, and the triumph of optimism and hope for the future over the reality of the past and the present on the part of their clients, that made divination so resistant to the sort of scepticism that he promoted.

Of Enchanters, Priests, and Physicians

'This Hebrue word *Habar*, being in Greeke *Epathin*, and in Latin *Incantare*, is in English, To inchant, or (if you had rather have it so) to bewitch.'[110]

In his book on cunning folk in English history, *Popular Magic*, Owen Davies informs us that, while in Britain in the nineteenth century there were tens of thousands of fortune-telling guides and dream books, there were scarcely any popular guides on learned magic. The one exception was an anonymous work entitled *Witchcraft Detected and Prevented: or the School of Black Art newly opened*.[111] Directed at the popular market, it was published at least three times during the 1820s. The subtitle of this work is of especial note: 'The greater part of this highly curious little volume is selected from the ancient and scarce works of the principal writers on these subjects, particularly from SCOTTS *Discovery of Witchcraft*, the book which supplied SHAKESPEARE with his Witch and Wizard Lore.'

But Scot's work had been used as a source for magic from shortly after its first publication. The earliest example of the use of Scot as a sourcebook for magic can be found in a manuscript in the Bodleian library in Oxford, Additional B.1, a later portion of which was copied from *The Discoverie of Witchcraft* probably before the end of the sixteenth century. As Frank Klassen and Christopher Phillips have pointed out, its author 'extracted selections from the magical operations and charms furnished as example by Scot, changing their language to strip out his antimagical perspective' returning them for use as originally intended.[112] Scot had stolen them from late medieval sources; this scribe stole them back.[113]

This is an important reminder that Scot's book was remembered in English culture, not only for its scepticism about witchcraft and demonology, but for its inclusion of long lists of magic charms and rituals, sufficient to enable any aspiring cunning person to set up shop in a professional way. Books twelve and fifteen in *The Discoverie of Witchcraft* are especially devoted to the detailed enumeration of charms, spiritual, angelic, and demonic. Book twelve is focused primarily on what we may call 'mundane' magic, focused more on 'this-worldly' outcomes; Book fifteen on spiritual 'preternatural' magic, the invocation, binding, and dismissal of spirits. For Scot, this was a distinction driven by his classification of magic and witchcraft in Biblical categories: in the case of Book twelve, *Habar* (to enchant); and in that of Book fifteen, *Iidoni* (conjurors).

It is clear though that Scot himself saw the distinction in terms of the superiority of the latter to the former, primarily in terms of their learning, eloquence, and nimbleness of hands. 'These are no small fooles,' he wrote, 'they go not to worke with a baggage tode, or a cat, as witches doo; but with a kinde of majestie, and with authoritie they call up by name, and have at their commandement seventie and nine principall and princelie divels, who have under them, as their ministers, a great multitude of legions of pettie divels.'[114]

It is less clear why Scot, particularly in Book twelve, elaborated magical charms in such detail. It is tempting to think that his 'publisher', Abraham Fleming, with an eye to the market, might have persuaded him that the inclusion of these would give the book a much broader audience. And he was right, as the subsequent use of Scot's book as a repository of magical practices bears witness. It is not improbable too that Fleming had provided Scot with at least some of his written sources. We know, for example, that Scot drew upon *The Beehive of the Romishe Churche* (1579) for some Catholic charms, a work which had been edited by Fleming.[115]

In addition to *The Beehive*, he drew upon many of his usual sources: Ovid, Virgil, Augustine, Weyer, the *Malleus Maleficarum*, Bodin, Danaeus, Nicolaus Hemingius, and Girolamo Cardano. But in addition to local knowledge which we can assume he had collected, he also drew on 'a Primer entituled the houres of our Ladie, after the use of the Church of *Yorke*, printed anno 1516.'[116] And he was particularly indebted to the Bishop of Pozzuoli Leonardus Vairus (1540–1603) and his *De Fascino Libri Tres* (Three Books on Fascination), published in Paris in 1583.

It was to Vairus that Scot owed his theory of how magic worked (or at least pretended to) through its 'deep structure', namely, that words, written or spoken, had the power to bring about specific effects in the world. For *L.Vairus* said, wrote Scot,

> That old women have infeebled and killed children with words, and have made women with child miscarrie; they have made men pine awaie to death; they have killed horsses, deprived sheepe of their milke, transformed men into beasts, flowne in the aire, tamed and staied wild beasts, driven all noisome cattell and vermine from corne, vines and hearbs, staied serpents, &c: and all with words. In so much as

> he saith, that with certeine words spoken in a bulles eare by a witch, the bull hath fallen downe to the ground as dead. Yea some by vertue of words have gone upon a sharpe sword, and walked upon hot glowing coles, without hurt; with words (saith he) verie heavie weights and burthens have been lifted up; and with words wild horsses and wild bulles have beene tamed, and also mad dogs; with words they have killed wormes, and other vermine, and staied all maner of bleeding and fluxes: with words all diseases in mans bodie are healed, and wounds cured; arowes are with wonderful strangenesse and cunning plucked out of mens bones. Yea (saith he) there be manie that can heale all bitings of dogs, or stingings of serpents or anie other poison: and all with nothing but words spoken.[117]

It was a theory that he saw imbedded in Catholicism, not least in the doctrine of the Mass whereby, in the words of consecration, bread and wine became the body and blood of Christ. It was, for Scot, an infringement of the doctrine of creation. The creative work of God by his word had been completed, and therefore no further new creation by words could be effected. 'For we,' he declared, 'neither all the conjurors, Cabalists, papists, soothsayers, inchanters, witches nor charmers in the world, neither anie other humane or yet diabolicall cunning can adde anie such strength to Gods workmanship, as to make anie thing anew, or else to exchange one thing into another.'[118]

Magic was an infringement, not only of the doctrine of creation, but also of the omnipotence of God. For magic entailed that priests, devils, and witches could outdo God by their magical cunning against his will. For Scot, the evidence was plain that witches at least could not do so. For they were unlearned women, poor and unable to provide metal or stones for natural magic, old and stiff and not able to deceive by legerdemain, heavy and often lame and not able to fly in the air or dance with the fairies, sad, melancholic, and sullen. And if they had been able to do what they were reputed to, whole households and countries would be killed, they would be rich and all others poor, and we would all be apes and they owls.

The formal distinction between what Scot calls 'Popish periapts, amulets and charmes' and more 'popular' forms of magic informs, in part, the structure of Book twelve. But it is a division that Scot himself was devoted to deconstructing. For, as he demonstrates, in both their forms and intentions, the distinction cannot be maintained. This collapsing of magic and Catholicism was not uncommon. Many medieval magical texts presented themselves as legitimate religion. But Scot's intention was the reverse, namely, to present Catholic practices as illegitimate magic. Scot was in fact reflecting what we have only more recently come to realise, namely, that in early modern Europe, the distinction between popular and elite forms of religion, and between magic and religion is a difficult one to draw, and this even in Scot's more apparently Protestant England. There was, as Eamon Duffy has argued, a symbiotic relationship between the official practice of the church and many apparently superstitious religious and magical practices.[119] Charms provided by Scot against rabies incurred from dog bite serve well as an example of this intimate connection:

> Put a silver ring on the finger, within the which these words are graven + Habay + habar + hebar + & saie to the person bitten with a mad dog, I am thy saviour, loose not thy life: and then pricke him in the nose thrise, that at each time he bleede. Otherwise: Take pilles made of the skull of one that is hanged. Otherwise: Write upon a peece of bread, *Irioni, khiriora, esser, khuder, feres*; and let it be eaten by the partie bitten. Otherwise: *O rex gloriae Jesu Christe, veni cum pace: In nomine patris max, in nomine filii max, in nomine spiritus sancti prax: Gaspar, Melchior, Balthasar + prax* + max + Deus I max +.[120]

Now without putting too fine a point on it, Scot's account of charms is difficult to comprehend. For it borders not merely on the unsystematic but on the incoherent. This is in part the consequence of his broadening the domain of magic way beyond that which had any formal connection to witchcraft to the multiple forms of engagement of the everyday with the preternatural with which most people would have been involved. In part too, it is the consequence of difficulties inherent then (as now) in imposing any form of order on such an enormous and inchoate mass of material. But we can map his account onto a number of sets of different practices: medical magic for the curing of illnesses; word magic, verbal and written, for medical and other reasons, and consisting of charms, prayers, blessings (and curses), and adjurations; and protective magic through the use of amulets, talismans, and so on.[121]

Medical magic, of the sort above for the cure of rabies, dominates Scot's account. And he provided detailed accounts of magical cures for a variety of early modern ailments – epilepsy, the pain of childbirth, the biting of a scorpion, toothache and headache, scrofula, sharp objects lodged in the body, runny eyes and constant coughs, issues of blood, and agues both occasional and chronic. The cures often involved various kinds of ritual act. Epilepsy could be cured by drinking water at a spring by night out of the skull of a man that had been hanged or eating a pig killed with a knife that had slain a man. Toothache could be stopped by scarifying the gums with a dead man's tooth, scrofula by touching the place with the hand of one that died an untimely death or of a fasting virgin, the pain of childbirth by throwing over the top of the house in which the woman lies 'a stone, or any other thing that hath killed three living creatures; namelie, a man, a wild bore, and a she beare.'[122]

Such ritual acts were also often accompanied by word magic, verbal and/or written. Thus, for example, if a woman were in the middle of child birth, the following was to be laid on her

Magic

stomach: '+ Jesus + Christus + Messias + Soter + Emmanuel + Sabbaoth + Adonai + Unigenitus + Majestas + Paracletus + Salvator noster + Agiros iskiros + Agios + Adanatos + Gasper + Melchior + & Balthasar + Matthaeus + Marcus + Lucas + Johannes.'[123] Such word magic would often use known languages such as Greek, Hebrew, or Latin, but also vernaculars. On occasion, what appears to be nonsense words (to us) are spoken or written, though they have a purported transcendent meaning as well as a performative power. Thus, 'This word, *Abra cadabra* written on a paper, with a certeine figure joined therewith, and hanged about ones necke, helpeth the ague'.[124] Multilingual chants with ritual acts no doubt had an additional magical cachet. Thus, to be delivered from evil, cut a hazel wand upon the Sabbath day before dawn saying,

> I cut thee O bough of this summers growth, in the name of him whome I meane to beate or maime. Then cover the table, and saie + *In nomine patris* + *& filii* + *& spiritus sancti* + *ter*. And striking thereon saie as followeth (english it he that can) *Drochs myroch, esenaroth,* + *betu* + baroch + ass + maaroth + : and then saie; holie trinitie punish him that hath wrought this mischiefe, & take it awaie by thy great justice, *Eson* + *elion* + *emaris, ales, age*; and strike the carpet with your wand.[125]

Word magic was also used for a variety of non-medical purposes: to open locks, to keep wine from turning into vinegar, to avoid pain in torture, to exorcise the self or others, to carry water in a sieve, in forms of counter magic against witchcraft, to find out a witch, to know who was talking about us behind our backs, to harm others through image magic, for the finding out of thieves.

If the number of charms provided by Scot was any indication of the prevalence of any particular early modern concerns, then theft was high on the list. Scot provided various charms to find out a thief – prayers to St. Helen, mother of the emperor Constantine, scrying with crystal or with glasses of water, divining with sheers and sieve while asking Saints Peter and Paul for the name of the thief. As one of many charms against thieves, Scot gave a long account of 'Saint Adelbert's cursse or charme against theeves,' which he had derived from Johannes Weyer. And, like Weyer, Scot used it to point to what he called the 'uncharitable impietie' of popish doctrine.[126] More curse than charm, it was an all purpose means to curse every part of any enemy from head to toe and to damn them to hell: 'Cursed be their navels, their spleenes, their bladder. Curssed be their thighs, their legs, their feete, their toes, their neckes, their shoulders. Curssed be their backs, curssed be their armes, curssed be their elbowes, curssed be their hands, and their fingers, curssed be both the nails of their hands and feete; curssed be their ribbes and their genitals, and their knees, curssed be their flesh, curssed be their bones, curssed be their bloud, curssed be the skin of their bodies, curssed be the marrowe in their bones, cursed be they from the crowne of the head, to the sole of the foote.'[127]

Such word magic could be applied not only to this-worldly matters but also to 'other-worldly' concerns, and notably to the adjuration or exorcism of spirits, not only of persons but of houses. Of particular note is the so-called 'Paracelsian charm', a Latin talisman for driving away spirits that haunt houses. Scot's version reads, 'Hang in everie of the four corners of your house this sentence written upon virgine parchment; *Omnis spiritus laudet Dominum: Mosen habent & prophetas: Exurgat Deus et dissipentur inimici ejus.*'[128]

The Paracelsian charm was as much a form of preventative as of curative magic, protecting houses preemptively against attack by spirits as much as expelling those who had taken up residence. It was a domestic version of the personal amulet, periapt, or talisman. Scot also gave a number of examples of protective magic through the wearing of such amulets: against lightning, drowning, and fire, an amulet known as an *Agnus Dei* containing the picture of a lamb carrying a flag on one side, Christ's head on the other, and containing a passage from St. John's Gospel within; against shot, a medieval 'bullet proof vest' made of flax spun on Christmas night by a virgin in the name of the Devil, with devil heads on the front side, and a cross on each side; against witchcraft, the first chapter of St. John's Gospel consecrated at a mass; the words 'Abra Cadabra' written on a paper and hung around the neck to help with the ague.

This is not to say that Scot was opposed to the wearing of all kinds of amulets. For he admitted that the wearing of such, if they consisted of herbs, roots, stones, or metal, might have beneficial medical outcomes as a consequence of the powers that were naturally inherent within them. And he endorsed the use of certain kinds of natural 'charms' for the healing of cattle.[129] As we will see later, the line between natural 'medicine' and 'natural' magic was, for Scot, hard to draw.

Scot was concerned to alert his readers to the dangers of having anything to do with the magical practices of witches and priests. But he was also committed to ridding the practice of medicine of any activities beyond what he construed as natural, and to exposing such practitioners as couseners. To this end, Scot told a long exemplary story which he had found in Weyer about a 'surgion' in the Duchy of Metz.[130] According to this, a gentleman named Elibert consulted a physician who proceeded to get him drunk, the better to 'con' him. When he was sufficiently drunk, the surgeon persuaded him that he was the victim of witchcraft and that, were it not prevented, it would spread throughout his household. Asked whom in his household he most trusted, he named his twenty-year-old daughter. And, at the physician's request, he and his wife persuaded their daughter to do all that the physician asked.

The physician asked the daughter to bring to his lodging samples of her parents' hair, and that of their cattle. When she arrived, he led her down to a cellar where he opened a book that lay on a table, and placed two knives across the volume 'with much circumstance of words.'[131] The young woman fainted from fear. When the physician had revived her, he sexually assaulted her. When she objected, he told her that, unless she was cooperative, her Father's destruction was certain. If she wished to save him, 'I must have carnall copulation with you, and therewithall [he] fell into hir bosome, and overthrew hir and hir virginitie.'[132] He did the same the following day, and tried unsuccessfully to do so again on the third day. In the meantime, he had administered such medicines to the Father as to keep him bedridden. Eventually, although she was reluctant to tell her Father, he persuaded her to tell him what had occurred, and later he informed Weyer. Scot fails to tell us the outcome of this sordid story, though Weyer does inform us that the surgeon went unpunished and continued his magical practices.

Though, as Scot and Weyer made plain, quackery and immorality went hand in hand, at least others were less naïve than the gentleman from Metz. Scot retold another story from Weyer about a cousening physician who persuaded a patient with a swollen stomach from a tumour that it was rather the consequence of vipers in his belly. There were sufficient sceptics present to forestall his intention to 'conveie vipers into his ordure and excrements.'[133] Not to be discouraged, the physician informed the patient that, if he wished to avoid pain equal to that of childbirth, he should allow him to place his hands in his trousers to rake out the worms there. The patient's Mother, having been forewarned, told the physician that she could do that herself. No happy ending here however. Although the cousener was prevented and fled the county, the patient died.[134] Scot's plain advice, from a country gentleman as it were, to all those who would seek out magical cures was quite simple. Read that passage from Paul's Epistle to the Ephesians 6.10-17, 'the charme of charmes', and put on the whole armour of God that you may stand against the assaults of the Devil. Alternatively, if you were unlearned and lacked friends, seek out the company of a learned, godly, and discreet preacher.

If you needed medical assistance, 'go to a learned physician, who by learning and experience knoweth and can discerne the difference, signes, and causes of such diseases, as faithlesse men and unskilful physicians impute to witchcraft.'[135] Above all, don't seek out priests, witches, or couseners.

Magic, Angelic and Demonic

'This word *Iidoni* is derived of *Iada*, which properlie signifieth to knowe: it is sometimes translated, *Divinus*, which is a divinor or soothsaier...; sometimes *Ariolus*, which is one that also taketh upon him to foretell things to come.'[136]

There are moments in *The Discoverie of Witchcraft* when the material with which Scot wished to deal failed to cohere with the structure into Biblical categories of a significant part of the work. Book fifteen is one such moment. For the relationship between *Iidoni* and the angelic and demonic magic focused upon in this Book is an attenuated one. However that may be, as I noted above, Scot did distinguish between unlearned magic and learned magic. Indeed, he went as far as to designate their practitioners differently as 'witches' in the former case and 'conjurors' in the latter. This latter group were distinguished from the former by their 'learning, eloquence, or nimblenesse of hands to accompany their confederacie,'[137] and by their superior activities – fetching devils out of Hell and angels out of Heaven, and souls out of both, together with the raising of tempests and earthquakes.

There was another distinction between them, though it is more implicit than explicit in the text. Here there is no mention of aging, uneducated, melancholic women in thrall to the devil. These conjurors were men of power, able to force the preternatural world of angels and demons to come and serve them, or apparently so. These were deluders rather than deluded. No Satanic cult here, they operated alone. And between conjurors and priests, Scot fixed no distance. Male conjurors predominate in the text. *The Discoverie of Witchcraft* refers to 'the maister', 'he', 'T.R. and

John Cokars', 'Colimannus and Stephanus Aterbatensis', 'Jacobus de Chusa'. And Book fifteen ends with the printing of a remarkable letter, sent to Scot by one 'T.E.', who had been condemned to death for conjuring, and who now admitted these 'wicked sciences' to be but 'meere cousenings and illusions'.[138] Moreover, T.E. referred Scot to a book 'written in the old Saxon toong, by one Sir John Malbourne a divine of Oxenford, three hundred yeares past; wherein he openeth all the illusions & inventions of those arts and sciences,'[139] which he had left with the parson of Slangham in Sussex. No doubt to Scot's chagrin, although the parson admitted to his possessing the book, he refused to lend it to Scot. Still, he was perhaps gratified to know that he was part of a long English tradition of debunking angelic and demonic magic.

Scot's sources for his detailed accounts of ritual magic are difficult to identify. Nevertheless, in a marginal note in the first chapter of Book fifteen, Scot does draw our attention to the *Pseudomonarchia Daemonum* (False Monarchy of Demons) of Johann Weyer. This was a work added to the 1563 first edition of Weyer's *De Praestigiis Daemonum*. It was essentially a catalogue of some sixty-nine demons, together with instructions on the hours in which the principal demons could be conjured (and restrained from doing harm), and the means by which they were constrained to arise and appear. Weyer's own source for this was listed by him as *Liber officiorum spirituum, seu Liber dictus Empto. Salomonis, de principibus & regibus dæmoniorum* (Book of the offices of spirits, or the Book of sayings of Empto. Solomon concerning the princes and kings of the demons).

Scot gave an English translation of it in chapters two to four of Book fifteen headed 'An inventarie of the names, shapes, powers, governement, and effects of divels and spirits, of their severall segniories and degrees: a strange discourse woorth reading.'[140] Between Scot's translation and Weyer's original, there was a number of minor differences. Prime among these was the absence in Scot's account of the description of the demon Pruflas, otherwise

Magic

known as Bufas, a great prince and duke whose mansion is around the Tower of Babylon. Others went to minor additions and omissions as well as variations in the spelling of some of the demons in Scot's account from that of Weyer.

These variations are best explained as errors occurring in the manuscript of the translation of Weyer which Scot was using. It was a translation made by an English magician whom we know only as 'T.R.' As Scot informs us in a marginal note, 'This was the work of one T.R. written in faire letters of red & blacke upon parchment, and made by him, Ann.1570...'[141] Moreover, we can assume that the better part of chapters six to twenty in Book fifteen of *The Discoverie of Witchcraft* was the work of T.R. and his collaborator, a John Cokars. 'As for these ridiculous conjurations, last rehearsed,' declared Scot, 'they are for the most part made by *T.R.* (for so much of his name he bewraieth) and *John Cokars*, invented and devised for the augmentation and maintenance of their living, for the edifieng of the poore, and for the propagating and inlarging of Gods glorie, as in the beginning of their booke of conjurations they protest.'[142]

The manuscript of these professional conjurors T.R. and John Cokars probably entitled *Secretum Secretorum* (Secret of Secrets),[143] as published in *The Discoverie of Witchcraft*, was of a kind with contemporary works of the same genre, the grimoire.[144] However, it is a 'no-nonsense' English version. As E.M. Butler remarks, 'But any adept of the school of Solomon would harbour an uneasy feeling, on perusing this text, that English magicians, like English statesmen, must have provoked disasters by being ill-prepared. The informal and happy-go-lucky nature of the preparations includes no daunting instructions about the forging of instruments, the tanning of skins or the mixing of inks; on the other hand neither is there any sinister talk of sacrificial victims or the letting of blood.'[145]

Nevertheless, Scot no doubt did provide sufficient details on a sufficient number of magical activities to satisfy at least the curiosity of what to many of his readers must have been fresh insights into an unknown more arcane world than that of unlearned magic. Thus, we find rituals for conjuring the spirits of the dead, fairies, and angels, for enclosing spirits in crystal stones, for binding and loosing spirits, and so on. A comprehensive set of rules was provided by Scot in the chapter entitled 'An experiment of Bealphares.' This ritual was intended to conjure a spirit in the likeness of a man or woman to be available to come when required for a variety of purposes, the finding of hidden treasures, the procuring of gold or silver, transportation from one country to another. It required the magician, not only to undertake a complex set of activities, but also to be a certain kind of person, to cultivate the persona of the Magus: 'Therefore he that will doo this worke, shall absteine from lecherousness and dronkennesse, and from false swearing, and doo all the abstinence that he may doo; and namelie three daies before he go to worke, and in the third daie, when the night is come, and when the starres doo shine, and the element faire and cleare, he shall bath himselfe and his fellowes (if he have anie) all together in a quicke welspring. Then he must be cloathed in cleane white cloathes... And he must have a drie thong of a lions or of a harts skin, and make thereof a girdle, and write the holie names of God all about, and in the end + Λ and Ω +.'[146]

It was Book fifteen of *The Discoverie of Witchcraft* that was considerably expanded in the 1665 edition of the work by the addition of nine chapters giving more detailed instructions on the consecrations of magical circles, fumigations, fire, magical garments and utensils, calling up the ghosts of those who have committed suicide by hanging, and the raising of spirits generally.[147] And it was probably inserted by the same person who was responsible for the additional book of 'A Discourse concerning Devils and Spirits' in that later version. In contrast to the philosophical bent of the Discourse of the first edition, this was little more than a continuation of the interests of Book fifteen, with further information on the varieties and natures of astral, aerial, watery, terrestrial,

Magic

and infernal spirits, together with additional detail on amulets, pentacles, conjurations, and so on.

Scot gives us no clue as to how he had come by the *Secretum Secretorum* of T.R. and John Cokars. But, he was clearly aware of the rich literary tradition of magic upon which 'conjurors', unlike 'witches', were wont to draw:

> And further, to adde credit to that arte, these conjurors carrie about at this daie, bookes intituled under the names of *Adam, Abel, Tobie,* & *Enoch*; which they repute the most divine fellow in such matters. They have also among them bookes that they saie *Abraham, Aaron,* and *Salomon* made. ... And for their further credit they boast, that they must be and are skilfull and learned in these arts; to wit, *Ars Almadell, ars Notoria,* ars *Bulaphiae,* ars *Athephii,* ars *Pomena,* ars *Revelationis, &c.*[148]

It was common in the period to attribute books of magic to such figures as Adam, Abel, Noah, Joseph, Moses, Solomon, Reuben, Enoch, and Paul. These were attributions that Scot was particularly concerned to rebut. Moses differed as much from a magician, he declared, 'as truth from falshood, and pietie from vanitie.'[149] Scot was aware too that Solomon was commonly seen as one of the key founders of the magical tradition. It was an attribution he was also concerned to deny.

By the third century AD, the image of Solomon the magician had emerged, as Pablo Torijano has demonstrated, 'a development based on both the exorcistic traditions that were linked with Solomon and the reinterpretation of the Biblical theme of his wisdom, first in Hermetic terms and afterwards in magical ones.'[150] It was the exorcist, Hermetic sage, and magician of late Antiquity who was looked to by medieval and early modern magicians as the founder of magic.

As Scot knew, the tradition of Solomon the exorcist could be traced as far back as the first century to the *Antiquities* of Josephus.

And Scot provided a paraphrase of 'a fable' from Josephus which purported to show the application of Solomon's methods in Josephus's day. According to this, a magician Eleazer, in the presence of the emperor Vespasian, his sons, and his army exorcised many: 'He did put unto the nose of the possessed a ring, under the seale wherof was inclosed a kind of roote, whose verture [sic] *Salomon* declared, and the savour thereof drewe the divell out at his nose; so as downe fell the man, and then *Eleazer* conjured the divell to depart, & to return no more to him... Which thing being doone, none there doubted how great *Salomons* knowledge and wisedome was.'[151] Eleazer was of course for Scot nothing but a cousener. And his strategy in relating the story of this 'knaverie or cousenage' done in the name of Solomon was to point to the similar use of Solomon in the cousenage of the Catholic Church, its endorsement of Solomon the magician in the liturgy on St. Margaret's day, and thus its support for the 'lies and fables' told as a result.

Scot devoted chapter twenty-three of Book fifteen to a translation of a passage detailing St. Margaret's skills as an exorcist, and a demon's apparent verification of King Solomon's exorcistic powers. It was a story that he told to prove 'the incredible, impossible, foolish, impious, and blasphemous matters conteined therein, and by the ridiculous circumstance thereof.'[152] According to Scot, having first defeated the devil in the form of a dragon, by making the sign of the cross upon which it burst in the middle, St. Margaret,

> [S]awe another man sitting like a Niger, having his hands abound fast to his knees, she taking him by the haire of the heade, threw him to the ground, and set hir foote on his heade; and hir praiers being made, a light shined from heaven into the prison where she was, and the cross of Christ was seene in heaven, with a doove sitting thereupon, who said; Blessed art thou O *Margaret*, the gates of paradise attend thy comming. Then she giving thanks to God, said to the

Magic

divell, Declare to me thy name. The divell said; Take awaie thy foote from my head, that I may be able to speake, and tell thee: which being done, the divell said, I am *Veltis*, one of them whom *Salomon* shut in the brasen vessell, and the *Babylonians* comming and supposing there had beene gold therein, brake the vessell, and then we flew out: ever since lieng in wait to annoie the just.[153]

Scot developed this theme in the following chapter in his retelling of a story that he drew from the late fifteenth-century *Speculum Exemplorum* (Mirror of Exempla), a collection of some twelve hundred stories for use in sermons. It told of a Lombard who was anxious to emulate St. Margaret in her victory over the Devil. Having withdrawn into the countryside to pray, he encountered a mute woman who, upon seeing him, was so afraid that 'she rored in such sort, as hir voice could not be understood, and with hir head and fists made threatning signes unto him.'[154] Convinced that she was a demon, he beat her and stabbed her almost to death. He was apprehended and imprisoned until she was cured both of her injuries and of her inability to speak by the intervention of St. Vincent.

For Scot, angels and demons, Catholic credulity, and clerical conjuring went hand in hand. And clerical conjurors, like their secular counterparts, were frauds. The realm of the occult, the esoteric, and the divinatory in general was deemed by Scot to be a chimera. He saw himself as bringing to light through the heat of his sun that which was hidden beneath the snow. He was fulfilling in his own work the words of Christ: 'Nothing is so secret, but it shall be knowne and revealed.'[155] For Scot, the Emperor of magic had no clothes:

> The conclusion therefore shall be this, whatsoever heeretofore hath gone for currant, touching all these fallible arts... be now counted counterfet, and therefore not to be allowed no not by common

sense, much lesse by reason, which should sift such cloked and pretended practises, turning them out of their rags and patched clowts, that they may appeere discovered, and shew themselves in their nakednesse.[156]

Chapter Five

Philosophy and Religion

Natural Magic

> 'The signification of the Hebrue word Hartummin...
> the inchanters of *Pharao*, being magicians of *Aegypt*
> were called *Hartummin*.'[1]

As we have seen, Scot was unimpressed by the notion that in Solomon was to be found the origins of spiritual magic, not least because one so wise could hardly be credited with something so foolish. But it was Solomon, nevertheless, that Scot did see as the founder of natural magic. And in his description of the wisdom of Solomon, he gives us clues to his perception of a domain in which, initially to the reader rather surprisingly, along with Solomon, Scot was a devoted and ardent traveller. For Solomon, declared Scot, was the greatest traveller in this art, especially in his *Ecclesiastes* and *The Wisdom of Solomon*. As a result, Solomon could justly claim that,

> God hath given me the true science of things, so as I knowe how the world was made, and the power of the elements, the beginning and the end, and the middest of times, how the times alter, and the change of seasons, the course of the yeare, and the situation of the starres, the nature of living things, and the furiousnesse of beasts, the power of the wind, and the imaginations of men, the diversities of plants, and the vertues of roots, and all things both secret and knowne, &c.[2]

In *The Discoverie of Witchcraft*, Scot limited the domain of natural magic in a way that was virtually guaranteed eventually to lead to its demise. In the passage above therefore, it is difficult to discern any difference between natural magic and the more general category of the natural order. This view is reinforced when we read that 'natural magicke is nothing else, but the worke of nature,'[3] and that in this art of natural magic, 'a man may learne the properties, qualities, and knowledge of all nature,'[4] so as be enabled to do things which appear to the common people to be miraculous. It was a theory of natural magic that Scot found in the *Magiae Naturalis* of Giambattista Della Porta, according to which natural magic was not only a part of, but also the perfection of, the sciences, and was clearly distinguished from those magical practices which involved the conjuration of spirits.

On the other hand, Scot appears also to mean by 'natural magic' those things that occur which provoke wonder, and which therefore are to be included in the realm, not of the natural, but of the preternatural. These were moments of experience which, by virtue of their not being within the realm of what habitually happened, were apparently unable to be brought within the domain of the natural order. As we know, Scot rejected the category of the supernatural, having argued that, since the time of the New Testament, miracles were no more. And he also rejected the category between those of the natural and the supernatural, namely the preternatural, at least to the extent that it involved the activities of any spiritual entities. But he did accept the reality of certain kinds of experiences – even if they are not simply or obviously reducible to the realm of the natural. Thus, he provided many examples of strange things 'brought to passe by naturall magicke'[5] – the taming of a bull by tying it to a fig tree, the properties of the load-stone, the virtues and qualities of stones, the sympathy between a fox and a serpent or the antipathy between a sheep and an elephant, the sympathies and antipathies of herbs and plants, the bewitching venom in the body of a harlot, the

Philosophy and Religion

virtues of bones and horns. In this sense, 'natural magic' translates as the 'magic' in nature. And the magic in nature is ultimately explicable in terms of nature. Natural magic declared the glory of God, both by the manifestation of his works, and by its capacity to apply these divine works to our use and service.

Scot's view can be illuminated in terms of the early modern distinction between 'occult' and 'manifest' qualities. It is not a distinction that he formally makes within the body of his work. But if it was not terminology with which he was familiar, it was no doubt a distinction which he knew, and one which underpinned his reduction of the preternatural to the natural, the wondrous to the mundane, and the portentous to the everyday.

The distinction between manifest and occult qualities was essentially an Aristotelian one between those qualities which were characterised as directly perceived as opposed to those which were insensible. It was a core distinction in Renaissance science at the time of *The Discoverie of Witchcraft*. As Daniel Sennert put it in the early seventeenth century,

> Qualities are divided in respect of our knowledge into *Manifest* and *Occult*. The manifest are those, which easily evidently and immediately are known to, and judged by the Senses. So light in the Stars, and Heaviness and Lightness.... But occult or hidden qualities are those, which are not immediately known to the Sences, but their force is perceived mediately by the Effect, but their power of acting is unknown. So we see the Load-stone draw the iron, but that power of drawing is to us hidden and not perceived by the Sences...So we perceive with our senses the evacuation caused by the purgative medicaments; but we do not perceive that quality by which the purging medicaments do work that effect. After the same manner, we perceive with our Senses the symptoms which Poysons do stir up in our Bodies; but the qualities whereby they cause the said symptoms we perceive not by the sense.... We

perceive the Actions but not the qualities whereby they are effected.[6]

Broadly speaking, among Christian Aristotelians, there was a recognition that occult qualities, even if real, were outside of the domain of that which could be studied, by virtue of the fact that they were outside of the realm of that which could be sensed. As Keith Hutchinson puts it, since only the *effects* of occult virtues could be sensed, their *causes* were outside of the range of the intellect.[7] Thus, the occult was outside of the range of the knowable.

For Scot, by contrast, 'the true science of things', of which Solomon was the exemplary practitioner, encompassed both manifest and occult qualities. The magic in nature was in the domain of the knowable, part of *scientia*, at least in principle. Moreover, knowledge of the magic in nature was sufficient to expel that essential mark of the preternatural – wonder. 'The dailie use and practise of medicine taketh awaie all admiration of the woonderful effects of the same.'[8] Natural magic, the domain of occult qualities, was a key part of how God bestowed his gifts and established order in his works.

In this inclination to accommodate occult qualities within the domain of the knowable, Scot was a genuine precursor of the later scientific revolution. Both seventeenth-century science and natural magic (of the sort defined by Scot) rejected the Aristotelian distinction between the occult and the manifest. And, as Keith Hutchinson concludes, 'in fact the two systems have in common a willingness to deal with occult qualities and a refusal to accept that insensibility implies spirituality: it is within natural magic that we can find precedents for the confidence with which seventeenth-century philosophy insisted that the insensible realms of human nature could be profitably entered by human thought.'[9]

For Scot, then, the meaning of the preternatural was located only in the natural, lacking any transcending 'human' meaning.

Signs, portents, and prodigies were divested of their meaning. The demonic was excluded, the divine diminished. Only the natural remained, albeit as powerful evidence of God's original creative and omnipotent handiwork. Explanation was to be found not in the realms above, but in the below, in natural explanation or human chicanery.

We can see Scot's method at work in his analysis of the witch's evil eye. He accepted the 'reality' of the evil eye, but only by giving it a completely natural explanation, albeit an obscure and complex one. On the one hand, for his account of 'fascination', Scot relied on Galenic humoural theory as mediated to him in this instance through Leonardus Vairus' *De Fascino Libri Tres* (Three Books on Fascination). According to this, the capacity to 'fascinate' others was intimately linked to an individual's emotional states, and in the case of witches, negative ones. As a result of hate, according to Vairus, there 'entereth a fierie inflammation into the eie of man, which being violentlie sent out by beams and streames, &c: infect and bewitch those bodies against whome they are opposed.'[10] This went also to the propensity of women to be witches more than men. For women naturally had greater inner rage than men, and were less able to moderate their fury. Their capacity to rage was exacerbated by their menstrual cycle. Thus,

> [U]pon everie trifling occasion, they (like brute beasts) fix their furious eies upon the partie whom they bewitch. Hereby it commeth to passe, that whereas women having a mervellous fickle nature, what greefe so ever happeneth unto them, immediatlie all peaceablenes of mind departeth; and they are so troubled with evill humors, that out go their venomous exhalations, ingendred thorough their ilfavoured diet, and increased by meanes of their pernicious excrements, which they expell. Women are also (saith he) monethlie filled full of superfluous humours, and with them the melancholicke bloud boileth; whereof spring vapours, and are carried up,

and conveied through the nosethrels and mouth, &c:
to the bewitching of whatsoever it meeteth.[11]

Scot also found support for this reading of the evil eye in the natural magic of Giambattista Della Porta. Della Porta, too, gave a naturalistic account of the evil eye. For him, it was the result of the gross vapours emanating from the eyes of post menopausal women unable naturally to rid themselves of their monthly excess of humours. And Scot appears to endorse Della Porta's account of how these vapours, emitted through the eyes, infected the air with the vapour of the corrupted blood, 'with the contagion whereof, the eies of the beholders are most apt to be infected.'[12]

Secular Enchantments

For Scot, natural magicians were learned men, thought by some to be practitioners of 'the verie absolute perfection of naturall philosophie.'[13] Moreover, since it involved the investigation of the nature, effects, and causes of things, it was not in itself evil. But it could become so when allied with fraud, prearranged trickery, and the use of confederates in order to hurt others, to profane God's name, or to support superstition or impiety. But Scot saw no harm in 'juggling' as he called it, intended for fun. He was no 'Puritan' (in the pejorative sense of that term): 'And so long as the power of almightie God is not transposed to the juggler, nor offense ministred by his uncomlie speech and behaviour, but the action performed in pastime, to the delight of the beholders, so as alwaies the juggler confesse in the end that these are no supernaturall actions, but devises of men, and nimble conveiances.'[14]

As his exemplars of natural magicians with deceit, illusion, and impiety added, Scot looked to the magicians of Pharaoh in their contest with Moses. These were for Scot the precursors of the contemporary art of juggling, 'consisting in fine and nimble conveiance, called legierdemaine.'[15] They were not to be compared with witches or conjurors who pretend to do with words and charms that

Philosophy and Religion

which Pharaoh's *Hartumin* did with their skills and their art. And in order to demonstrate the analogies between Pharaoh's magicians and the jugglers of Scot's time, chapters twenty-two to thirty-four of Book thirteen of *The Discoverie of Witchcraft* were devoted to the discovering or uncovering of legerdemain and illusion, and to the demonstrating that the jugglers of Scot's time, like those of the Pharaoh's, depended 'upon manual dexterity to deceive onlookers' eyes; verbal dexterity to confuse their minds; and the preparation of special effects to baffle their understanding.'[16] In so doing, Scot produced the first English work to expose 'secular enchantments'. His intention in doing so is clear. It was to expose as legerdemain that which Bodin, Spinaeus, Vairus, and their supporters took as the work of devils and familiars. 'But truelie,' he wrote, 'my studie and travell herein hath onelie beene employed to the ende I might proove them fooles, as whereby they may become wiser, and God may have that which to him belongeth.'[17]

There can be no doubt that Scot did the hard yards in his investigation into juggling, both by study and travel. And we can conclude that he himself became quite good at juggling. His was no mere book learning: 'for if time, place, and occasion serve, I can shewe so much herein, as I am sure *Bodin*, *Spinaeus*, and *Vairus*, would sweare I were a witch, and had a familiar divell at commandement.'[18] He was certainly familiar with the tricks of a number of the main jugglers of his day. Thus, for example, in the course of these chapters on legerdemain, he mentioned Brandon, Bomelio Feates, Steeven Tailor and his confederate Pope, Clarvis, and Kingsfield.[19] And he seems to have been particularly reliant upon conversations held with a London juggler by the name of John Cautares, a Frenchman by birth who lived in St. Martin's. Although Cautares worked for a living and practised magic only on an amateur basis, Scot claimed that he had 'the best hand and conveiance (I thinke) of anie man that liveth this daie.'[20]

As one of his core contemporary examples of 'juggling', Scot looked to 'Brandon's pigeon'. Brandon was one of the early sixteenth century's most well known conjurors. He was identified as 'the Lord king's juggler' ('Joculatori domini Regis') in the early 1520s, and was admitted as a freeman of the City of London in 1522. He held the position of 'King's juggler' until at least 1536/7. Contemporary records show him as having toured in Kent and Sussex, Cornwall, Devon, Oxford, Shrewsbury, and Worcester, as well as Norfolk, Suffolk, and Cambridge.[21] Scot's account of 'Brandon's pigeon', which he labelled as an 'Example of a ridiculous wonder', indicates that Brandon not only held the position of juggler to Henry VIII, but performed before him.

Scot's description of the trick is the main evidence that we have of the nature of Brandon's work. According to Scot, Brandon painted on a wall a picture of a dove. And seeing a dove on top of a nearby house said to the King, 'Lo now your Grace shall see what a juggler can doo, if he be his craftes maister.'[22] He then pricked the picture with a knife with accompanying words with the result that the pigeon fell from the top of the house stone dead. Brandon, Scot informs us, was forbidden to do the trick again, lest he employed it in any other murder, 'as though he, whose picture soever he had pricked, must needs have died.'[23] Having himself experimented on crows and magpies, Scot explained how the trick was done. The pigeon was in the hands of the juggler before hand and had been administered a dram of *Nux vomica* (strychnine), or some other such poison, sufficient for it not to live beyond half an hour. Let loose, it always resorted to the top of the next house. After a short time, it fell down, either dead or comatose. In the meantime, 'the juggler useth words of art, partlie to protract the time, and partlie to gaine credit and admiration of the beholders.'[24] As Scot rather aptly concluded, 'If this or the like feate should be done by an old woman, everie bodie would crie out for fier and faggot to burne the witch.'[25]

Of the jugglers mentioned by Scot, he was especially familiar with Bomelio Feates, also known as Hilles. Like Brandon, he was quite well known in the mid-sixteenth century. For Scot, he was

Philosophy and Religion

in every way a cousener: 'his qualities and feats were to me and manie other well knowne and detected.'[26] Feates worked with a trained dog, and Scot admired his ability, like that of other jugglers, to train animals: 'in so much as they [vipers] be not by mans industrie or cunning to be made familiar, or traind to doo anie thing, whereby admiration maie be procured: as *Bomelio Feates* his dog could doo; or *Mahomets* pigeon, which would resort unto him, being in the middest of his campe, and picke a pease out of his eare.'[27] And amongst those who worked by prearranged tricks or with the assistance of confederates, Scot believed that Feates was preeminent.

We can analyse Scot's account of legerdemain in terms of five categories: conveyance, private and public confederacy, appearances and disappearances, substitutions, words, and stage tricks. Conveyance was for Scot of the essence of juggling: 'Such are the miracles wrought by jugglers,' he wrote, 'consisting in fine and nimble conveiance, called legierdemaine: as when they seeme to cast awaie, or to deliver to another that which they reteine still in their owne hands; or conveie otherwise.'[28] It consisted in the hiding and conveying of balls, the alteration of money, and in the shuffling of cards, the purpose of all of which was to 'abuse mens eies and judgements.'[29] As Scot remarked in a marginal note, it required the practitioner to be 'close and slie: or else you discredit the art.'[30] And it required considerable dexterity. Nimble conveyance was required 'To cut halfe your nose asunder, and to heale it againe presentlie without anie salve.'[31] And no mistake could be made in inserting a nail or a fine pointed knife into that part of a chicken's head between its comb and brain to ensure it did not come to harm.[32] All this was to ensure that 'the eies of the beholders may not discerne or perceive the drift.'[33]

Secular enchantments relied too on prearranged trickery, the help of confederates, or both. Scot expressed these in terms of the distinction between private and public confederacy. Brandon's pigeon was a clear example of the former. 'Private confederacie

I meane,' declared Scot, 'when one (by a special plot made by himselfe, without any compact made with others) persuadeth the beholders, that he will suddenlie and in their presence doo some miraculous feat which he hath alreadie accomplished privillie.'[34] Brandon's pigeon may have also involved public confederacy, with the aid of 'a confederate, who standing at some window in a church steeple, or other fir place, holding the pigeon by the leg in a string, after a signe given by his fellowe, pulleth downe the pigeon, and so the wonder is wrought.'[35]

Scot was aware too of the means by which appearances and disappearances were often managed by the use of false bottoms and partitions.[36] And he gives us a long account, together with a diagram entitled 'To cut off ones head, and to laie it in a platter, which the jugglers call the decollation of John Baptist,' of the substitution involved in one of the sixteenth century's most well known illusions. Scot himself had most likely seen the trick performed, for he tells us that it was done by a London juggler called Kingsfield on 24 August 1582. With the addition of a small boy to be decapitated, smoke from brimstone, and bullock's blood, little wonder the beholders were astonished.[37]

Scot also introduced his readers to a number of stage tricks involving protective stomach plates, false bladders of blood, and hollow daggers. These tricks were often dangerous: 'An other miracle may be shewed touching counterfet executions; namelie, that with a bodkin or a dagger you shall seeme to kill your selfe, or at the least make an unrecoverable wound in your bellie: as (in truth) not long since a juggler caused himself to be killed at a tavern in cheapside, from whence he presentlie went into Powles churchyard and died. Which misfortune fell upon him through his owne follie, as being then drunken, and having forgotten his [protective stomach] plate which he should have had for his defense.'[38]

Scot saw language as a tool of the juggler to direct and misdirect the onlookers, and to persuade them that in the words used was 'power'. With words or charms, you will 'seeme to conveie the same ball from under the same candlesticke';[39] 'use words of course, and suddenlie open your hand';[40] 'use certeine words over it'; 'you must ever remember to use (with words, countenance, and gesture) such a grace, as may give grace to the action, and moove admiration in the beholders'.[41] And he gives us several marginal lists of words most effective to these ends: Hey, fortuna furie, numquam credo, passe, when come you sirra, Ailif, casyl zaze, hit mel meltat, Saturnus, Jupiter, Mars, Sol, Venus, Mercurie, Luna, droch myroch, senaroth betu baroch assmaaroth, roûsee farounsee, and so on.[42]

'Of the Art of Alchumystrie'

It is no coincidence that Scot placed his analysis of alchemy in Book fourteen immediately after that of juggling. For linguistic mystification was also at the very heart of the practices of the alchemists. Scot was part of a satirical tradition reaching back to Chaucer that, with some good reason, scorned alchemy's predilection to explain the unknown by the totally incomprehensible.[43] According to Scot, in order to be thought wise, learned, and cunning, alchemists had invented words of art, and sentences and epithets obscure and confectious, so as to confuse the capacities of all and to bring credit to what was for him nothing but cousenage: 'subliming, amalgaming, engluting, imbibing, incorporating, cementing, ritrination, terminations, mollifications, and indurations of bodies, matters combust and coagulat, ingots, tests, &c.'[44] He poured scorn on their drugs, simples, and confections: 'orpiment, sublimed *Mercurie*, iron squames, *Mercurie* crude, groundlie large, bole armoniake, verdegrece, borace, boles, gall, arsenicke, sal armoniake, brimstone, salt, paper, burnt bones, unsliked lime, claie, saltpeter, vitriall, saltartre, alcalie, sal preparat, claie made with horsse doong, mans haire, oil of tartre, allum, glasse, woort, yest, argoll, resagor, gleir of an eie, powders, ashes, doong, pisse, &c.'[45]

Unusually, Scot provided his readers with little analysis of alchemy. And, if he had read much by its proponents, it isn't evident within the body of *The Discoverie of Witchcraft*. He was content with the following summary:

> Now you must understand that the end and drift of all their worke, is, to atteine unto the composition of the philosophers stone, called Alixer, and to the stone called Titanus; and to Magnatia, which is a water made of the foure elements... And by these they mortifie quicke silver, and make it malleable, and to hold touch: heereby also they convert any other mettall (but speciallie copper) into gold. This science (forsooth) is the secret of secrets; even as *Salomons* conjuration is said among the conjurors to be so likewise. And thus, when, when they chance to meete with yong men, or simple people, they boast, brag, and saie with *Simon Magus*, that they can worke miracles, and bring mightie things to passe.[46]

So Scot knew that alchemy was part science, part magic, or perhaps better, partly natural, partly preternatural. But he ignored the former and focused almost completely on the latter. He read alchemy as nothing but a particularly sophisticated form of cousening. And he viewed its practitioners 'as ranke couseners, and consuming cankers to the common wealth, and therefore to be rejected and excommunicated from the fellowship of all learned men.'[47] His main source for his knowledge of alchemy was Geoffrey Chaucer, and his *The Canon's Yeoman's Tale*.[48] Although not as sympathetic to alchemy as Chaucer was in the final fifty or so lines of *The Canon's Yeoman's Tale*, Scot's summary above is clearly a 'prosified' version of these lines which present alchemy as a science, 'the secree of secrees'[49], an ending that has led many to believe that it was not so much alchemy that was in Chaucer's sights, as its fraudulent misusers. Moreover, Scot's 'technical' knowledge of alchemy was also drawn from this work. Indeed,

Philosophy and Religion

virtually all the activities and ingredients mentioned by Scot in the passages above can be found in Chaucer.[50]

Chaucer can certainly be read as opposed not so much to alchemy itself as to its fraudulent misuse. But if these were Chaucer's intentions, they were not Scot's. He was certainly not interested in alchemy as 'science', not even as a possible candidate for a 'natural magic'. He viewed it solely as a form of cousening magic. His marginal notes left the reader in no doubt: 'The Alchymists bait to catch a foole,' 'A cousening devise by running awaie to save the credit of the art,' 'Here the Alchimyster uttereth a point of cousening knaverie.'[51]

After a summary of *The Canon's Yeoman's Tale*, Scot exemplified its fraudulent nature with a series of three exemplary tales calculated to expose alchemists as charlatans who prey, not only on simple yeomen, but also on kings and priests. The first of these concerned a simple and pretty gullible fellow Kentishman. The alchemists and his confederates had chosen their mark carefully. They gained the simple yeoman's confidence through his daughter 'to whome he made love cunninglie in words,'[52] eventually persuading him that he could use his alchemical skills to turn one angel into two or three. This was a simple 'conveyancing' trick with 'angels' within balls of wax, whereby a ball of wax with one angel within was substituted with one with three. This was the kind of son-in-law which any simple yeoman would want to have. The sting was now in, and the yeoman ready to be played. The alchemist then suggested that, just as he had increased the angels, so he could increase amounts of gold. 'This yeoman, in hopes of gaines and preferment, &c: consented to this sweete motion, and brought out and laid before his feete, not the one halfe of his goodes, but all that he had, or could make or borrowe anie maner of waie.'[53] The alchemist wrapped the money in a ball of wax, and 'conveieng the same into his bosome or pocket, delivered another ball...of the like quantitie unto the yeoman' to place in his chest.[54] Each had a key to the locks on the chest so that neither could defraud the other. The alchemist then told the yeoman that they could go about their business until the time when the gold would have multiplied. The alchemist failed to turn up, neither to the hour, the day, nor the year he was supposed to. Eventually, although the yeoman did not wish to violate his promise to the alchemist, he forced open the chest to find the ball of wax still within the chest, though no clear signs of its having multiplied. 'So as he thought (if the hardest should fall) he should find his principall: and while not as good increase hereof now, as of the other before. But alas! When the wax was broken, and the metal discovered, the gold was much abased, and beecame perfect lead.'[55]

The second of Scot's stories was the story of a king who was the victim of an alchemist's deceit. The third was a long retelling of one of Erasmus's colloquies, namely, 'The Alchymist'.[56] Like the first two stories, it was another that went to the capacity of alchemists to 'milk' their clients of funds, most of which went into the alchemists' deep pockets. Scot's conclusion to this story was an apt one for his position on alchemy generally. 'By this discourse,' he wrote,

> *Erasmus* would give us to note, that under the golden name of Alcumystrie there lieth lurking no small calamitie; wherein there be such severall shifts and sutes of rare subtilties and deceipts, as that not onelie welthie men are thereby manie times impoverished, and that with the sweete allurement of this art, through their owne covetousness; as also by the flattering baits of hoped gaine: but even wise and learned men hereby are shamefullie overshot, partlie for want of due experience in the wiles and subtilties of the world, and partlie through the softenes and pliablenesse of their good nature, which cousening knaves doo commonlie abuse to their owne lust and commoditie, and to the others utter undooing.[57]

Philosophy and Religion

To support his conclusion, Scot looked to a number of additional authorities. Following Albertus Magnus's *Mineralium* (The Book of Minerals), he reported on the belief of the Arabic philosopher Avicenna (*c*. AD 980–1037) that alchemy cannot change the nature of things but only their external appearance.[58] He looked also to the Italian Renaissance humanist Petrarch (AD 1304–74) for support for his claim that the only gold that alchemists could make came from the pockets of others: 'Alcumysters are a beggerlie kind of people, who though they confesse themselves bare and needie, yet will they make others rich and welthie: as though others povertie did more molest and pitie them than their owne.'[59] And finally, Scot drew on an ancient writer of a religious order who lived more than a thousand years before, who called alchemists '*Falsificantes metallorum & mineralium*, witches and counterfetters of metals and minerals.'[60]

The vain hope for undreamt-of wealth was what drove otherwise sensible men into the arms of the alchemists. This was no virtuous hope for Scot. On the contrary, if the nature of any action can be determined by its consequences, then the hope for gold was not holy but cursed. For those afflicted by it, the outcomes were inevitable: 'they have nothing left in lieu of lucre, but onelie some few birned brickes of a ruinous fornace, a pecke or two of ashes, and such light stuffe, which they are forced peradventure in fine to sell, when beggerie hath arrested and laid his mace on their shoulders.'[61] Covetousness, just another form of idolatry, was at its core. The currency was devalued by it, wisemen were bewitched, con men increased, princes abused, the rich impoverished, the poor beggared, and the multitude made fools of.

A Devilish and Spiritual Discourse

It is perhaps unfortunate that the most read modern edition of Scot's *The Discoverie of Witchcraft*, that of Montague Summers first published in 1930, does not contain the final section of Scot's work, 'A Discourse upon divels and spirits'.[62] Summers was himself a conservative Catholic who held what amounted to the kind of supernatural worldview that Scot was determined to critique. As a consequence, he was no supporter of Scot. Indeed, he ended his introduction to Scot's work by quoting an earlier judgement upon Scot made by an anonymous person whom he called 'a cautious and circumstantial investigator.' According to this, 'Scot was naturally sceptical, and in religion he would be now-a-days a pseudo-scientific modernist. That is to say, he was utterly without imagination, a very dull, narrow, and ineffective little soul...had he dared, Scot would have openly denied the supernatural, of that there can be no doubt.'[63] It was an opinion, Summers declared, that 'is temperately and fairly stated.' We are not surprised by this judgement when we realise that the authority that Summers was quoting was none other than himself in one of his earlier works.[64] However that may be, had Summers included 'A Discourse upon divels and spirits' in his edition, many modern readers may have been less inclined to conclude with him that Scot was nothing but an atheistic pseudo-scientific modernist. For a careful reading of the Discourse would lead most readers to conclude that, whatever Scot was, he was not this.

In fact, Scot went out of his way at the beginning of the Discourse to distance himself, not only from those Classical and modern authors who, in support of the doctrine of devils and spirits, 'write so ridiculouslie in these matters, as if they were babes fraied with bugges', but also from the Sadducees and Peripatetics who 'denie that there are any divels or spirits at all.'[65]

What is clear is that, as we have seen, at the centre of Scot's critique of witchcraft and demonology was his denial, not of the existence of spirits, but of the possibility of their being able to assume bodies and to interact with us *physically*. That is to say, they exist, but as *essentially non-corporeal beings*. Thus, Scot was putting forward, not a new form of natural philosophy that

Philosophy and Religion

denied the reality of angels and demons, but rather one that *only* removed them from the realm of physical nature. This was still, however, a radically innovative manoeuvre on Scot's part. As Stuart Clark remarks, had Scot's view of the non-corporeal nature of spirits become general, 'it would not merely have preempted the intricate and inconclusive task of separating the demonic from the non-demonic, and the actual from the illusory; it would also have destroyed at one blow the very essence of magic and witchcraft.'[66] In short, the reality of witchcraft and demonology depended upon the possibility of physical interactions between humans and embodied spirits, and the impossibility of the former destroyed the reality of the latter. In sum, Scot's was an extreme view, sufficiently so to have nothing but a negative impact upon his contemporaries.

However, Scot's denial of the corporeality of spirits was more a radical theological position than a radical 'scientific' one. And it necessitated too a radical re-reading of the Scriptures. For Scripture, at least with respect to its apparent endorsement of the corporeal reality of angels and spirits, could not be read literally. To do so led to absurdity: 'If we have onelie respect to the bare word, or rather to the letter, where spirits or divels are spoken of in the scriptures, we shall run into as dangerous absurdities as these are. For some are so carnallie minded, that a spirit is no sooner spoken of, but immediatelie they thinke of a blacke man with cloven feete, a paire of hornes, a taile, clawes, and eies as broad as a bason, &c.'[67] Scripture was written to suit the needs of its audience, both now and especially then, 'that could not otherwise conceive of spirituall things, than by such corporall demonstrations.'[68] It was not intended to be read 'corporally', but figuratively. And the true sense and meaning of the text was therefore to be found beneath the apparent literal meaning.

This was not simply, not even, a reassertion of medieval modes of spiritual, mystical, or allegorical reading of the Scriptures. In the first place, as we will see later, Scot's distinction between 'corporeal' and 'spiritual' reading of the texts was one which went, not to the method of Biblical reading, but to the personae of the readers. The carnal man read 'corporeally', the spiritual man 'spiritually'. In the second place, at least with respect to matters to do with spirits and devils, Scot's 'spiritual' reading was not one in addition to the literal or the historical, but *in place of it*. Scot read the Bible, not as an historical text, but as a set of stories which needed to be interpreted 'spiritually'.

Thus, for example, he radically re-read the story in Isaiah chapter fourteen of the fall of Lucifer. According to Scot, the witchmongers read this chapter as telling literally how the angel Lucifer was cast out of Heaven, together with his confederates, by God as a result of the angel's desire to be equal with him. It was a story which, read literally, led to many intellectual battles among those scholars who wished to be seen 'to have crept out of wisedomes bosome, who rather crawled out of follies breeches.'[69] According to Scot, God knows there is no such thing mentioned in or meant by the text. And he read it parabolically as a story about the folly of pride and the fall of King Nebuchadnezzar who, like the morning star Lucifer who was exiled for pride in its glorious appearance, esteemed himself to be above all others.

More importantly, he radically retold the story of the Fall of Man. This was a key demonological text. For central to its traditional reading was the belief that Satan had assumed the corporeal form of a serpent in order to tempt Eve. 'They that contend so earnestlie for the divels assuming of bodies and visible shapes, doo thinke they have a great advantage by the words uttered in the third of *Genesis*, where they saie, the divell entered into a serpent or snake.'[70] That the serpent had literally done so can be found within the Jewish tradition for the first time around the first century in *The Book of the Secrets of Enoch*. Thence it became part of the Rabbinic tradition. By the time of Augustine, the belief that Satan had insinuated himself into the serpent was a central feature of Christian doctrine.[71]

Philosophy and Religion

For Scot, the story of Eve and the serpent is no more than that, a story, and the serpent is no more than a metaphor for the Devil:

> How those words are to be considered may appeare, in that it is of purpose so spoken, as our weake capacities may thereby best conceive the substance, tenor, and true meaning of the word, which is there set downe *in the manner of a tragedie*, in such humane and sensible forme, as woonderfullie informeth our understanding; though it seeme contrarie to the spirituall course of spirits and divels, and also to the nature and divinitie of God himselfe; who is infinite, and whome no man ever saw with corporall eies, and lived.[72]

By the same token, the curse that was placed upon the serpent by God, which condemned the serpent to crawl upon his belly, is also to be taken metaphorically of Satan: 'But although I abhorre that lewd interpretation of the familie of love, and such other heretikes, as would reduce the whole bible into allegories: yet (me thinkes) the creeping there is rather metaphoricallie or significativelie spoken than literallie.'[73] As a serpent creeps upon us to annoy our bodies, so did the Devil creep into the conscience of Eve to deceive her.

Thus, whenever spirits are mentioned in the Biblical texts, Scot believed that they should be read 'spiritually', sometimes for infirmities of the body, sometimes for the vices of the mind, sometimes also for the gifts of both of them. 'I denie not therefore that there are spirits and divels,' he declared, 'of such substance as it hath pleased GOD to create them. But in what place soever it be found or read in the scriptures, a spirit or divell is to be understood spirituallie, and is neither a corporall nor a visible thing.'[74] Thus when the New Testament spoke of seven devils who were cast out of Mary Magdalen (Mark 16.9), this was a metaphor for 'a great multitude, and an uncerteine number of vices.'[75] To have turned such a woman from vice to virtue was no less a miracle than making the blind to see, the lame to walk, and the dead to rise again.

In general, of those said in the Bible to be possessed by spirits, this was no more than to say that they were lunatic or frantic, 'which disease in these daies is said to proceed of melancholie.'[76] Indeed, in spite of Scot's claims that he did not deny the reality of spirits, there are passages in the Discourse which do suggest that, at least in some instances, they are nothing more than imaginations: 'Also where it is said; If the spirit of gelosie come upon him: it is as much to saie as; If he be mooved with a gelous mind, and not that a corporall divell assaulted him.'[77]

The Secret Sadducee?

Was Scot a secret Sadducee? This was certainly the conclusion of Sydney Anglo in his important study of Scot in 1977. 'The truth of the matter is,' he concluded, 'that Scot no more accepted the reality of spirits and demons than he accepted the reality of witches...Thus Scot's spirits and witches are defined out of existence. And in this sense Scot was, indeed, the Sadducee his enemies have always considered him to be.'[78] It is a position more recently endorsed by James Sharpe in his *Instruments of Darkness*. Sharpe was more attuned than Anglo to what Scot actually meant by 'spirit'. But he nonetheless still felt able to conclude that 'In effect (and despite his disavowals), the logic of Scot's arguments led to a denial of the reality of the spirit world as surely as it did to a denial of the reality of witchcraft.'[79]

However, accepting Anglo's and Sharpe's view does entail that we read Scot's claims that he did not deny the existence of spirits as disingenuous, and it does imply that to deny the possibility of the corporeality of spirits is tantamount to an implicit denial of their reality. This is not a path down which we need to go if we cease to read Scot as a secret Sadducee.

Leland L. Estes is right to draw our attention to the fact that Scot's overall impulse was a religious one rather than a

Philosophy and Religion

proto-scientific one. As he puts it, 'Behind the façade of scientific rationality that modern commentators have imposed on Scot there lies a deeply religious man. His opposition to the witch craze found its source, not in a deeper and more sophisticated construal of the facts, but in a theology that rejected the very possibility of witchcraft because, more fundamentally, it rejected the corporeal activity of created spirit.'[80]

I can see no strong reasons for doubting the genuineness of Scot's claim that he does not deny the existence of spirits in spite of his denial of the possibility of their being embodied. The assertion of the reality of the realm of 'spirits' together with the denial of their possible embodiment is at the very centre of Scot's theology. Indeed, in one particular passage, in direct opposition to the Sadducees' claims that spirits and devils are only motions and affections, and that angels are but tokens of God's power, he declared, 'I will not sticke to saie, that they are living creatures, ordeined to serve the lord in their vocation. And although they abode not in their first estate, yet that they are the Lords ministers, and executioners of his wrath, to trie and tempt in this world, and to punish the reprobate in hell fier in the world to come.'[81] Even here however, we need to take into account that Scot may be speaking of 'spirits' to the 'uneducated', conforming his language to the 'corporal', as had the Biblical texts.

So perhaps it would be better to say that it was the reality of 'spirit' rather than of 'spirits' that Scot did not deny. For he was not unaware that, granting the impossibility of their being embodied, the notion of 'multiple' spirits was a conceptually problematic one. It was a problem that, a century later, was to draw the Cambridge Platonist Henry More to an assertion that souls (and by extension 'spirits') were embodied (in bodies of matter, air or ether). For More recognised that unembodied souls could not in principle be plural if they could not be embodied and therefore capable of a specific location in physical space.[82]

Scot too recognised that this problem of the locatability of spirits was present in the Bible. And he drew attention to the fact that, in the Scriptures, it was on occasion said that one spirit entered into many men, whereas on other occasions many thousands of devils were said to possess one man. The problem of a plurality of souls had been solved by Henry More by the notion of the 'bodies' of the soul. Scot's rejection of the possibility of spirits having bodies ruled out such an answer. His solution was to reject the question of 'singularity' or 'plurality' of spirits as a genuine one: 'So as, though the spirits, as well good as bad, are said to be given by number and proportion; *yet the qualitie and not the quantitie of them* is alwaies thereby ment and presupposed.'[83] And as a consequence, the domain of interaction between the realm of 'spirit' (rather than of 'spirits) and the human realm is not that of the spatial and the physical but of the non-spatial and (what we would call) the psychological. And the realm of the immaterial spirit went both to good and evil. Scot left us in no doubt that all of those whom he had criticised in *The Discoverie of Witchcraft* were, as far as he was concerned, in thrall to the force of darkness. Thus Scot's definition of 'spirit':

> In summe, this word [Spirit] dooth signifie a secret force and power, wherewith our minds are mooved and directed; if unto holie things, then is it the motion of the holie spirit, of the spirit of Christ and of God: if unto evill things, then is it the suggestion of the wicked spirit, of the divell, and of satan. Whereupon I inferre, by the waie of a question, with what spirit we are to suppose such to be mooved, as either practise anie of the vanities treated upon in this booke, or through credulitie addict themselves thereunto as unto divine oracles, or the voice of angels breakeing through the clouds? We cannot impute this motion unto the good spirit; for then they should be able to discerne betweene the nature of spirits, and not swarve in judgement: it followeth therefore, that

Philosophy and Religion

> the spirit of blindnes and error dooth seduce them; so that it is no mervell if in the alienation of their minds they take falshood for truth, shadowes for substances, fansies for verities, &c: for it is likewise that the good spirit of God hath forsaken them, or at leastwise absented it selfe from them: else would they detest these divelish devises of men, which consist of nothing but delusions and vaine practices, whereof (I suppose) this my booke to be a sufficient discoverie.[84]

Ironically, for Scot himself, his *Discoverie of Witchcraft* was as much a demonology as a theology. Those whom he had criticised were in league with the Devil. He had uncovered the genuine witches. It was they who had been forsaken by the good spirit of God. He was in this sense the demonologist's demonologist, the one who had 'discovered' those in whom the spirit of evil really did work.

Still, if the overarching thematic of Scot's work is a theology of the spirit, how does it square away with his commitment to natural magic? We may recall that Scot's account of the magic in nature could be illuminated by the contemporary distinction between manifest and occult qualities – between those which were characterised as directly perceived, or capable of being so, as opposed to those which were insensible. In Aristotelianism, by virtue of their insensibility, the existence of occult qualities was denied. But natural magic, as we saw earlier, demonstrated the confidence with which seventeenth-century philosophy insisted that the insensible realms of human nature could be profitably entered by human thought. For Scot, his view of natural magic took the realm of the natural beyond the sensible to the realm of occult causes. So too in theology, Scot had denied the possibility of 'sensible' interactions between realm of the spiritual and the human as a consequence of his denial of the possible embodiment of spirit. But this did not entail that reality was limited to the possibility of such 'sensible' interactions. The domain of the interaction between the human and spiritual was beyond the sensible but, as in natural magic, no less real for that. In short Scot's account of natural magic is, in form if not in content, of a kind with his theology of the spirit. And, in both cases, the realm of the real extended beyond that of sense perception.

Scot's rejection of the 'external' operations of spirits in the world was a radical one. But his locating of the activities of the 'spiritual realm' within the 'internal' world of the mind was of a piece with mainstream Protestant theology. The demonism imbedded in the liturgy, in sermons, conduct books, pulp press pamphlets, in diaries and commonplace books, and in autobiographies and popular lives centered above all on the notion of the 'internal temptation' of the Protestant soul. As Nathan Johnstone notes, 'Whereas the medieval remit of the Devil had included temptation as one of a variety of activities with which he might afflict mankind, Protestants elevated it into the single most important aspect of his agency, which virtually eclipsed all others.'[85] And for Scot, it was to all intents and purposes, his only activity.

Moreover, the internalisation of the Devil's work was crucial in the development of Protestant self regulation for it problematised the origin of the individual's innermost thoughts. Were they of the Spirit of God or of the Devil, as Scot was asking above? Thus was relief from the demonic only possible through the most rigorous introspection, self-regulation and examination of the conscience. Scot's Devil was no longer an exotic 'other' in the outer world of compacts with Satan, witches' Sabbaths, and the possessed. The norms of Satanism were no longer to be found in the Devil hidden in thunderstorms, or appearing in the shape of a black dog, or as an incubus. The Devil in Scot, as in Protestantism more generally, was normalised. He was present in the inner life of all Christians. For Scot, the Devil was no longer the inverter (à la Stuart Clark) of the external world,[86] but, more crucially, the subverter of the inner world of the individual.

Carnal and Spiritual Men

Along with Scot's theology of the Spirit went a strong Trinitarian commitment, and especially to the full divinity of the Holy Spirit, 'the spirit of spirits'.[87] His was a theology that also rejected not only the opinion of the Sadducees who denied the realm of spirit altogether, but also the opinion of the fourth-century heretics, the Pneumatochi, 'a sect so injurious to the holie spirit of God, that contemning the sentence of Christ, wherein he foretelleth that the sinne against the holie spirit is never to be pardoned, neither in this world nor in the world to come, they doo not onelie denie him to be God, but also pull from him all being.'[88] Scot went on to provide a lengthy debate for and against the divinity of the Holy Spirit in which ten arguments against were met with ten arguments for. It is not insignificant that *The Discoverie of Witchcraft* ends with a declaration that it is the presence of the Holy Spirit which enables us to discern true from false spirits: 'for the illumination of this inlightning spirit, which as it bringeth light with it to discover all spirits, so it giveth such a fierie heate, as that no false spirit can abide by it for feare of burning.'[89]

What was motivating Scot to end his work with this apparent lengthy rejection of fourth century anti-Trinitarianism? David Wootton has recently and provocatively suggested that Scot was only apparently arguing against it, and was in reality subtly attempting to persuade his readers of the worth of the Pneumatochi's arguments.[90] This is part of Wootton's argument that Scot was in fact a member of the Family of Love, a Protestant sect founded by Hendrick Niclaes (AD c.1502-1580) which had entered England as early as 1561, and that Scot, like the Familists, was in reality anti-Trinitarian.

This is a long bow to draw, not merely because we need to accept that Scot's argument for the centrality of the Holy Spirit within his general theology of the Spirit is a disingenuous one, but also because we would have to accept (as Wootton does) as similarly insincere his abhorrence of 'that lewd interpretation of the *familie of love*, and such other heretikes, as would reduce the whole bible into allegories.'[91] And it is worth noting too, as Wootton does, that Scot's patron, Sir Thomas Scot, to whom Scot dedicated his work, is held 'to have been a Puritan opponent of the Family of Love because he was a member of the Parliamentary committee charged with introducing a Bill against them.'[92]

This is not to deny that there may be links between Scot's collaborator and publisher Abraham Fleming and the Familists or that Scot's Dutch publisher, Thomas Basson, was a Familist. But this is perhaps no more than to say that Scot's work was more likely to find marginal somewhat 'edgy' collaborators, and does not go to Scot's own personal commitment to the Familist cause. Nor is it to deny that Scot may have picked up Familist ideas through his voluminous reading, though there is no evidence of Familist sympathisers among the English writers noted by him at the beginning of his work. Moreover, as we have seen throughout this study, Scot was not averse to use the works of any, opponents and supporters, to make his case. He was eclectic, syncretic, and a genuine *bricoleur*. As we have seen, Scot found support for his case where he could, often by selectively choosing, judiciously omitting, or even carefully revising the opinions of those whose works he mined.

Crucially perhaps, were Scot's theology of the Holy Spirit disingenuous, it would effectively destroy his core argument. For were he not genuine in this, he would not be able to sustain his argument for the reality of the realm of the non-corporeal spirit. The spirit of spirits is, of its essence non-corporeal: 'I will in no case have it thought, that the holie spirit is in us, as a bodie placed in a place terminablie; but to attribute thereunto, as dulie belongeth to the deitie, an ubiquitie, or universall presence; not corporallie and palpablie; but effectuallie, mightilie, mysticallie, divinelie. &c.'[93] It is no coincidence that this is the second to last sentence of *The Discoverie of Witchcraft*. Thus, the non-corporeality of spirit made possible the omnipresence of the spirit of spirits. Its omnipresence

Philosophy and Religion

in the world (both the 'external' and 'internal' world) was that which, according to Scot, the ancient philosophers were drawing attention to, albeit in a 'somewhat mistie, darke, lame and limping' way,[94] with their doctrine of the *anima mundi*, the spirit or soul of the world.

There is, however, a decidedly unorthodox 'perfectionist' strain in Scot's theology, to which Wootton rightly draws attention, and which does find resonances in the doctrines of the Family of Love for whom the person illuminated by the Holy Spirit within had vanquished sin.[95] For Scot, the story of the fall of Adam and Eve was to be read, not as history but as a metaphor for that which occurs in the life of each and everyone. The spirit of evil has entered all of us. Those who practised any of the vanities within *The Discoverie of Witchcraft* or were addicted to them through credulity had been forsaken by the spirit of God and seduced by 'the spirit of blindness and error.'[96] Redemption too occurred within the life of each, and the action of the Holy Spirit made possible the perfection of the individual. The Holy Spirit, wrote Scot, 'doth purifie and cleanse the whole man from top to toe, it doth burne out the soile and drosse of sinnes, and setteth him all in a flaming and hot burning zeale to preferre and further Gods glorie.'[97]

As a consequence, Scot's theology entailed an anthropology that divided humanity into two kinds, the carnal and the spiritual. And the latter were those who, enlivened by the Spirit, were able to discern spiritual things: 'That which is spirituall onelie discerneth spirituall things: for no carnall man can discerne the things of the spirit.'[98] And he adjures his readers to seek the illumination of the Spirit: 'And therefore let us,' he wrote, 'if we will discerne and trie the spirits whether they be of God or no, seeke for the illumination of this inlightning spirit, which as it bringeth light with it to discover all spirits, so it giveth such a fierie heate, as that no false spirit can abide by it for fear of burning. Howbeit the holie spirit must be in us, otherwise this prerogative of trieng spirits will not fall to our lot.'⁹⁹ This enables us, finally, to make sense of the Biblical text that Scot included on the title page of his work: 'Beleeve not everie spirit, but trie the spirits, whether they are of God; for manie false prophets are gone out into the world, &c.'

The Spiritual Demonologist

Scot believed himself to be among those men who have the Holy Spirit within and are consequently capable of discerning good from evil. There is no doubt that, for Scot, good and evil were intimately related to Catholicism and Protestantism. This, for Scot, was the focus of the carnal and the spiritual. As for most of his Elizabethan Protestant contemporaries, to be Protestant was to be above all vehemently anti-Catholic and anti-clerical. Catholics were carnal and Protestants, or at least some of them, were spiritual.

Scot nowhere elaborated what all this might mean for the everyday life of the Christian, either in theory or practice. He was not, after all, a theologian. On the key issues that separated Protestant from Catholic, and Protestant from Protestant, he had virtually nothing to say. But he was a demonologist. He knew the demonic when he saw it. It was present within all of those theories and practices which *The Discoverie of Witchcraft* set out to critique.

He knew it when he saw it because he was a spiritual and not a carnal man. The Holy Spirit, declared Scot, was called the spirit of truth,

> For that it is the touchstone to trie all counterfet devises of mans braine, and all vaine sciences, prophane practises, deceitfull arts, and circumventing inventions; such as be in generall all sorts of witchcrafts and inchantments, within whose number are comprehended all those wherewith I have had some dealing in this my discoverie; to wit, charmes or incantations, divinations, augurie, judiciall astrologie, nativitie casting, alcumystrie, conjuration, lotshare, poperie which is mere paltrie, with diverse

other: not one whereof, no nor all together are able to stand to the triall and examination which this spirit of truth shall and will take of those false and evill spirits.[100]

That Scot's discovery of witchcraft was driven by a theology of the Holy Spirit was not recognised by *his* contemporaries any more than by ours. The denial of the miraculous, at least since the time of Christ, the rejection of the preternatural, the medical reductionism of his account of witchcraft, his consistent questioning of the evidences for the truth of witchcraft, his denial of the possibility of the corporeality of spirits – all these pointed to a sceptical naturalism which denied the reality of the spiritual realm altogether.

Orthodoxy, both Protestant and Catholic, required the possibility of corporeal interaction between the spiritual and the natural. His own contemporaries, not surprisingly, found it hard to read him otherwise than as a *denier* of the whole realm of spirit, so radical were his claims relative to the orthodoxies of his time, and so unorthodox his exclusion of the domain of the spirit from the realm of the physical. Scot's denial of the possibility of the corporeality of spirit would have looked as odd to his contemporaries as its assertion looks to us. So it is perhaps a matter of little surprise that our contemporaries, admiring both his humanism and his scepticism, have been inclined to applaud in Scot that which his contemporaries abhorred – his denial of the corporeality of spirit – at least as a significant moment in the history of purely natural explanations of seemingly supernatural or preternatural events.

Without doubt, among his contemporaries, Scot was by far the most radically sceptical. But Scot would have been the least surprised by the failure of most of his contemporaries to endorse his arguments. For his was a radical scepticism grounded in the certainty that only a man, illuminated by the Holy Spirit, could discern the good from the evil, the true from the false, and the genuinely divine from the really demonic. And his theology entailed that such men were few and far between. He might have ended his life as a man disappointed that his ideas did not receive a sympathetic hearing, though he could hardly have been surprised at that. He would have been genuinely surprised though, had he known that his critique of witchcraft and demonology would come to be valued most by those who, far from endorsing his theology of the Spirit, would be equally sceptical of *its* intellectual coherency and cogency.

Notes

One 'The Discoverie of Witchcraft'

1. James R., *Daemonologie, in Forme of a Dialogue, Divided into Three Bookes* (Edinburgh, 1597), the Preface.
2. *Ibid.*
3. *Ibid.*
4. The most accessible modern edition of Scot's *Discoverie*, edited by Montague Summers, and first published in 1930, does not contain the 'Discourse'. It also omits Scot's four Prefatory Epistles to Sir Roger Manwood, to his cousin Sir Thomas Scot, to 'his loving friends' John Coldwell Dean of Rochester and William Redman Archdeacon of Canterbury, and finally to his readers. See Montague Summers, *The Discoverie of Witchcraft by Reginald Scot* (London: John Rodker, 1930).
5. See Cyndia Susan Clegg, 'Burning Books as Propaganda in Jacobean England,' in Andrew Hadfield (ed.), *Literature and Censorship in Renaissance England* (Hampshire: Palgrave Macmillan, 2001), p. 176. See also David Cressy, 'Book Burning in Tudor and Stuart England,' *The Sixteenth Century Journal* 36 (2005), pp. 359–74. And see especially Philip C. Almond, 'King James I and the Burning of Reginald Scot's *The Discoverie of Witchcraft*: The Invention of a Tradition,' *Notes and Queries* 56 (2009), pp. 209–213.
6. Thomas Ady, *A Candle in the Dark: Or, a Treatise Concerning the Nature of Witches & Witchcraft* (London, 1656), sig. A.3.r.
7. John Webster, *The Displaying of Supposed Witchcraft* (London, 1677), p. 9.
8. Alexander B. Grosart, *The Works of Gabriel Harvey* (London: The Huth Library, 1884–5), ii. 291.
9. See Ronald B. McKerrow, *The Works of Thomas Nashe* (London: A.H. Bullen, 1904–10), i. 309. See also i. 351.

10 See John Deacon and John Walker, *Dialogicall Discourses of Spirits and Divels* (London, 1601), p. 125. The Biblical passage is 1 Samuel 28. See also Reginald Scot, *The Discoverie of Witchcraft* (London, 1584), pp. 139-51.
11 See Samuel Harsnett, *A Declaration of Egregious Popish Impostures* (London, 1603) in F.W. Brownlow (ed.), *Shakespeare, Harsnett, and the Devils of Denham* (Newark: University of Delaware Press, 1993), pp. 305, 306, 307, 309.
12 George Gifford, *A Discourse of the Subtill Practises of Devilles by Witches and Sorcerers* (London, 1587), title page. In chapter 7, Gifford takes on Scot's analysis of Pharaoh's magicians and the witch of Endor as cousenors or tricksters. See also George Gifford, *A Dialogue Concerning Witches and Witchcraftes* (London, 1593), sig. B.4.v. On George Gifford, see Alan Macfarlane, 'A Tudor Anthropologist: George Gifford's *Discourse* and *Dialogue*, in Sydney Anglo (ed.), *The Damned Art: Essays in the Literature of Witchcraft* (London: Routledge and Kegan Paul, 1977), pp. 140-55.
13 See William Perkins, *A Discourse of the Damned Art of Witchcraft* (London, 1608), epistle dedicatory.
14 See John Cotta, *The Triall of Witch-Craft* (London, 1616), p. 62.
15 See Richard Bernard, *A Guide to Grand-Jury Men* (London, 1627), pp. 6, 134, 145, 146, 177, 180, 188.
16 See Francis Hutchinson, *An Historical Essay Concerning Witchcraft* (London, 1718), pp. 19, 25, 26, 27, 30, 31, 175, 189-93.
17 See Joseph Glanvill, *Some Philosophical Considerations Touching the Subject of Witches and Witchcraft* (London, 1667), pp. 41-3. On Glanvill and the vehicles of the soul, see Philip C. Almond, *Heaven and Hell in Enlightenment England* (Cambridge: Cambridge University Press, 1994), pp. 4-37.
18 See Scot, *The Discoverie of Witchcraft*, sig. B. 6.r-v. Though it should be noted that his knowledge of many of these sources was sometimes only indirect.
19 *Ibid.*, p. 124. The work to which Scot refers is *De Fascino Libri Tres* (Paris, 1583).
20 See Elizabeth Story Donno, 'Abraham Fleming: A Learned Corrector in 1586-87,' *Studies in Bibliography* 42 (1989), p. 202.
21 See *Holinshed's Chronicles of England, Scotland, and Ireland* (London: J. Johnson *et al.*, 1807-8), iv. 846-68.

Notes

22   The project focused on the construction of a dam in the harbour with a sluice gate, the releasing of water through which was intended to keep the harbour free of silt. See Eric H. Ash, '"A Perfect and an Absolute Work:" Expertise, Authority, and the Rebuilding of Dover Harbor, 1579-83,' *Technology and Culture* 41 (2000), pp. 239-68. For an analysis of Scot's account, see Annabel Patterson, *Reading Holinshed's* Chronicles (Chicago: University of Chicago Press, 1994), pp. 95-8, 201-11.

23   Francis Peck, *Desiderata Curiosa* (London, 1732-5), Liber V, p. xvii. Cited by William E. Miller, 'Abraham Fleming: Editor of Shakespeare's Holinshed,' *Texas Studies in Language and Literature* 1 (1959), pp. 93-4.

24   The likely first printing of the 1651 edition was annotated 'London, printed by Richard Cotes'; the second in 1651, 'Printed by R. C. and are to be sold by *Giles Calvert*, dwelling at the Black Spread-Eagle at the West-end of *Pauls*, 1651'; the third in 1654, with a minor variation to the title page, 'London, Printed by E. Cotes, and are to be sold by *Thomas Williams* at the Bible in *Little-Britain*, 1654'.

25   Stylistically, they are of a piece, and no doubt from the same hand.

26   In this third edition, the two Discourses are paged separately from the main body of the work, and consecutively, the first from pp. 1-38, the second from pp. 39-72.

27   See pp. 215-28 of the third edition.

28   Heinrich Cornelius Agrippa von Nettesheim, *Three Books of Occult Philosophy Written by Henry Cornelius Agrippa of Nettesheim...; Translated out of Latin into the English Tongue by J.F.* (London, 1651).

29   Heinrich Cornelius Agrippa von Nettesheim, *Henry Cornelius Agrippa's Fourth Book of Occult Philosophy... Translated into English by Robert Turner* (London, 1655).

30   For this material on Ann Watts, I am indebted to James Sharpe, *Instruments of Darkness: Witchcraft in England 1550-1750* (London: Hamish Hamilton, 1996), p. 218; and Owen Davies, *Popular Magic: Cunning-Folk in English History* (London: Hambledon Continuum, 2007), pp. 126-7.

31   Simon During, *Modern Enchantments: The Cultural Power of Secular Magic* (Cambridge, Massachusetts: Harvard University Press, 2002), p. 76.

32   See Scot, *The Discoverie of Witchcraft*, pp. 349-50.

33   *Ibid.*, p. 352.

34   *Ibid.*, p. 344.

35   It continued to be re-published into the 20th century.

36 This work was reprinted in 1576 and 1578, and was incorporated in 1640 into [Mascall, Leonard], *The Country-mans Recreation, or the Art of Planning, Graffing, and Gardening, in three Bookes* (London, 1640).
37 Reginald Scot, *A Perfite Platforme of a Hoppe Garden, and Necessarie Instructions for the Making and Mayntenaunce thereof* (London, 1574), sig. B.2.r-v.
38 See *Holinshed's Chronicles of England, Scotland, and Ireland*, iv. 865-6.
39 Scot, *The Discoverie of Witchcraft*, sig. B.4.r.
40 See Peter Clark, *English Provincial Society from the Reformation to the Revolution: Religion, Politics and Society in Kent 1500-1640* (Hassocks, Sussex: The Harvester Press, 1977).
41 Scot, *The Discoverie of Witchcraft* , sig. A.8.r.
42 *Ibid.*, sig. A.2.r. On the philanthropy of Roger Manwood, see Claire Bartram, ' "Melancholic Imaginations": Witchcraft and the Politics of Melancholia in Elizabethan Kent,' *Journal of European Studies* 33 (2003), pp. 203-11.
43 Scot, *The Discoverie of Witchcraft*, sig. B.3.r.
44 *Ibid.*, sig. B.5.r.
45 *Ibid.*, sig. A.6.r.
46 A transcript of Scot's will may be found in Brinsley Nicholson (ed.), *The Discoverie of Witchcraft by Reginald Scot, Esquire* (London: Elliot Stock, 1973), pp. xxvii-viii.
47 The abstract of an inquisition taken at Maidstone on the death of Lady Wynifred Rainsford on 30 March 1576 notes Reginald Scot as '38 years of age et amplius.' See Nicholson (ed.), *The Discoverie of Witchcraft by Reginald Scot, Esquire*, p. xxix.
48 His death is mentioned in the will of his brother, Sir Reginald Scot, who died on 16 December 1554. Mary is buried in St. Etheldreda's church in Hatfield, Hertfordshire, together with Fulke Onslow.
49 See Anthony A. Wood, *Athenae Oxonienses* (London, 1691), i. 257-8.
50 *Ibid.*, i. 258.
51 Alice may have been Alice Collyar for Scot left 'my daughter in Lawe Marie Collyar six poundes thirteene shillings foure pence to be paide unto her within one quarter after my decease.' However, Collyar may have been Marie's husband's name.
52 Scot, *The Discoverie of Witchcraft*, p. 48.
53 For a table of persecutions in Kent from 1565-1657, see Malcolm Gaskill, 'Witches and Witchcraft Prosecutions, 1560-1660,' in

Notes

Michael Zell (ed.), *Early Modern Kent 1540-1640* (Woodbridge: The Boydell Press and Kent County Council, 2000), pp. 274-7.

54   John Ayre (ed.), *The Works of John Jewel, Bishop of Salisbury* (Cambridge: Cambridge University Press, 1845-50), iv. 1217.

55   On the date of this sermon, see Wallace Notestein, *A History of Witchcraft in England from 1558 to 1718* (Washington: American Historical Association, 1911), pp. 16-17, n. 22.

56   Ayre, *The Works of John Jewel, Bishop of Salisbury*, ii. 1028.

57   See Norman Jones, 'Defining Superstitions: Treasonous Catholics and the Act against Witchcraft of 1563,' in Charles Carlton (ed.), *State, Sovereigns & Society in Early Modern England: Essays in Honour of A.J. Slavin* (Gloucestershire: Sutton Publishing, 1998), pp. 187-203.

58   Quoted by James Sharpe, *Witchcraft in Early Modern England* (Harlow: Longman, 2001), p. 99.

59   See Scot, *The Discoverie of Witchcraft*, pp. 126-31. Wallace Notestein sees this as the conviction of 'old Alice', the woman who putatively sent the devils to Mildred. The context of the story in *The Discoverie of Witchcraft* suggests that it is Mildred who is arraigned. See Notestein, *A History of Witchcraft in England from 1558 to 1718*, p. 386. *The Discoverie of Witchcraft* is our only source for this story.

60   See Scot, *The Discoverie of Witchcraft*, pp. 51, 543. And see anon., *A Rehearsall Both Straung and True, of Hainous and Horrible Actes Committed by Elizabeth Stile, alias Rockingham, Mother Dutten, Mother Devell, Mother Margaret, Fower Notorious Witches, Apprehended at Windsor in the Countie of Barks. And at Abbington Arraigned, Condemned, and Executed, on the 26. daye of Februarie laste Anno 1579* (London, 1579); Richard Galis, *A Brief Treatise Containing the Most Strange and Horrible Cruelty of Elizabeth Stile alias Rockingham and her Confederates* (London, 1579).

61   Scot, *The Discoverie of Witchcraft*, p. 542.

62   W.W., *A True and Just Recorde, of the Information, Examination, and Confession of all the Witches taken at S.Oses in the Countie of Essex*, sig. A.3.v.

63   Notestein believes that this refers to the above mentioned John Jewel, as does Brinsley Nicholson. See Notestein, *A History of Witchcraft in England from 1558 to 1718*, p. 18, n. 24; and Nicholson (ed.), *The Discoverie of Witchcraft by Reginald Scot, Esquire*, p. xxxii. The gap of twenty three or so years between Jewel's return and Darcy's presumed mention of the person as 'come over lately' makes this

unlikely. Neither of them was aware of the visit of Bodin. Kittredge recognises the improbability of 'come over lately' referring as far back as the return of Jewel. He puts it down to 'a bugbear of Brian Darcy's [sic] own manufacture.' See George Lyman Kittredge, *Witchcraft in Old and New England* (Cambridge, Massachusetts: Harvard University Press, 1929), p. 265.

64   The preface of *A True and Just Recorde* opens with a paraphrase of a passage from it. See Marion Gibson, *Early Modern Witches: Witchcraft Cases in Contemporary Writing* (London: Routledge, 2000), p. 76, n. 6.

65   The question of authorship is disputed as to whether it is by Kramer with the participation of Sprenger or by the former alone. For an argument in favour of the former, see Christopher S. Mackay (ed. & trans.), *Malleus Maleficarum* (Cambridge: Cambridge University Press, 2006), i. 103–21. I will assume in the remainder of this work that Kramer was the primary author and attribute the work to him.

66   See *ibid.*, i. 170-1. There were a further nine editions between 1588 and 1669.

67   Mora (ed.), *Witches, Devils, and Doctors in the Renaissance: Johann Weyer, De Praestigiis Daemonum* (Binghamton, New York: Medieval and Renaissance Texts and Studies, 1991). This contains an English translation of *De Praestigiis Daemonum.*

68   Hugh R. Trevor-Roper in *The European Witch-Craze of the Sixteenth and Seventeenth Centuries and Other Essays* (New York: Harper and Row, 1969), pp. 146–9 argues wrongly that Scot was doing little more than adopting Weyer's theory. Weyer, in contrast to Scot, was a firm believer in the capacity of demons to act in the world, an ability the denial of which was the core component of Scot's critique. This is not to suggest that Scot denied the existence of spirits.

69   On extracts from Weyer in Scot, see Nicholson (ed.), *The Discoverie of Witchcraft by Reginald Scot, Esquire*, pp. 553–63.

70   Mora (ed.), *Witches, Devils, and Doctors in the Renaissance*: *Johann Weyer, De Praestigiis Daemonum*, p. 93.

71   *Ibid.*, p. 93.

72   Scot, *The Discoverie of Witchcraft*, p. 109.

73   *Ibid.*, p. 109.

74   In his edition of Scot, Brinsley Nicholson points out a number of seemingly careless errors in Scot of which his description of the Pharaoh as a Persian and Nebuchadnezzar as an Egyptian King are notable. He puts these down to 'a feverous haste of composition,'

excited by his outrage at the excesses of the St. Osyth's trial. It is perhaps too much a 19th-century reading of Scot as 'the outraged Victorian gentleman' for the modern reader. See Nicholson (ed.), *The Discoverie of Witchcraft by Reginald Scot, Esquire*, pp. xxxv–vi; and Scot, *The Discoverie of Witchcraft*, p. 174. Nicholson was not incorrect, however, in his recognition that Scot could be wayward. Scot will later, following Weyer, call one of his categories 'Iidoni', rather than 'Idoni', as in the above quotation. See Scot, *The Discoverie of Witchcraft*, p. 376.
75 Scot, *The Discoverie of Witchcraft*, p. 110.
76 *Ibid.*, p. 472.
77 *Ibid.*, p. 483.

Two   Witchcraft

1 John Dove, *A Sermon…Intreating of the Second Coming of Christ, and the Disclosing of Antichrist* (London, 1594), sig. A.3.r.
2 Thomas Cranmer, *Catechismus* (London, 1648), fol. ccii. Quoted by Stuart Clark, *Thinking with Demons: The Idea of Witchcraft in Early Modern Europe* (Oxford: Oxford University Press, 2005), pp. 346–7.
3 Scot, *The Discoverie of Witchcraft*, p. 4.
4 *Ibid.*, p. 5.
5 *Ibid.*, p. 5. I am conscious that the identification of 'French pox' with our modern syphilis is difficult. The context is highly suggestive though that by 'French pox' is here intended a sexually acquired disease. On such difficulties, see Claudia Stein, 'The Meaning of Signs: Diagnosing the French Pox in Early Modern Augsburg,' *Bulletin of the History of Medicine* 80 (2006), pp. 617–48
6 See Malcolm Gaskill, *Crime and Mentalities in Early Modern England* (Cambridge: Cambridge University Press, 2000), pp. 50–5.
7 See C. L'Estrange Ewen, *Witchcraft and Demonianism* (London: Heath Cranton, 1933), p. 154.
8 Scot, *The Discoverie of Witchcraft*, p. 6.
9 *Ibid.*, pp. 152–3.
10 *Ibid.*, sig. B.5.r.
11 *Ibid.*, p. 1.
12 Ralph Walker, *A Learned and Profitable Treatise of Gods Providence* (London, 1608), pp. 332–3. And see Alexandra Walsham, *Providence in Early Modern England* (Oxford: Oxford University Press, 1999), pp. 25–8.

13 Gifford, *A Dialogue Concerning Witches and Witchcraftes*, sig. D.1.r.
14 See Scot, *The Discoverie of Witchcraft*, sig. A.3.r-v.
15 Gifford, *A Dialogue Concerning Witches and Witchcraftes*, sig. H.3.v.
16 Macfarlane, Alan, 'A Tudor Anthropologist: George Gifford's *Discourse* and *Dialogue*,' in Sydney Anglo (ed.), *The Damned Art: Essays in the Literature of Witchcraft* (London: Routledge and Kegan Paul, 1977), p. 150.
17 Scot, *The Discoverie of Witchcraft*, sig. A.3.r.
18 Perkins, *A Discourse of the damned Art of Witchcraft*, pp. 174–5.
19 Leland L. Estes, 'Good Witches, Wise Men, Astrologers, and Scientists: William Perkins and the Limits of the European Witch-Hunts,' in Ingrid Merkel and Allen G. Debus, *Hermeticism and the Renaissance: Intellectual History and the Occult in Early Modern Europe* (Washington: Folger Books, 1988), p. 160.
20 Cotta, *The Triall of Witch-Craft*, p.78. Quoted by *ibid.*, p.160.
21 Mackay (ed. and trans.), *Malleus Maleficarum*, pt. 2, qu. 1, ch. 2, 95D.
22 Scot, *The Discoverie of Witchcraft*, p. 9.
23 See Mackay (ed. and trans.), *Malleus Maleficarum*, pt. 2, qu. 1, ch. 2, 96A-C.
24 Johannes Nider (*c.* AD 1380–1438), the author of the *Formicarius* (AD 1437–8), one of the sources used by the *Malleus Maleficarum*.
25 This is the inquisitor named in the *Malleus Maleficarum* as 'the inquisitor of Como'. He has been identified as the Northern Italian Dominican Inquisitor Lorenzo Soleri Da Sant'Agata. See Mackay (ed. and trans.), *Malleus Maleficarum*, ii. 163, n. 453.
26 Lambert Daneau (1530–1595), French Calvinist minister and author of *Dialogus de veneficiis* (1564).
27 Andreas Hyperius [Gerhard] (1511–64), Protestant theologian of Marburg. Scot was probably familiar with the English publication *Two Common Places Taken Out of Andreas Hyperius* (London, 1581). See especially, 'Whether that the Devils have bene the Shewers of magicall Artes; and by their helpe, evill men do woorke signes and wonders,' pp. 75ff. In this work, he argued that the Devil, with God's permission and within the laws of nature, works either directly or through magicians.
28 Niels Hemmingsen (1513–1600), Danish Protestant theologian, and author of the 1575 work *Admonitio de superstitionibus magicis vitandis* (*Warning About the Tricks of Superstitious Magicians*).

Notes

29 Bartolomeo della Spina (1475/1479–1546), Dominican inquisitor and author of *Quaestio De Strigibus* (An Investigation On Witches) (1523). His most cited source is the *Malleus Maleficarum*.
30 Scot, *The Discoverie of Witchcraft*, pp. 9–10.
31 The only surviving copy of this pamphlet is in the Bodleian Library at Oxford. Its title page is missing.
32 Scot, *The Discoverie of Witchcraft*, p. 17.
33 I take the marginal reference 'Confessio Windesor' on Scot *The Discoverie of Witchcraft*, p. 10 to be a reference to this work. Scot mentions Elizabeth Stile on p. 51 with the marginal note 'in a little pamphlet of the acts and hanging of four witches, in anno. 1579'.
34 John Roche Dasent (ed.), *Acts of the Privy Council of England* (London: Eyre and Spottiswoode, 1890–5), xi. 22.
35 *Ibid.*, x. 309.
36 Mendoza to Zayas, 8 September 1578, State Papers, Spanish, 1568–79, no. 524, p. 611. Quoted by Kittredge, *Witchcraft in Old and New England*, p. 88.
37 John Roche Dasent (ed.), *Acts of the Privy Council of England*, xi. 22.
38 Barbara Rosen, *Witchcraft* (London: Edward Arnold, 1969), p. 86, n. 4 fails to recognise that the author of *A Brief Treatise* is a different Richard Galis to that 'killed' by Elizabeth Stile and her colleagues.
39 Anon., *A Rehearsall Both Straung and True*.
40 Scot, *The Discoverie of Witchcraft*, p. 10.
41 *Ibid.*, p. 10.
42 *Ibid.*, p. 543.
43 Richard Galis, *A Brief Treatise*, sig. A.4.r.
44 Mother Dutton in *A Rehearsall Both Straung and True*.
45 Galis, *A Brief Treatise*, sig. B.1.v.
46 Mother Devell in *A Rehearsall Both Straung and True*.
47 Galis, *A Brief Treatise*, sig. B. 3.r.
48 Scot, *The Discoverie of Witchcraft*, p. 176.
49 Galis, *A Brief Treatise*, sig. C.1.v.
50 *Ibid.*, sig. C.2.r.
51 Father Rosimond in *A Rehearsall Both Straung and True*.
52 Galis, *A Brief Treatise*, sig. C.4.v. See also Scot, *The Discoverie of Witchcraft*, p. 24.
53 A different version of her confession to that of *A Rehearsall Both Straung and True* is presented by Galis at the end of *A Brief Treatise*.

54 Scot, *The Discoverie of Witchcraft*, p. 542. I can find no child witnesses mentioned in *A True and Just Recorde* younger than six years of age.
55 See Rosen, *Witchcraft*, pp. 103–4.
56 See W.W., *A True and Just Recorde*, sig. F.8.v.
57 Gibson, *Early Modern Witches*, p. 73. She has isolated some eighteen documents missing from the story.
58 Grace Thurlowe was a servant of a relative of Brian Darcy and the head of the local family, Thomas, Lord Darcy of Chiche (i.e. St. Osyth). The Preface of *A True and Just Recorde* was addressed to him.
59 W.W., *A True and Just Recorde*, sig. 2A.2.r.
60 *Ibid.*, sig. 2A.3.r.
61 *Ibid.*, sig. 2A.7.r.
62 Scot, *The Discoverie of Witchcraft*, p. 117; see also p. 451.
63 Randy A. Scott (trans.), *On the Demon-Mania of Witches* (Toronto: Centre for Reformation and Renaissance Studies, 1995), iv. 1.
64 W.W., *A True and Just Recorde*, sig. 2.A.8.r.
65 Scot, *The Discoverie of Witchcraft*, sig. A.3.v–A.4.r.
66 W.W., *A True and Just Recorde*, sig. B.6.v. Justices of the Peace did not at this time have authority to try witches. Still, the Privy Council did on occasion send letters to Justices of the Peace to round up conjurors. See Dasent (ed.), *Acts of the Privy Council of England*, xii. 23, 29, 34.
67 W.W., *A True and Just Recorde*, sig. A.4.r.
68 *Ibid.*, fold out table.
69 Of the fifteen in *A True and Just Recorde*, Henry Selles, the only male accused, appears not to have been sent to trial. However, in the August 1582 Assizes, he is in court charged with arson, though found innocent. There is no legal record of Joan Robinson who denied all charges. Margery Sammon may have appeared under the name of Margery Barnes at the Assizes in March 1584. See Rosen, *Witchcraft*, p. 156, n. 45.
70 See Ewen, *Witchcraft and Demonianism*, p. 155.
71 On John Darcy, see *Oxford DNB*.
72 Scot, *The Discoverie of Witchcraft*, sig. B.5.v.
73 *Ibid.*, p. 12.
74 See *Ibid.*, p. 11.
75 *Ibid.*, p. 11.
76 See Scott (trans.), *On the Demon-Mania of Witches*, iv. 5. On Bodin, witchcraft, and the state see Clark, *Thinking with Demons*, ch. 44. On the coherence in Bodin's *corpus*, see E. William Monter, 'Inflation

and Witchcraft: The Case of Jean Bodin,' in Theodore K. Rabb, and Jerrold E. Seigel (eds.), *Action and Conviction in Early Modern Europe* (Princeton: Princeton University Press, 1969), pp. 371-389.
77   *Ibid.*, iv. 5.
78   *Ibid.*, iv. 5.
79   *Ibid.*, iv. 5.
80   *Ibid.*, iv. 5. See also *Ibid.*, ii. 7.
81   *Ibid.*, iv. 5.
82   Scot treated as impossible the crime of 'incestuous adulterie with spirits' (p. 33). This was a misreading of Bodin for whom the relevant crime was the having of children born of 'natural' incest, to be distinguished from the crime of copulation with the Devil.
83   See John L. Teall, 'Witchcraft and Calvinism in Elizabethan England: Divine Power and Human Agency,' *Journal of the History of Ideas* 23 (1962), p. 23.
84   See Scot, *The Discoverie of Witchcraft*, p. x.
85   Charles William Bingham (transl.), *Commentaries on the Four Last Books of Moses Arranged in the Form of a Harmony* (Grand Rapids, Michigan: Baker Book House, 1984), i. 430-1. See also Peter Jensen, 'Calvin and Witchcraft,' *The Reformed Theological Review* 34 (1975), pp. 76-86; and Teall, 'Witchcraft and Calvinism in Elizabethan England,' pp. 21-36. I am indebted to Jensen for his discussion of Calvin and witchcraft.
86   Bingham (transl.), *Commentaries on the Four Last Books of Moses*, i. 428 (my italics).
87   See Susan E. Schreiner, 'Exegesis and Double Justice in Calvin's Sermons on Job,' *Church History* 58 (1989), pp. 322-38.
88   Scot here means 'before the courts'. He is not referring to the technical sense of *coram nobis*, or 'in our presence', by which is meant a petition to the court to correct a previous error.
89   Scot, *The Discoverie of Witchcraft*, p. 106.
90   Thomas Cooper, *Thesaurus Linguae Romanae & Britannicae* (London, 1584), sig. 6C.4.v.
91   See Kittredge, *Witchcraft in Old and New England*, p. 550; and Scot, *The Discoverie of Witchcraft*, p. 473. There are no extant trial records of Mother Bungie.
92   *Mother Bombie*, III.i.31-5. Quoted by A. Harriette Andreadis, *Mother Bombie by John Lyly* (Salzburg: Institut für englische Sprache und Literatur, 1975), p. 27.

93 See Gibson, *Early Modern Witches*, p. 150, n. 22.
94 Scot, *The Discoverie of Witchcraft*, p. 473.
95 *Ibid.*, pp. 473-4.
96 These were priests who said the first mass of the day.
97 See Scot, *The Discoverie of Witchcraft*, pp. 471-2. See also sig. B.3.r-v.
98 *Ibid.*, sig. A.6.v.
99 See here Clark, *Thinking with Demons*, ch. 31.
100 Scot, *The Discoverie of Witchcraft*, sig. B.5.r-v.
101 *Ibid.*, sig. A.6.r.
102 See *ibid.*, sig. A.4.r.
103 See *ibid.*, sig. A.6.r.
104 *Ibid.*, sig. A.6.v.
105 Keith Thomas, *Religion and the Decline of Magic* (Harmondsworth: Penguin, 1984), pp. 660-1.
106 See Alan Macfarlane, *Witchcraft in Tudor and Stuart England* (London: Routledge and Kegan Paul, 1970), pp. 200-06.
107 See here, Marion Gibson, 'Understanding Witchcraft? Accusers' Stories in Print in Early Modern England,' in Stuart Clark (ed.), *Languages of Witchcraft: Narrative, Ideology and Meaning in Early Modern Culture* (Houndsmill, Basingstoke: Macmillan, 2001), pp. 41-54.
108 *Ibid.*, p. 7.
109 John Gaule, *Select Cases of Conscience Touching Witches and Witchcraft* (London, 1646), pp. 4-5, Quoted by Malcolm Gaskill, 'Witchcraft in Early Modern Kent: Stereotypes and the Background to Accusations,' in Jonathan Barry (ed.), *Witchcraft in Early Modern Europe: Studies in Culture and Belief* (Cambridge: Cambridge University Press, 1998), p. 260.
110 L[aurence] P[rice], *The Witch of the Woodlands* (London, 1655), quoted in Gaskill, 'Witchcraft in Early Modern Kent: Stereotypes and the Background to Accusations', p. 260.
111 Quoted by Alan Macfarlane, *Witchcraft in Tudor and Stuart England*, p. 159.
112 See Scot, *The Discoverie of Witchcraft*, p. 38.
113 See Michael Bailey, 'From Sorcery to Witchcraft: Clerical Conceptions of Magic in the Later Middle Ages,' *Speculum* 76 (2001), pp. 960-990.
114 Alexander Roberts, *A Treatise of Witchcraft* (London, 1616), p. 43.
115 Henry Holland, *The Historie of Adam, or the Foure-fold State of Man* (London, 1606), p. 7. See also Philip Almond, *Adam and Eve in*

Notes

   Seventeenth-Century Thought (Cambridge: Cambridge University Press, 1999), pp. 187–90.
116 Robin Robbins (ed.) *Sir Thomas Browne's Pseudodoxia Epidemica* (Oxford: Clarendon Press, 1981), i.bk.1, ch.1.
117 John Stearne, *A Confirmation and Discovery of Witchcraft* (London, 1648), p. 11.
118 See Tommaso Garzoni, *The Hospitall of Incurable Fooles* (London, 1600), p. 16.
119 On melancholy, see Angus Gowland, 'The Problem of Early Modern Melancholy,' *Past and Present* 191 (2006), pp. 77–120. I am especially indebted to Gowland's comprehensive analysis. See also, Lawrence Babb, *The Elizabethan Malady: A Study of Melancholia in English Literature from 1580 to 1642* (East Lansing: Michigan State College Press, 1951).
120 Scot, *The Discoverie of Witchcraft*, p. 52.
121 *Ibid.*, p. 53.
122 Mora (ed.), *Witches, Devils, and Doctors in the Renaissance: Johann Weyer, De Praestigiis Daemonum*, p. 181.
123 *Ibid.*, p. 186.
124 Montague Summers (ed.), *Francesco Maria Guazzo: Compendium Maleficarum* (New York: Dover, 1988), p. 105.
125 *Ibid.*, p. 106.
126 Mora (ed.), *Witches, Devils, and Doctors in the Renaissance: Johann Weyer, De Praestigiis Daemonum*, p. 189.
127 See Gregory Zilboorg, *The Medical Man and the Witch During the Renaissance* (Baltimore: The Johns Hopkins Press, 1935), p. 138. See also Sydney Anglo, 'Melancholia and Witchcraft: The Debate between Wier, Bodin, and Scot,' in A. Gerlo (ed.), *Folie et déraison à la Renaissance* (Brussels: Editions de l'Université de Bruxelles, 1976), pp. 209–28.
128 Scot, *The Discoverie of Witchcraft*, p. 54.
129 See Patricia Crawford, 'Attitudes to Menstruation in Seventeenth-Century England,' *Past and Present* 91 (1981), p. 54.
130 *Ibid.*, p. 54.
131 James, R., *Daemonologie*, p. 30.
132 Thomas Erastus (aka Thomas Lüber or Lieber) is best known as the putative Father of Erastianism, the theory of state control of the Church (though this was never advocated by Erastus).
133 Scot, *The Discoverie of Witchcraft*, p. 58.

134 See *ibid.*, p. 318. The marginal reference in Scot is 'Erast. in disputat. de lamaiis'. We cannot tell from this with which of Erastus's works on witchcraft Scot is familiar and other references to Erastus in Scot are not sufficiently specific. See *ibid*, sig. A.4.v, 10, 135, 170.
135 *Ibid.*, sig. A.4.r-v.
136 *Repetitio disputationis de lamiis*, pp. 33–4 quoted by Charles D. Gunnoe Jr., 'The Debate between Johann Weyer and Thomas Erastus on the Punishment of Witches,' in James Van Horn Melton (ed.), *Cultures of Communication from Reformation to Enlightenment: Constructing Publics in the Early Modern German Lands* (Aldershot, Hampshire: Ashgate, 2002), p. 274. I am particularly indebted to Gunnoe for his insightful analysis of Erastus.
137 Scot, *The Discoverie of Witchcraft*, p. 49.
138 *Ibid.*, p. 49.
139 *Ibid.*, p. 57.
140 *Ibid.*, pp. 56–7.
141 *Ibid.*, p. 56. On the Ransom or Classic theory of the atonement see Gustav Aulen, *Christus Victor: An Historical Study of the Three Main Types of the Idea of the Atonement* (New York: Macmillan, 1977). In this work Aulen argues for a modernised form of the Classic theory.
142 *Ibid.*, p. 56.
143 *Ibid.*, p. 56.
144 *Ibid.*, p. 57.
145 *Ibid.*, p. 57.
146 *Ibid.*, p. 57.
147 *Ibid.*, p. 68.
148 *Ibid.*, p. 63.

Three   Demonology

1 For an excellent account of the transition from sorcery to witchcraft around the year 1400, see Bailey, 'From Sorcery to Witchcraft: Clerical Conceptions of Magic in the Later Middle Ages,' pp. 960–990.
2 Henry Charles Lea, *Materials Toward a History of Witchcraft* (New York: Thomas Yoseloff, 1957), i. 224.
3 The first English witchcraft text, to my knowledge, which includes the suggestion of the witches' Sabbath is Thomas Potts, *The wonderfull Discoverie of Witches in the Countie of Lancaster* (London, 1613). The text itself was significantly influenced by the *Daemonologie*

Notes

of King James. See Jonathan Lumby, *The Lancashire Witch-Craze: Janet Preston and the Lancashire Witches, 1612* (Lancaster: Carnegie, 1995), and Stephen Pumfrey, 'Potts, Plots and Politics: James I's *Daemonologie* and *The Wonderfull Discoverie of Witches*,' in Robert Poole (ed.), *The Lancashire Witches: Histories and Stories* (Manchester: Manchester University Press, 2002), pp. 22–41.

4 See Scot, *The Discoverie of Witchcraft*, p. 45.
5 See Mackay, (ed. and trans.), *Malleus Maleficarum*, pt. 2, qu. 1, ch. 2, 97B–98B.
6 Scot has three marginal notes in *The Discoverie of Witchcraft* to the *Formicarius*. See Scot, *The Discoverie of Witchcraft*, pp. 74, 82, 280 where the reference is 'in fornicario'. Two of these occur without reference to any other work. But the parallel passage to the first of these may be found in the *Malleus Maleficarum* pt. 2, qn. 1, ch. 4, 108A–B; and the second may be found in part 2, qn. 1, 90D–91A. The third citation of the *Formicarius* is also derived from the *Malleus Maleficarum* for it is combined with a citation of the *Malleus Maleficarum* part 2, qn 2, ch. 7. At this point Scot also cites Nider's other work which treats of witchcraft, the *Preceptorium Divine Legis*. Scot's reference here to 'praecept 1. ca.11' is suggestive of his having read the *Preceptorium*, except for the fact that this specific citation also occurs in the *Malleus Maleficarum*. The relevant passage in that work (in part. 2, qn. 2, ch. 7, 180A) reads: 'Also, Nider says in his *Praeceptorium* (Precept 1, Chapter 11) that it is also lawful to bless domestic animals like sick people with written chants and sacred words...'
7 In keeping with his emphasis on the female gender of witches, Scot here has 'the mistresse of that profession'. See Scot, *The Discoverie of Witchcraft*, p. 8.
8 Mackay (ed. and trans.), *Malleus Maleficarum*, part. 2, qn. 1, ch. 2, 97D–98A.
9 See David Keck, *Angels and Angelology in the Middle Ages* (New York: Oxford University Press, 1998), p. 73.
10 *Ibid.*, p. 91.
11 Alexis Bugnolo (trans. and ed.), *Peter Lombard's Sententiarum Liber Secundus, De Rerum Creatione et Formatione Corporalium et Spiritualium*, http://www.franciscan-archive.org/lombardus/II, distinction 3, ch.2.
12 *Ibid.*, distinction 6, ch. 1.
13 *Ibid.*, distinction 8, ch. 1.

14 Henry Bettenson (trans.), *Concerning the City of God Against the Pagans* (Harmondsworth: Penguin, 1972), book 21, chapter 10, p. 985.
15 See Almond, *Heaven and Hell in Enlightenment England*, ch. 1.
16 See Walter Stephens, *Demon Lovers: Witchcraft, Sex, and the Crisis of Belief* (Chicago: The University of Chicago Press, 2002), p. 62.
17 Fathers of the English Dominican Province (trans.), *Thomas Aquinas, Summa Theologica* (London: Burns Oates and Washbourne, 1920-), http://www.newadvent.org/summa/, part 1, question 51, article 1.
18 *Ibid.*, part 1, question 51, article 2.
19 *Ibid.*, part 1, question 51, article 3. See Stephens, *Demon Lovers*, pp. 61-3. See also, Charles Edward Hopkin, *The Share of Thomas Aquinas in the Growth of the Witchcraft Delusion* (Philadelphia: University of Pennsylvania Press, 1940), ch. 1.A.
20 Stephens, *Demon Lovers*, p. 27.
21 See Augustine, *De Doctrina Christiana*, book 2, ch. 23.
22 See Norman Cohn, *Europe's Inner Demons* (Frogmore, St. Albans, Herts.: Paladin, 1976), p. 176.
23 John Gaule, *Select Cases of Conscience Touching Witches and Witchcrafts* (London, 1646), pp. 39-40. Quoted by Clark, *Thinking with Demons*, p. 487.
24 Mackay (ed. and trans.), *Malleus Maleficarum*, pt. 1, qn. 1, 10D.
25 See Scot, *The Discoverie of Witchcraft*, p.40. Compare Mackay (ed. and trans.), *Malleus Maleficarum*, pt. 2, qn. 1, ch. 2, 96C.
26 See Scot, *The Discoverie of Witchcraft*, p.46; and see Mackay (ed. and trans.), *Malleus Maleficarum*, pt. 2, qn. 1, ch. 2, 98B.
27 Neither Scot nor the *Malleus Maleficarum* use the term 'Sabbath' to describe these public ceremonies of commitment to the Devil, though no doubt the descriptions of these public vows to Satan were imbedded in later more elaborated accounts of the Sabbath. Scot does, however, have witches singing 'Sabbath, Sabbath' at their meetings.
28 The *Malleus Maleficarum* speaks of the women present, rather than of witches, and of a female novice or male disciple. It only mentions renouncing the Christian faith and worship of the Blessed Virgin Mary, and not rejection of sacraments, spitting at Host, and rejecting fasting. See Mackay (ed. and trans.), *Malleus Maleficarum*, pt. 2, qn. 1, ch. 2, 96C-D.
29 The *Malleus Maleficarum* speaks only of the woman giving herself eternally in body and soul to the devil. There is no mention of torment in everlasting fire (as Scot paraphrases it).

Notes

30 Mackay (ed. and trans.), *Malleus Maleficarum*, pt. 2, qn. 1, ch. 2, 97C–D.
31 See Scot, *The Discoverie of Witchcraft*, pp. 41, 42.
32 See Scot, *The Discoverie of Witchcraft*, p. 42. Scot gives as his reference 'cap.1. in novo Mal.malef.' Bartolomeo della Spina published two other works on witchcraft in addition to *Quaestio de Strigibus*. These were *Tractatus de Praeeminentia Sacrae Theologiae* (1525) and *Quadruplex Apologia de Lamiis Contra Ponzinibium* (1525). These three works were often published together, the most well known edition being in 1576. They were republished in 1581 under the title *Novus Malleus Maleficarum sub Quaestione de Strigibus seu Maleficis*. This is no doubt the edition in which Scot accessed Spina's work.
33 Scot, *The Discoverie of Witchcraft*, p. 42. See also Scott (trans.), *On the Demon-Mania of Witches*, ii. 4. Bodin adds the detail that he was condemned on Christmas Eve 1543, and that the Devil was in the form of a goat.
34 Scot, *The Discoverie of Witchcraft*, p. 42. See also Scott (trans.), *On the Demon-Mania of Witches*, ii. 4.
35 Scot was relying on the English translation of this work, *A Dialogue of Witches* ([London], 1575).
36 Scot, *The Discoverie of Witchcraft*, p. 43.
37 Daneau, *A Dialogue of Witches*, sig. F.4.v.
38 See Jeffrey Burton Russell, *Witchcraft in the Middle Ages* (Ithaca and London: Cornell University Press, 1972), pp. 242–3.
39 See E. William Monter, *Witchcraft in France and Switzerland: The Borderlands During the Reformation* (Ithaca and London: Cornell University Press, 1976), pp. 157–9.
40 On the life of Daneau, see Olivier Fatio, 'Lambert Daneau 1530–1595,' in Jill Raitt (ed.), *Shapers of Religious Traditions in Germany, Switzerland, and Poland, 1560–1600* (New Haven and London: Yale University Press, 1981), pp. 105–19.
41 See Christina Larner, *Enemies of God: The Witch-hunt in Scotland* (London: Blackwell, 1981), pp. 110–12.
42 Michael Dalton, *The Countrey Justice Containing the Practice of the Justices of the Peace out of their Sessions* (London, 1630), p. 273.
43 Thus, the nipple was often sought for in the genital regions. For an early example of this at the popular level, see Anon., *The Most Strange and Admirable Discoverie of the Three Witches of Warboys, Arraigned, Convicted, and Executed at the Last Assises at Huntington*

(London, 1593), sig. O.3.v–O.4.r. See also Philip C. Almond, *The Witches of Warboys: An Extraordinary Story of Sorcery, Sadism and Satanic Possession* (London: I.B.Tauris, 2008).

44 Anon., *The Examination and Confession of Certaine Wytches at Chensforde in the Countie of Essex* (n.p., 1566), sig. 2.A.7.v.
45 Scot, *The Discoverie of Witchcraft*, p. 10.
46 See W.W., *A True and Just Recorde*, sig. C.2.v–C.3.r.
47 Michael Dalton, *The Countrey Justice* (London, 1697), p. 384.
48 Bernard, *A Guide to Grand-Jury Men*, p. 218. See also pp. 110–111, 219. The passage in Dalton drawn from Bernard first appeared in the 1630 edition of *The Countrey Justice*.
49 James, R., *Daemonologie*, p. 80.
50 Anon., *The Witches of Northamptonshire* (London, 1612), sig. C.2.r (my italics).
51 Scot, *The Discoverie of Witchcraft*, p. 47.
52 *Ibid.*, p. 48.
53 *Ibid.*, p. 50.
54 *Ibid.*, pp. 46–7. See also Scott (trans.), *On the Demon-Mania of Witches*, ii. 4. I cannot find this story in the *Malleus Maleficarum*.
55 As it was by Scot. His marginal note reads, 'Concil.Acquirens [sic] in decret.26.quae5. can.episcopi. August. de spiritu & anima cap.8. Franc. Ponzivib. [sic] tract de lam. numero 49 Grillandus de sort. Numero. 6. See Scot, *The Discoverie of Witchcraft*, p. 66. The last two references are to the Italian demonologist Paolo Grillando (fl. In the first half of the sixteenth century) and his *Tractatus de hereticis et sortilegiis eorum poenis* (Treatise on Heretics and Sorcerors and their Punishments) written around 1524, and the Italian lawyer Giovanni Francesco Ponzinibio (fl. In the first half of the sixteenth century) and his *Tractatus subtilis, et elegans, de lamiis, et excellentia utriusque iuris* (Subtle and Elegant Treatise on Witches and the Excellence of Both Civil and Canon Law) written in 1519–20. Grillando was initially a sceptic on the question of the bodily transportation of witches, though he came to change his mind. Ponzinibio concluded that transportation occurs in the imagination of the witch and not in reality, following the canon *Episcopi*. On Grillando and Ponzinibio, see Lea, *Materials toward a History of Witchcraft*, i. 395–412, i. 377–82. On pseudo-Augustine's use of the *Decretum*, see Lea, *Materials Toward a History of Witchcraft*, i. 181. Scot and Weyer both assume this work is by St. Augustine. See Mora (ed.), *Witches, Devils, and*

Notes

    Doctors in the Renaissance: Johann Weyer, De Praestigiis Daemonum, pp. 191–2.
56 Lea, *Materials Toward a History of Witchcraft*, i. 178–80. The phrases in square brackets are additions to the canon *Episcopi* in the *Decretum*.
57 *Ibid.*, i. 179. This explanation would have suited Weyer to a tee. In fact, Weyer does cite the pseudo-Augustinian *Liber de spiritu et anima*'s quotation of the *Decretum* in support of his account of demonic illusions. See Mora (ed.), *Witches, Devils, and Doctors in the Renaissance: Johann Weyer, De Praestigiis Daemonum*, pp. 191–2. Scot does leave in his abbreviated version the statement that the wicked women were, in his translation, 'following sathans provocations, being seduced by the illusion of divels.' See Scot, *The Discoverie of Witchcraft*, p. 66.
58 See Bartolomeo della Spina, *Quaestio de Strigibus* (Venice, 1523), chs. 21–26. See also Lea, *Materials Toward a History of Witchcraft*, i. 390–1.
59 Scot, *The Discoverie of Witchcraft*, p. 66.
60 See Johannes Nider, *Formicarius* (Cologne, 1480), 71b-72b. Werner Tschacher, *Der Formicarius des Johannes Nider von 1437/38* (Aachen: Shaker Verlag, 2000), pp. 344–5.
61 See Granger Ryan and Helmut Ripperger (trans.), *The Golden Legend of Jacobus de Voragine* (New York: Arno Press, 1969), p. 397.
62 Mackay (ed. and trans.), *Malleus Maleficarum*, pt. 2, qn. 1, ch. 3, 105C.
63 *Ibid.*, pt. 2, qn. 1, ch. 2, 100D.
64 *Ibid.*, pt. 2, qn. 1, ch. 3, 104A.
65 *Ibid.*, pt. 1, qn. 1, 10C–D (my italics).
66 *Ibid.*, pt. 2, qn. 1, ch. 3, 105A (my italics).
67 *Ibid.*, pt. 2, qn. 1, ch. 3, 105A–B. And see also pt. 1, qn. 3, 79B–C.
68 *Ibid.*, pt. 2, qn. 1, ch. 3, 105C.
69 See Mora (ed.), *Witches, Devils, and Doctors in the Renaissance: Johann Weyer, De Praestigiis Daemonum*, pp. 225–6.
70 Scot, *The Discoverie of Witchcraft*, p. 185.
71 *Ibid.*, p. 185.
72 Scot has only Mt. 4.8 and Lk. 3.9 (wrongly) as his marginal references. See Scot, *The Discoverie of Witchcraft*, p. 103.
73 Mora (ed.), *Witches, Devils, and Doctors in the Renaissance: Johann Weyer, De Praestigiis Daemonum*, p. 197.
74 Scot, *The Discoverie of Witchcraft*, p. 103.
75 *Ibid.*, p. 104.

76 E[usebius] P[aget], *A Harmonie upon the three Evangelists, Matthew, Mark, and Luke, with the Commentarie of M. John Calvine* (London, 1584), p. 131.
77 See James, R., *Daemonologie*, pp. 41–2.
78 Scot, *The Discoverie of Witchcraft*, p. 89.
79 *Ibid.*, p. 97.
80 Scot makes him an Englishman.
81 See Mackay (ed. and trans.), *Malleus Maleficarum*, pt. 2, qn. 2, ch. 4, 166C-167C; see also Scot, *The Discoverie of Witchcraft*, pp. 94–6.
82 See Mackay (ed. and trans.), *Malleus Maleficarum*, pt. 1, qn. 10, 59C–63C.
83 *Ibid.*, pt. 2, qn. 2, ch. 4, 167A–167B.
84 Quoted by Joyce E. Salisbury, *The Beast Within: Animals in the Middle Ages* (New York and London: Routledge, 1994), p. 160.
85 Bettenson (trans.), *Concerning the City of God Against the Pagans*, Bk. 18, ch. 18, p. 783.
86 See Thomas Aquinas, *Summa Theologica*, pt. 1, qn. 114, art. 4. See also *De Potentia Dei* qn. 6, art. 5
87 See Dennis M. Kratz, 'Fictus Lupus: The Werewolf in Christian Thought,' *Classical Folia* 30 (1976), pp. 57–79.
88 Scot, *The Discoverie of Witchcraft*, p. 97. In fact Scot seems to have quite misread Augustine's claim that these stories are so incredible that credence should be withheld.
89 Daneau, *A Dialogue of Witches*, sig. F.1.r. See also Scot, *The Discoverie of Witchcraft*, pp. 98–9.
90 See *Ibid.*, sig. F.1.v–F.2.v. To muddy the waters further, Daneau combined his explanation of transformation as 'true' demonic illusions with a medical account of them as 'false' illusions.
91 Scot, *The Discoverie of Witchcraft*, p. 100.
92 *Ibid.*, p. 101.
93 See Almond, *Adam and Eve in Seventeenth-Century Thought*, pp. 27–32.
94 See Daniel 4. 28–37. And see Scott (trans.), *On the Demon-Mania of Witches*, ii. 6, p. 129.
95 See David Lyle Jeffrey (ed.), *A Dictionary of Biblical Tradition in English Literature* (Grand Rapids, Michigan: Eerdmans, 1992), pp. 544–5.
96 Scot, *The Discoverie of Witchcraft*, p. 102. And see Mora (ed.), *Witches, Devils, and Doctors in the Renaissance: Johann Weyer, De Praestigiis*

Notes

Daemonum, p. 343. Scot appears to be the first person in England to use the term 'lycanthropy'.
97   James, R., *Daemonologie*, p. 61.
98   *Ibid.*, p. 62.
99   Scot, *The Discoverie of Witchcraft*, p. 72.
100 See Mackay (ed. and trans.), *Malleus Maleficarum*, pt. 2, qn. 1, chs. 4–7.
101 Though the *Malleus Maleficarum* cites Nider and Thomas.
102 Scot, *The Discoverie of Witchcraft*, p. 75. And see Mackay (ed. and trans.), *Malleus Maleficarum*, pt. 2, qn. 1, ch. 4, 109B–D.
103 *Ibid.*, p. 76. And see Mackay (ed. and trans.), *Malleus Maleficarum*, pt. 2, qn. 1, ch. 4, 110D–111A.
104 Scot, *The Discoverie of Witchcraft*, p. 77. And see Mackay (ed. and trans.), *Malleus Maleficarum*, pt. 2, qn. 1, ch. 6, 115A.
105 *Ibid.*, p. 78. And see Mackay (ed. and trans.), *Malleus Maleficarum*, pt. 2, qn. 1, ch. 7, 117D–118A.
106 Mackay (ed. and trans.), *Malleus Maleficarum*, pt. 2, qn. 1, ch. 7, 115D.
107 Mackay (ed. and trans.), *Malleus Maleficarum*, pt. 2, qn. 1, ch. 7, 118A.
108 Scot, *The Discoverie of Witchcraft*, p. 78.
109 Mackay (ed. and trans.), *Malleus Maleficarum*, pt. 2, qn. 1, ch. 7, 118C. See also, pt. 1, qn. 2, 56A–58B.
110 *Ibid.*, pt. 2, qn. 1, ch. 9, 121D.
111 *Ibid.*, pt. 2, qn. 1, ch. 7, 118A.
112 *Ibid.*, pt. 2, qn. 1, ch. 7, 118B–C.
113 Scot, *The Discoverie of Witchcraft*, p. 86.
114 Ludwig Lavater, *Of Ghostes and Spirites, Walking by Nyght* (London, 1596), pp. 6, 12–13. See also Owen Davies, 'The Nightmare Experience, Sleep Paralysis, and Witchcraft Accusations,' *Folklore* 114 (2003), pp. 181–203.
115 See Mora (ed.), *Witches, Devils, and Doctors in the Renaissance: Johann Weyer, De Praestigiis Daemonum*, pp. 232–3.
116 Scot, *The Discoverie of Witchcraft*, pp. 83–4.
117 Scot gives as his source 'vita Hieronym' ('Life of Jerome'). See Scot, *The Discoverie of Witchcraft*, p. 79. He has taken this from the attribution of the story in the *Malleus Maleficarum* to a 'John of Andrea in the *Book of Jerome*' I have not been able to trace this work.
118 Mackay (ed. and trans.), *Malleus Maleficarum*, pt. 2, qn. 1, ch. 11, 131B.

119 Scot, *The Discoverie of Witchcraft*, p. 79.
120 See Andreas Hyperius, *Methodi Theologiae, sive Praecipuorum Christianiae Religionis* (Basel, 1563), pp. 304–6
121 Scot, *The Discoverie of Witchcraft*, p. 85. See also p. 219. The notion of Merlin as fathered by an incubus first appeared in Geoffrey of Monmouth's *Historia Regum Britanniae* in *c.* AD 1136.
122 See Walter Stephens, *Giants in Those Days* (Lincoln and London: University of Nebraska Press, 1989), ch. 2.
123 See Bettenson (trans.), *Concerning the City of God Against the Pagans*, bk. 15, ch. 23, pp. 637–42.
124 Thomas Aquinas, *Scriptum Super Sententiis*, http:www.corpus homisticum.org/snp2005, bk.2, dist.8, qn.1, art.4.
125 Mackay (ed. and trans.), *Malleus Maleficarum*, pt. 1, qn. 3, 26C.
126 *Ibid.*, pt. 2, qn. 1, ch. 4, 109A.
127 Scot, *The Discoverie of Witchcraft*, p. 74. Both the *Malleus Maleficarum* and (consequently) Scot wrongly cite the passage in Aquinas' commentary on the *Sentences* as bk. 2, dist. 4, art. 4 rather than bk. 2, dist. 8, qn. 1, art. 4. Scot's irony is rather lost by virtue of his translating the phrase in the *Malleus Maleficarum* to do with corporeal strength and size (*fortes et magni corpore*) by 'greatnesse and excellencie'.
128 See Scot, *The Discoverie of Witchcraft*, p.8 7. And see also Robert C. Hill (trans.), *Saint John Chrysostom: Homilies on Genesis 18–45* (Washington D.C.: The Catholic University of America Press, 1990), Homily 22.
129 See Scot, *The Discoverie of Witchcraft*, p.87. And see also Hyperius, *Methodi Theologiae, sive Praecipuorum Christianiae Religionis*, p. 306.
130 *Ibid.*, p. 87.
131 Mackay (ed. and trans.), *Malleus Maleficarum*, pt. 2, qn. 1, ch. 4, 105D-107D.
132 *Ibid.*, pt. 2, qn. 1, ch. 4, 107D.
133 Scot, *The Discoverie of Witchcraft*, p. 85.
134 See *Ibid.*, p. 131.
135 *Ibid.*, p. 85. This was the most familiar name for a fairy in Elizabethan England. He was often thought of as the offspring of a spirit and a female. Scot's account includes the common motif that when he is given a waistcoat instead of a bowl of milk he disappears for ever. Robin Good-fellow was soon to make a comeback thanks to William Shakespeare. He is the model for Puck in *A Midsummer*

Night's Dream. See especially act 2, scene 1. Robert Burton included him in his list of terrestrial devils in his *The Anatomy of Melancholy*.
136   *Ibid.*, p. 86.

Four   Magic

1   Scot, *The Discoverie of Witchcraft*, p. 111.
2   *Ibid.*, p. 109. Elsewhere, Scot argued that there were three kinds. The veneficiae were just 'plaine poisoners'. Apart from them, he declared, there were only two sorts: the one sort being such by imputation, as so thought of by others (and these are abused, and not abusors) the other by acceptation, as being willing so to be accompted (and these be mere cousenors.)' These four biblical categories all fit within the veneficiae and those who are witches by acceptation. See Scot, *The Discoverie of Witchcraft*, sig. A.4.r.
3   *Ibid.*, p. 112.
4   *Ibid.*, p. 112.
5   *Ibid.*, p. 111. This was the case with Wycliffe's Bible (1382), Tyndale's Pentateuch (1530), The Miles Coverdale Bible (1535), The Geneva Bible (1560), and The Bishop's Bible (1568). The one slight exception was the Douai-Rheims version (1582) which substituted 'wizard' for 'witch'. The Latin Vulgate had set the pattern for the translation 'witch' with its rendition of Exodus 22.18, 'maleficos non patieris vivere.'
6   The Septuagint reads, 'φαρμακους οὐ περιποιήσετε'. Scot has 'Φάρμακους ὀυκ ἐπιζεώσετε'. He must not have had a copy of the Septuagint at hand.
7   William Whiston (trans.), *Flavius Josephus, The Antiquities of the Jews*, http://www.gutenberg.org/files/2848/2848-h, book 4, ch. 8, v. 34. See Scot, *The Discoverie of Witchcraft*, p. 111. Scot found the reference in Weyer. See Mora (ed.), *Witches, Devils, and Doctors in the Renaissance: Johann Weyer, De Praestigiis Daemonum*, p. 545.
8   Scot's suggestion that Veneficiae were both poisoners and cousennot;ers is again derived from Weyer. See Mora (ed.), *Witches, Devils, and Doctors in the Renaissance: Johann Weyer, De Praestigiis Daemonum*, pp. 93-4.
9   Scot, *The Discoverie of Witchcraft*, p. 115.
10 *Ibid.*, p. 116.
11 *Ibid.*, p. 114.

12 *Ibid.*, p. 124. See also Mora (ed.), *Witches, Devils, and Doctors in the Renaissance: Johann Weyer, De Praestigiis Daemonum*, pp. 274–5.
13 *Ibid.*, p. 117.
14 *Ibid.*, p. 120. There is also a brief account of a monk who poisoned King John. It was a common belief at the time that John had died as a result of poisoning. Scot probably knew of the story from its telling in Foxe's *Book of Martyrs*, a work with which he was familiar.
15 *Ibid.*, p. 119.
16 *Ibid.*, p. 116.
17 See Randall Martin, *Women, Murder, and Equity in Early Modern England* (USA: Routledge, 2008.), ch. 4.
18 Scot, *The Discoverie of Witchcraft*, p. 126.
19 Richard Church (ed.), *William Lambarde: A Perambulation of Kent* (Bath: Adams and Dart, 1970), p. 170. On Elizabeth Barton, see Diane Watt, *Sectaries of God: Women Prophets in Late Medieval and Early Modern England* (Cambridge: D.S. Brewer, 1997), ch. 3.
20 *Ibid.*, p. 171.
21 *Ibid.*, pp. 171–2.
22 See L. E. Whatmore, 'The Sermon against the Holy Maid of Kent and her Adherents, delivered at Paul's Cross, November 23rd, 1533, and at Canterbury, December the 7th,' *The English Historical Review* 58 (1943), p. 466.
23 John Cox (ed.), *The Works of Thomas Cranmer* (Cambridge: Cambridge University Press, 1844–6), ii. 273.
24 Church (ed.), *William Lambarde: A Perambulation of Kent*, p. 174.
25 *Ibid.*, p. 175.
26 Whatmore, 'The Sermon against the Holy Maid of Kent and her Adherents, delivered at Paul's Cross, November 23rd, 1533, and at Canterbury, December the 7th,' p. 469.
27 Scot, *The Discoverie of Witchcraft*, p. 126.
28 See *ibid.*, p. 132.
29 See Philip C. Almond, *Demonic Possession and Exorcism in Early Modern England: Contemporary Texts in their Cultural Contexts* (Cambridge: Cambridge University Press, 2004), ch. 2.
30 See Scot, *The Discoverie of Witchcraft*, pp. 127–9.
31 *Ibid.*, p. 129.
32 *Ibid.*, p. 130. Wallace Notestein read Scot this way. See Notestein, *A History of Witchcraft in England from 1558 to 1718*, p. 386.

Notes

33 *Ibid.*, p. 131. Thomas Wotton (c. AD 1521–87) was a Justice of the Peace and Sheriff of Kent from 1558–9 and again from 1578–9. Thomas Lambarde's *The Perambulation of Kent* was dedicated to him.

34 See *ibid.*, p. 136. It was a piece of information that he probably drew from Weyer. See Mora (ed.), *Witches, Devils, and Doctors in the Renaissance: Johann Weyer, De Praestigiis Daemonum*, p. 141.

35 Mora (ed.), *Witches, Devils, and Doctors in the Renaissance: Johann Weyer, De Praestigiis Daemonum*, p. 141. Weyer attributes this passage to a work by Chrysostom entitled *Concerning the Pythian Woman or the Oracle of Apollo*. It comes in fact from a homily by Chrysostom on I Corinthians, 12.1–2. See Philip Schaff (ed.), *Saint Chrysostom: Homilies on the Epistles of Paul to the Corinthians* (Grand Rapids, Michigan: Eerdmans, 1969), p. 170. The early Church Fathers generally regarded the Ventriloqui as possessed by demons. See David E. Aune, *Prophecy in Early Christianity and the Ancient Mediterranean World* (Grand Rapids, Michigan: Eerdmans, 1983), pp. 40–1.

36 See Michael Slusser (trans.), *St. Gregory Thaumaturgus: Life and Works* (Washington, D.C.: The Catholic University of America Press, 1998), pp. 56–7.

37 Scot, *The Discoverie of Witchcraft*, p. 137.

38 Again, apart from local knowledge, Scot was reliant on Lambarde's *The Perambulation of Kent* for his knowledge of the rood of grace and St. Rumwald. See Scot, *The Discoverie of Witchcraft*, pp. 137–8,

39 Quoted by Margaret Aston, *Faith and Fire: Popular and Unpopular Religion* (London: Hambledon Press, 1993), p. 268.

40 Scot, *The Discoverie of Witchcraft*, p. 139. See also, p. 155. Both in the text and in the margin Scot here gives the Biblical source as 2 Samuel 28. It is in fact 1 Samuel 28. Elsewhere he correctly cites 1 Samuel.

41 1 Sam. 28.7. The Hebrew text (transliterated) has *'ba'alath 'obh'* ('a woman with a spirit'). The Vulgate reads 'mulier habens pythonem' ('a woman having a divining spirit'). The Septuagint reads 'γυνη έγγαστρίμυθος' ('a ventroloquising woman'). Both the Geneva Bible and the King James version connect the woman at Endor with English witchcraft through the translation 'familiar spirit.'

42 1 Sam. 28.19.

43 For early interpretations, see K.A.D. Smelik, 'The Witch of Endor: 1 Samuel 28 in Rabbinic and Christian Exegesis till 800 A.D.', *Vigiliae Christianae* 33 (1979), pp. 160–79.

44 The eleventh century Rabbi Samuel ben Hofni read her as a fraud. See *ibid.*, p. 163.
45 Scot would have been horrified by the claim made in the second book of 'A Discourse Concerning Devils and Spirits' appended to the 1665 edition of *The Discoverie of Witchcraft*, and written by an occult supporter in which it was claimed that Samuel appeared in his 'Sydereal Spirit'. See Brinsley Nicholson (ed.), *The Discoverie of Witchcraft by Reginald Scot, Esquire*, p. 504.
46 See Scott (trans.), *On the Demon-Mania of Witches*, p. 105.
47 See Jean Bodin, *De la Demonomanie des Sorciers* (Paris, 1580), p. 70v.
48 Anthonie Marten (trans.), *The Common Places of the Most Famous and Renowned Diviner Doctor Peter Martyr* (London, 1583). Scot did not read them as carefully as he might have. On p. 140 of *The Discoverie of Witchcraft*, Scot refers to a distinction of Peter Martyr with 'me thinks' in parentheses. The passage which follows is clearly derived from Lavater. See Ludwig Lavater, *Of Ghostes and Spirites walking by Nyght* (London, 1572), pp. 127–8.
49 On Augustine's uncertainty on the issue, see Smelik, 'The Witch of Endor: 1 Samuel 28 in Rabbinic and Christian Exegesis till 800 A.D.,' p. 173.
50 Lloyd E. Berry (ed.), *The Geneva Bible: A Facsimile of the 1560 Edition* (Madison, Wisconsin: University of Wisconsin Press, 1969), Fol. 134v.
51 Scot, *The Discoverie of Witchcraft*, p. 134.
52 His real name was Burchard Kranich (d.1578). See *Oxford D.N.B.*, and F.E. Halliday, 'Queen Elizabeth and Dr Burcot,' *History Today* 5 (1955), pp. 542–4.
53 See Scot, *The Discoverie of Witchcraft*, pp. 252, 309.
54 *Ibid.*, p. 146.
55 *Ibid.*, p. 150.
56 *Ibid.*, p. 152.
57 John Hooper, 'A Brief and Clear Confession of the Christian Faith,' in Charles Nevinson (ed.), *Later Writings of Bishop Hooper* (Cambridge: Cambridge University Press, 1852), pp. 44–5. Quoted by Jane Shaw, *Miracles in Enlightenment England* (New Haven and London: Yale University Press, 2006), p. 26.
58 See Lorraine Daston and Katherine Park, *Wonders and the Order of Nature* (New York: Zone, 2001), p. 121.
59 Lorraine Daston, 'Marvellous Facts and Miraculous Evidence in Early Modern Europe,' in Peter G. Platt (ed.), *Wonders, Marvels, and*

Notes

Monsters in Early Modern Culture (Newark, New Jersey: University of Delaware Press, 1999), p. 81.
60 John Baptista Porta, *Natural Magic* (London, 1658), pp. 1–2. This passage is translated from the 1584 edition of *Magiae Naturalis*. We do not know if Scot had a copy of this edition, though the thoughts expressed are in line with those in the 1558 first edition which he did know.
61 See Chapter five.
62 Scot, *The Discoverie of Witchcraft*, p. 159.
63 *Ibid.*, pp. 160–1. The biblical allusion here is to 1 Corinthians 15. 25–8.
64 *Ibid.*, p. 166.
65 *Ibid.*, p. 167.
66 *Ibid.*, p. 171.
67 *Ibid.*, pp. 167–8.
68 See Patrick Curry, *Prophecy and Power: Astrology in Early Modern England* (Princeton, New Jersey: Princeton University Press, 1989), p. 8.
69 See Thomas, *Religion and the Decline of Magic*, ch. 10.
70 Curry, *Prophecy and Power*, p. 11.
71 G[oddred] G[ylby] (trans.), *An Admonicion against Astrology judiciall... by Jhon Calvine* (London, 1561), sig. A.7.r. See also Christine McCall Probes, 'Calvin on Astrology,' *Westminster Theological Journal* 37 (1974), pp. 24–33.
72 *Ibid.*, sig. D.1.v.
73 See *Ibid.*, sig. B.1.r.
74 See *Ibid.*, sig. D.7.r.
75 See *Ibid.*, sigs. C.2.r., C.3.r.
76 Scot, *The Discoverie of Witchcraft*, p. 169.
77 *Ibid.*, p. 171.
78 See Allan Chapman, 'Astrological Medicine' in Charles Webster (ed.), *Health, Medicine and Mortality in the Sixteenth Century* (Cambridge: Cambridge University Press, 1979), pp. 275–300.
79 G[ylby] (trans.), *An Admonicion*, sigs. A.8.v-B.1.r.
80 See *Ibid.*, sig. B.1.r-v.
81 *Ibid.*, sig. B.5.r.
82 See *Ibid.*, sig. B.7.r.
83 See Scot, *The Discoverie of Witchcraft*, pp. 169–70. The marginal note reads 'The ridiculous art of nativitie casting.' This note does not reflect Scot's ambivalence in the text.

84 *Ibid.*, p. 177.
85 Thomas, *Religion and the Decline of Magic*, p. 151.
86 Scot, *The Discoverie of Witchcraft*, p. 187.
87 Thomas Hill, *The Moste Pleasaunte Arte of the Interpretation of Dreames* (London, 1576), Epistle Dedicatory. The date of Hill's work is uncertain. The earliest complete copies are dated 1576, though Scot refers to the work as published in 1568. See Scot, *The Discoverie of Witchcraft*, p. 180. On this issue, and early modern dream interpretation generally, see Peter Holland, '"The Interpretation of Dreams" in the Renaissance,' in Peter Brown (ed.), *Reading Dreams: The Interpretation of Dreams from Chaucer to Shakespeare* (Oxford: Oxford University Press, 1999), pp. 125-46.
88 See Robert J. White (trans. and comm.), *The Interpretation of Dreams: Oneirocritica by Artemidorus* (Park Ridge, New Jersey: Noyes Press, 1975), bk. 1.1-2. See also S. R. F. Price, 'The Future of Dreams: From Freud to Artemidorus,' *Past and Present* 113 (1986), pp. 3-37.
89 Scot, *The Discoverie of Witchcraft*, p. 178.
90 *Ibid.*, p. 182.
91 *Ibid.*, p. 183.
92 *Ibid.*, p. 180.
93 *Ibid.*, p.179. And see Holland, '"The Interpretation of Dreams" in the Renaissance,' pp. 131-2, n. 13. There were numerous editions of this published in England in the sixteenth century.
94 *Ibid.*, p. 177.
95 *Ibid.*, p. 189.
96 *Ibid.*, p. 194.
97 Thomas, *Religion and the Decline of Magic*, pp. 282-3.
98 Scot, *The Discoverie of Witchcraft*, p. 197.
99 *Ibid.*, p. 208.
100 *Ibid.*, p. 203.
101 *Ibid.*, p. 201.
102 *Ibid.*, p. 191.
103 [Richard Roussat], *The Most Excellent Profitable, and Pleasaunt Booke of the Famous Doctor and Expert Astrologian Arcandum* (London, 1578), sub-title.
104 *On Occult Philosophy* was first published from 1531-1533, though began some twenty years earlier.
105 J.F. (trans.), *Three Books of Occult Philosophy, written by Henry Cornelius Agrippa, of Nettesheim* (London, 1651), p. 162. By 'naturall

Notes

signification' was meant the notion that there was a 'real', rather than an arbitrary, relation between the sign and the thing signified, and hence the efficacy of Hebrew (as the language of God – and of Adam) as a natural language in magic. On Hebrew as the Adamic language and the early modern quest for a 'natural language', see Almond, *Adam and Eve in Seventeenth-Century Thought*, pp. 128–42.

106 Henrich Cornelius Agrippa, *Of the Vanitie and Uncertaintie of Arts and Sciences* (London, 1575), sig. B.1.r. See also Philip Beitchman, *Alchemy of the Word: Cabala of the Renaissance* (New York: State University of New York Press, 1998), ch. 2. Here Beitchman argues that in *Of the Vanitie and Uncertaintie of Arts and Sciences* Agrippa, far from rejecting Cabala, was in effect endorsing a higher form of it, one that was accessible to everyone. He sees its outcomes in the radical mysticism of the Anabaptists. I suspect it played out more widely, not only in the 'cabalistic' or 'mystical' readings of Scripture within Reformation radicals but in neo-Platonic conservatives like Henry More. In Henry More's understanding of Cabala, all specifically Jewish understandings of the term have disappeared. In More, a Cabalistic reading is no more than a 'mystical' one in the broadest neo-Platonic sense.

107 Scot, *The Discoverie of Witchcraft*, p. 199.
108 Agrippa, *Of the Vanitie and Uncertaintie of Arts and Sciences*, p. 61.
109 It was an idea that Scot had probably taken from one of the Latin poems of Sir Thomas More. See J. H. Marsden, *Philomorus: A Brief Examination of the Latin Poems of Sir Thomas More* (London: Pickering, 1842), pp. 68–9.
110 Scot, *The Discoverie of Witchcraft*, p. 216.
111 See Davies, *Popular Magic: Cunning-Folk in English History*, p. 131; and anon., *Witchcraft detected and prevented: or, the School of Black Art newly opened* (Peterhead: P. Buchan, 1824).
112 Frank Klaassen and Christopher Phillips, 'The Return of Stolen Goods: Reginald Scot, Religious Controversy, and Magic in Bodleian Library, Additional B.1.' in *Magic, Ritual, and Witchcraft* 1 (2006), p. 142.
113 See *Ibid.*, p. 142.
114 Scot, *The Discoverie of Witchcraft*, p. 377.
115 [Philips van Marnix van St. Aldegonde], *The Bee Hive of the Romishe Churche* (London, 1579). And see Scot, *The Discoverie of Witchcraft*, pp. 230, 236.

116 This is *Horae Eboracenses*. See Christopher Wordsworth (ed.), *Horae Eboracenses: The Prymer or Hours of the Blessed Virgin Mary, According to the Use of the Illustrious Church of York* (Durham: Surtees Society, 1920). See Scot, *The Discoverie of Witchcraft*, p. 234. See also Eamon Duffy, *The Stripping of the Altars: Traditional Religion in England 1400–1580* (New Haven and London: Yale University Press, 1992), p. 274.
117 Scot, *The Discoverie of Witchcraft*, pp. 279–80.
118 *Ibid.*, p. 218.
119 See Duffy, *The Stripping of the Altars: Traditional Religion in England 1400*, ch. 8.
120 Scot, *The Discoverie of Witchcraft*, p. 243.
121 See Richard Kieckhefer, *Magic in the Middle Ages* (Cambridge: Cambridge University Press, 2000), ch. 4.
122 Scot, *The Discoverie of Witchcraft*, p. 244.
123 *Ibid.*, p. 232. The names of the three Magi: Gaspar, Melchior, and Balthasar were commonly used in talismanic or word magic. See *ibid.*, pp. 231–2 for a charm against epilepsy using their names.
124 *Ibid.*, p. 272.
125 *Ibid.*, pp. 269–70.
126 See *ibid.*, p. 265. Mora (ed.), *Witches, Devils, and Doctors in the Renaissance: Johann Weyer, De Praestigiis Daemonum*, pp. 381–3.
127 *Ibid.*, p. 264.
128 *Ibid.*, pp. 246–7. It translates as 'Let every spirit praise the Lord: They have Moses and the Prophets: Let God arise and let his enemies be scattered.' The sections of the prayer come from the Biblical passages, Psalm 150.6, Luke 16.29, and Psalm 68.1. Scot's marginal note gives Psalm 150, Luke 16, and (incorrectly) Psalm 64. Scot takes the passage from Psalm 150 from the version of the Vulgate in use in his time (reflecting the *Clementine Vulgate* of 1592) which reads *Omnis spiritus laudet Dominum*. The passage from Psalm 150 in the modern critical edition, *Nova Vulgata* (1979) has 'omne quod spirat, laudet Dominum' ('Let everything which breathes praise the Lord').
129 He referred his readers to '*B.Googe* his third booke' and to '*Vegetius*, his foure bookes thereupon' or the illiterate to 'some cunning bullocke leech.' See Scot, *The Discoverie of Witchcraft*, p. 283. The first reference is to Conrad Heresbach, *Foure Bookes of Husbandry, collected by M. Conradus Heresbachius ... newely Englished, and increade,*

Notes

by Barnabe Googe, Esquire (London, 1577), Book 3, pp. 111–56. The second is to Publius Renatus Vegetius (fl.450–500), the author of *Artis Veterinariae, sive Mulomedicinae*. This was the first veterinary medicine book of the Christian era, and among the first printed veterinary works. Scot was probably familiar with the edition published in 1574.

130 See Mora (ed.), *Witches, Devils, and Doctors in the Renaissance: Johann Weyer, De Praestigiis Daemonum*, pp. 408–10.
131 Scot, *The Discoverie of Witchcraft*, p. 274.
132 *Ibid.*, p. 275.
133 *Ibid.*, p. 276.
134 See Mora (ed.), *Witches, Devils, and Doctors in the Renaissance: Johann Weyer, De Praestigiis Daemonum*, p. 410.
135 Scot, *The Discoverie of Witchcraft*, p. 284.
136 *Ibid.*, p. 376.
137 *Ibid.*, p. 376.
138 *Ibid.*, p. 468.
139 *Ibid.*, p. 468.
140 *Ibid.*, p. 377.
141 *Ibid.*, p. 393. There is one addition to the manuscript clearly made by Scot: 'And note how this agreeth with popish charmes and conjurations.' See *ibid.*, p. 394.
142 *Ibid.*, pp. 430–1.
143 See *ibid.*, p. 393. A magical work with the same title was traditionally ascribed to Aristotle.
144 On the place of the *Pseudomonarchia daemonum* in the genre of the grimoire, and on the use of Scot in later such lists, see E.M. Butler, *Ritual Magic* (Cambridge: Cambridge University Press, 1949).
145 *Ibid.*, p. 236.
146 Scot, *The Discoverie of Witchcraft*, p. 415.
147 Thus Book fifteen, chapter one of the first edition became chapter ten in the 1665 version. For a detailed description of these chapters, see Butler, *Ritual Magic*, pp. 242–53.
148 Scot, *The Discoverie of Witchcraft*, p. 451. He adds 'the art of Paule' to this list on p. 466. We can assume that, although Scot knew of these works, he had not read them. None of them appear in his list of 'forren authors used in this Booke' at the beginning of *The Discoverie of Witchcraft*.
149 *Ibid.*, p. 452.

150 Pablo A. Torijano, *Solomon, the Esoteric King: From King to Magus, Development of a Tradition* (Leiden: Brill, 2002), p. 223.
151 Scot, *The Discoverie of Witchcraft*, pp. 454–5. Scot gives chapter twenty-two of Book five of the *Antiquities* as his source for this story. It occurs in fact in Book eight, chapter two.
152 *Ibid.* p. 459.
153 *Ibid.* p. 456. This was the 'mythical' St. Margaret of Antioch, also known as Marina. On the lives of St. Margaret, see Mary Clayton and Hugh Magennis, *The Old English Lives of St Margaret* (Cambridge: Cambridge University Press, 1994). One of the most popular medieval saints, she is one of those whose voices Joan of Arc was supposed to have heard. Although Scot does not tell us so, she defeats the Devil. Her life also appears in *The Golden Legend*. See Ryan and Ripperger (trans.), *The Golden Legend of Jacobus de Voragine*, pp. 351–4.
154 *Ibid.*, p. 457.
155 See *ibid.*, p. 469. The reference is to Matthew, 10.26, Mark 4.22, and Luke 8.17.
156 *Ibid.*, p. 469.

Five Philosophy and Religion

1 Scot, *The Discoverie of Witchcraft*, p. 287.
2 *Ibid.*, p. 289.
3 *Ibid.*, p. 290.
4 *Ibid.*, p. 290.
5 *Ibid.*, p. 291.
6 Daniel Sennert, *Thirteen Books of Natural Philosophy* (London, 1661), pp. 29, 431. Quoted by Keith Hutchinson, 'What Happened to Occult Qualities in the Scientific Revolution?,' *Isis* 73 (1982), p. 234.
7 See Hutchinson, 'What happened to Occult Qualities in the Scientific Revolution?,' p. 236.
8 Scot, *The Discoverie of Witchcraft*, p. 291.
9 Hutchinson, 'What Happened to Occult Qualities in the Scientific Revolution?,' p. 250.
10 Scot, *The Discoverie of Witchcraft*, p. 278.
11 *Ibid*, pp. 278–9. Scot ignores Vairus' belief that the power of fascination was dependent also upon either a tacit or express compact with Satan.

Notes

12 *Ibid.*, p. 486. And see Porta, *Natural Magic*, Book eight, chapter fourteen.
13 *Ibid.*, p. 288.
14 *Ibid.*, p. 351. See also p. 307.
15 *Ibid.*, p. 307.
16 Anglo, 'Reginald Scot's *Discoverie of Witchcraft*: Scepticism and Sadduceeism', p. 123.
17 Scot, *The Discoverie of Witchcraft*, p. 352.
18 *Ibid.*, p. 352.
19 See *Ibid.*, pp. 144, 252, 308, 309, 330, 339, 343–4, 349.
20 *Ibid.*, p. 352.
21 See Philip Butterworth, *Magic on the Early English Stage* (Cambridge: Cambridge University Press, 2005), pp. 9–13. I am particularly indebted to this work for information on juggling.
22 Scot, *The Discoverie of Witchcraft*, p. 308.
23 *Ibid.*, p. 308.
24 *Ibid.*, p. 309.
25 *Ibid.*, p. 309.
26 *Ibid.*, p. 144.
27 *Ibid.*, p. 252. The account of Muhammad and his pigeon was common in sixteenth and seventeenth-century England. According to the legend, Muhammad taught the pigeon to pick a pea out of his ear, informing his followers that it was the Holy Spirit telling him what God would have him do. Although Scot does not mention Sebastian Muenster in his list of authors, he may well have read the legend in Sebastian Muenster, *A Brief Collection...Gathered out of the Cosmographye of Sebastian Muenster* (London, 1572), p. 64.
28 *Ibid.*, p. 307.
29 *Ibid.*, p. 321.
30 *Ibid.*, p. 326.
31 *Ibid.*, p. 348. And see *ibid.*, p. 339 for an account of Steeven Tailor and Pope on 'how to tell where a stolen horse is become', to which the short answer was to steal them yourselves first.
32 See *Ibid.*, p. 346.
33 *Ibid.*, p. 324.
34 *Ibid.*, p. 308.
35 *Ibid.*, p. 309.
36 See *Ibid.*, pp. 340–1.
37 See *Ibid.*, pp. 349–50.

38 *Ibid.*, p. 350.
39 *Ibid.*, p. 323.
40 *Ibid.*, p. 329.
41 *Ibid.*, p. 350.
42 See *ibid.*, pp. 147, 323, 329, 339.
43 See Stanton J. Linden, *Darke Hieroglyphics: Alchemy in English Literature from Chaucer to the Restoration* (Lexington, Kentucky: The University Press of Kentucky, 1996).
44 Scot, *The Discoverie of Witchcraft*, p. 354.
45 *Ibid.*, p. 354.
46 *Ibid.*, p. 355.
47 *Ibid.*, p. 375.
48 See Maurice Hussey (ed.), *The Canon's Yeoman's Prologue and Tale* (Cambridge: Cambridge University Press, 1966).
49 *Ibid.*, p. 54, l.894.
50 I can only find two terms in Scot not mentioned in Chaucer, namely, 'terminations' and 'yest'.
51 Scot, *The Discoverie of Witchcraft*, pp. 357, 359, 365.
52 *Ibid.*, p. 357.
53 *Ibid.*, p. 358.
54 *Ibid.*, pp. 358–9.
55 *Ibid.*, p. 359.
56 See N. Bailey (trans.), *The Colloquies of Erasmus* (London: Reeves & Turner, 1878), i. 402–11.
57 *Ibid.*, p. 368.
58 Scot has accurately described Avicenna's position. See E. J. Holmyard, *Alchemy* (Harmondworth: Penguin, 1957), pp. 90–5.
59 *Ibid.*, p. 369. Scot's marginal note here reads, 'Franc. Petrarch. lib. de remed. utr. fort. I. cap. 10.' The reference is to Petrarch's *De Remediis utriusque Fortune*. Scot's reference to I. cap.10 is incorrect. The section on alchemy, 'De alchimia', is Dialogue 111. See Conrad H. Rawski (trans.), *Petrarch's Remedies for Fortune Fair and Foul* (Bloomington and Indianapolis: Indiana University Press, 1995), i. 299–301.
60 *Ibid.*, p. 369.
61 *Ibid.*, p. 372.
62 See Summers, *The Discoverie of Witchcraft by Reginald Scot*. A Dover edition of this work has been regularly published since 1972.
63 Montague Summers, *The Discoverie of Witchcraft by Reginald Scot* (Mineola, New York: Dover, 1972), p. xxxii.

Notes

64 See Montague Summers, *The Geography of Witchcraft* (London: Kegan and Paul, 1927), pp. 128-9.
65 Scot, *The Discoverie of Witchcraft*, p. 491.
66 Clark, *Thinking with Demons*, p. 212.
67 Scot, *The Discoverie of Witchcraft*, p. 507.
68 *Ibid.*, p. 515.
69 *Ibid.*, p. 502.
70 *Ibid.*, p. 536.
71 See Almond, *Adam and Eve in Seventeenth-Century Thought*, pp. 180-7.
72 Scot, *The Discoverie of Witchcraft*, p. 536 (my italics).
73 *Ibid.*, p. 539.
74 *Ibid.*, p. 510.
75 *Ibid.*, p. 511.
76 *Ibid.*, p. 512.
77 *Ibid.*, p. 510.
78 Anglo, 'Reginald Scot's *Discoverie of Witchcraft:* Scepticism and Sadduceeism', p. 129.
79 Sharpe, *Instruments of Darkness*, p. 55.
80 Leland L. Estes, 'Reginald Scot and his "Discoverie of Witchcraft": Religion and Science in the Opposition to the European Witch Craze,' *Church History* 52 (1983), p. 446.
81 Scot, *The Discoverie of Witchcraft*, p. 540.
82 See Almond, *Heaven and Hell in Enlightenment England*, pp. 29-37. For More, the Cartesian view that the soul was unextended entailed that it was nowhere, that it was incorporeal entailed that it was everywhere. His account of the bodies of the soul was intended to ensure that souls (and, by extension, spirits) could be said to be somewhere.
83 *Ibid.*, p. 515. My italics.
84 *Ibid.*, pp. 547-8.
85 Nathan Johnstone, *The Devil and Demonism in Early Modern England* (Cambridge: Cambridge University Press, 2006), p. 16. I am indebted to Johnstone for his analysis of Protestant demonism.
86 See Stuart Clark, 'Inversion, Misrule and the Meaning of Witchcraft,' *Past and Present* 87 (1980), pp. 98-127.
87 Scot, *The Discoverie of Witchcraft*, p. 545.
88 *Ibid.*, p. 548.
89 *Ibid.*, p. 560.

90 See David Wootton, 'Reginald Scot/Abraham Fleming/The Family of Love,' in Stuart Clark (ed.), *Languages of Witchcraft: Narrative, Ideology and Meaning in Early Modern Culture* (Hampshire: Macmillan, 2001), pp. 119–38.
91 *Ibid.*, p. 539 (my italics).
92 Wootton, 'Reginald Scot/Abraham Fleming/The Family of Love,' p. 135. Though Wootton cavils at the truth of this.
93 Scot, *The Discoverie of Witchcraft*, p. 560.
94 *Ibid.*, p. 557.
95 See Wootton, 'Reginald Scot/Abraham Fleming/The Family of Love,' p. 124. See also Christopher W. Marsh, *The Family of Love in English Society, 1550–1630* (Cambridge: Cambridge University Press, 1994), ch. 2
96 *Ibid.*, p. 549.
97 *Ibid.*, p. 545.
98 *Ibid.*, p. 508.
99 *Ibid.*, pp. 560–1.
100 *Ibid.*, p. 546.

Bibliography

Ady, Thomas, *A Candle in the Dark: Or, a Treatise Concerning the Nature of Witches & Witchcraft* (London, 1656).

Agrippa, Henrie Cornelius, *Of the Vanitie and Uncertaintie of Arts and Sciences* (London, 1575).

Agrippa von Nettesheim, Heinrich Cornelius, *Three Books of Occult Philosophy written by Henry Cornelius Agrippa of Nettesheim...; translated out of Latin into the English Tongue by J.F.* (London, 1651).

Almond, Philip C., *Heaven and Hell in Enlightenment England* (Cambridge: Cambridge University Press, 1994).

Almond, Philip C., *Adam and Eve in Seventeenth-Century Thought* (Cambridge: Cambridge University Press, 1999).

Almond, Philip C., *Demonic Possession and Exorcism in Early Modern England: Contemporary Texts in their Cultural Contexts* (Cambridge: Cambridge University Press, 2004).

Almond, Philip C., *The Witches of Warboys: An Extraordinary Story of Sorcery, Sadism and Satanic Possession* (London: I.B.Tauris, 2008).

Almond, Philip C., 'King James I and the Burning of Reginald Scot's *The Discoverie of Witchcraft*: The Invention of a Tradition,' *Notes and Queries* 56 (2009), pp. 209-213.

Andreadis, A. Harriette, *Mother Bombie by John Lyly* (Salzburg: Institut für englische Sprache und Literatur, 1975).

Anglo, Sydney 'Melancholia and Witchcraft: The Debate between Wier, Bodin, and Scot,' in A. Gerlo (ed.), *Folie et Déraison à la Renaissance* (Brussels: Editions de l'Université de Bruxelles, 1976), pp. 209-28.

Anglo, Sydney, 'Reginald Scot's *Discoverie of Witchcraft*: Scepticism and Sadduceeism,' in Sydney Anglo (ed.), *The Damned Art: Essays in the Literature of Witchcraft* (London: Routledge and Kegan Paul, 1977), pp. 106-139.

Anon., *A Rehearsall both Straung and True, of Hainous and Horrible Actes Committed by Elizabeth Stile, alias Rockingham, Mother Dutten, Mother*

Devell, Mother Margaret, Fower notorious Witches, Apprehended at Windsor in the Countie of Barks. And at Abbington Arraigned, Condemned, and Executed, on the 26. daye of Februarie laste Anno 1579 (London, 1579).

Anon., *The Most Strange and Admirable Discoverie of the Three Witches of Warboys, Arraigned, Convicted, and Executed at the Last Assises at Huntington* (London, 1593).

Anon., *Witchcraft Detected and Prevented: or, the School of Black Art newly opened* (Peterhead: P. Buchan, 1824).

Aquinas, Thomas, *Scriptum super Sententiis*, http: www.corpus homisticum.org/snp2005.

Ash, Eric H., ' "A perfect and an absolute work:" Expertise, Authority, and the Rebuilding of Dover Harbor, 1579-83,' in *Technology and Culture* 41 (2000), pp. 239-68.

Aston, Margaret, *Faith and Fire: Popular and Unpopular Religion 1350-1600* (London: Hambledon Press, 1993).

Aulen, Gustav, *Christus Victor: An Historical Study of the Three Main Types of the Idea of Atonement* (NewYork: Macmillan, 1977).

Aune, David E., *Prophecy in Early Christianity and the Ancient Mediterranean World* (Grand Rapids, Michigan: Eerdmans, 1983).

Ayre, John (ed.), *The Works of John Jewel, Bishop of Salisbury* (Cambridge: Cambridge University Press, 1845-50).

Babb, Lawrence, *The Elizabethan Malady: A Study of Melancholia in English Literature from 1580 to 1642* (East Lansing: Michigan State College Press, 1951).

Bailey, Michael, 'From Sorcery to Witchcraft: Clerical Conceptions of Magic in the Later Middle Ages,' *Speculum* 76 (2001), pp. 960-990.

Bartram, Claire, ' "Melancholic Imaginations": Witchcraft and the Politics of Melancholia in Elizabethan Kent,' *Journal of European Studies* 33 (2003), pp. 203-11.

Beitchman, Philip, *Alchemy of the Word: Cabala of the Renaissance* (New York: State University of New York Press, 1998).

Bernard, Richard, *A Guide to Grand-Jury Men* (London, 1627).

Berry, Lloyd E. (ed.), *The Geneva Bible: A Facsimile of the 1560 Edition* (Madison, Wisconsin: University of Wisconsin Press, 1969).

Bettenson, Henry (trans.), *Concerning the City of God Against the Pagans* (Harmondsworth: Penguin, 1972).

Bingham, Charles William (transl.), *Commentaries on the Four Last Books of Moses Arranged in the Form of a Harmony* (Grand Rapids, Michigan: Baker Book House, 1984).

Bibliography

Bugnolo, Alexis (trans. and ed.), *Peter Lombard's Sententiarum Liber Secundus, De Rerum Creatione et Formatione Corporalium et Spiritualium*, http://www.franciscan-archive.org/lombardus/II.

Butler, E. M., *Ritual Magic* (Cambridge: Cambridge University Press, 1949).

Butterworth, Philip, *Magic on the Early English Stage* (Cambridge: Cambridge University Press, 2005).

Chapman, Allan, 'Astrological Medicine,' in Charles Webster (ed.), *Health, Medicine and Mortality in the Sixteenth Century* (Cambridge: Cambridge University Press, 1979), pp. 275–300.

Church, Richard (ed.), *William Lambarde: A Perambulation of Kent* (Bath: Adams and Dart, 1970).

Clark, Peter, *English Provincial Society from the Reformation to the Revolution: Religion, Politics and Society in Kent 1500–1640* (Hassocks, Sussex: The Harvester Press, 1977).

Clark, Stuart, 'Inversion, Misrule and the Meaning of Witchcraft,' *Past and Present* 87 (1980), pp. 98–127.

Clark, Stuart, *Thinking with Demons: The Idea of Witchcraft in Early Modern Europe* (Oxford: Oxford University Press, 1997).

Clayton, Mary and Hugh Magennis, *The Old English Lives of St Margaret* (Cambridge: Cambridge University Press, 1994).

Clegg, Cyndia Susan, 'Burning Books as Propaganda in Jacobean England,' in Andrew Hadfield (ed.), *Literature and Censorship in Renaissance England* (Hampshire: Palgrave MacMillan, 2001), pp. 165–86.

Cohn, Norman, *Europe's Inner Demons* (Frogmore, St. Albans, Herts.: Paladin, 1976).

Cooper, Thomas, *Thesaurus Linguae Romanae et Britannicae* (London, 1584).

Cotta, John, *The Triall of Witch-Craft* (London, 1616).

Cox, John (ed.), *The Works of Thomas Cranmer* (Cambridge: Cambridge University Press, 1844–6).

Crawford, Patricia, 'Attitudes to Menstruation in Seventeenth-Century England,' *Past and Present* 91 (1981), pp. 47–73.

Cressy, David, 'Book Burning in Tudor and Stuart England,' in *The Sixteenth Century Journal* 36 (2005), pp. 359–74.

Curry, Patrick, *Prophecy and Power: Astrology in Early Modern England* (Princeton, New Jersey: Princeton University Press, 1989).

Dalton, Michael, *The Countrey Justice containing the Practice of the Justices of the Peace out of their Sessions* (London, 1630).

Dalton, Michael, *The Countrey Justice: Containing the Practice of the Justices of the Peace out of their Sessions* (London, 1697).

Daneau, Lambert, *A Dialogue of Witches* ([London], 1575).
Dasent, John Roche (ed.), *Acts of the Privy Council of England* (London: Eyre and Spottiswoode, 1890–5).
Daston, Lorraine, 'Marvellous Facts and Miraculous Evidence in Early Modern Europe,' in Peter G. Platt (ed.), *Wonders, Marvels, and Monsters in Early Modern Culture* (Newark, New Jersey: University of Delaware Press, 1999), pp. 76–104.
Daston, Lorraine and Katherine Park, *Wonders and the Order of Nature* (New York: Zone, 2001).
Davies, Owen, 'The Nightmare Experience, Sleep Paralysis, and Witchcraft Accusations,' *Folklore* 114 (2003), pp. 181–203.
Davies, Owen, *Popular Magic: Cunning-Folk in English History* (London: Hambledon Continuum, 2007).
Deacon, John and John Walker, *Dialogicall Discourses of Spirits and Divels* (London, 1601).
Donno, Elizabeth Story 'Abraham Fleming: A Learned Corrector in 1586–87,' *Studies in Bibliography* 42 (1989), pp. 200–11.
Dove, John, *A Sermon...Intreating of the Second Coming of Christ, and the Disclosing of Antichrist* (London, 1594).
Duffy, Eamon, *The Stripping of the Altars: Traditional Religion in England 1400–1580* (New Haven and London: Yale University Press, 1992).
During, Simon, *Modern Enchantments: The Cultural Power of Secular Magic* (Cambridge, Massachusetts: Harvard University Press, 2002).
Estes, Leland L., 'Reginald Scot and his "Discoverie of Witchcraft": Religion and Science in the Opposition to the European Witch Craze,' *Church History* 52 (1983), pp. 444–56.
Estes, Leland L., 'Good Witches, Wise Men, Astrologers, and Scientists: William Perkins and the Limits of the European Witch-Hunts,' in Ingrid Merkel and Allen G. Debus, *Hermeticism and the Renaissance: Intellectual History and the Occult in Early Modern Europe* (Washington: Folger Books, 1988), pp. 154–65.
Ewen, C. L'Estrange, *Witchcraft and Demonianism* (London: Heath Cranton, 1933).
F., J. (trans.), *Three Books of Occult Philosophy, written by Henry Cornelius Agrippa, of Nettesheim* (London, 1651).
Fatio, Olivier, 'Lambert Daneau 1530–1595,' in Jill Raitt (ed.), *Shapers of Religious Traditions in Germany, Switzerland, and Poland, 1560–1600* (New Haven and London: Yale University Press, 1981), pp. 105–19.

Bibliography

Galis, Richard, *A Brief Treatise Conteyning the most Strange and Horrible Crueltye of Elizabeth Stile alias Bockingham & hir Confederates Executed at Abington upon Richard Galis* (London, 1579).

Garzoni, Tommaso, *The Hospitall of incurable Fooles* (London, 1600).

Gaskill, Malcolm, *Crime and Mentalities in Early Modern England* (Cambridge: Cambridge University Press, 2000).

Gaskill, Malcolm, 'Witchcraft in Early Modern Kent: Stereotypes and the Background to Accusations,' in Jonathan Barry (ed.), *Witchcraft in Early Modern Europe: Studies in Culture and Belief* (Cambridge: Cambridge University Press, 1998), pp. 257-287.

Gaskill, Malcolm, 'Witches and Witchcraft Prosecutions, 1560-1660,' in Michael Zell (ed.), *Early Modern Kent 1540-1640* (Woodbridge: The Boydell Press and Kent County Council, 2000), pp. 245-77.

Gibson, Marion, *Early Modern Witches: Witchcraft Cases in Contemporary Writing* (London: Routledge, 2000).

Gibson, Marion, 'Understanding Witchcraft? Accusers' Stories in Print in Early Modern England,' in Stuart Clark (ed.), *Languages of Witchcraft: Narrative, Ideology and Meaning in Early Modern Culture* (Houndsmill, Basingstoke: Macmillan, 2001), pp. 41-54.

Gifford, George, *A Discourse of the Subtill Practises of Devilles by Witches and Sorcerers* (London, 1587).

Gifford, George, *A Dialogue Concerning Witches and Witchcraftes* (London, 1593).

Glanvill, Joseph, *Some Philosophical Considerations Touching the Subject of Witches and Witchcraft* (London, 1667).

Gowland, Angus, 'The Problem of Early Modern Melancholy,' *Past and Present* 191 (2006), pp. 77-120.

Grosart, Alexander B., *The Works of Gabriel Harvey* (London: The Huth Library, 1884-5).

Gunnoe, Charles D. Jr., 'The Debate between Johann Weyer and Thomas Erastus on the Punishment of Witches,' in James Van Horn Melton (ed.), *Cultures of Communication from Reformation to Enlightenment: Constructing Publics in the Early Modern German Lands* (Aldershot, Hampshire: Ashgate, 2002), pp. 257-85.

Halliday, F. E., 'Queen Elizabeth and Dr Burcot,' *History Today* 5 (1955), pp. 542-4.

Harsnett, Samuel, *A Declaration of Egregious Popish Impostures* (London, 1603) in F.W.Brownlow (ed.), *Shakespeare, Harsnett, and the Devils of Denham* (Newark: University of Delaware Press, 1993).

Heresbach, Conrad, *Foure Bookes of Husbandry, collected by M. Conradus Heresbachius ... newely Englished, and increade, by Barnabe Googe, Esquire* (London, 1577).

Hill, Robert C. (trans.), *Saint John Chrysostom: Homilies on Genesis 18–45* (Washington D.C.: The Catholic University of America Press, 1990).

Hill, Thomas, *The Moste Pleasaunte Arte of the Interpretation of Dreames* (London, 1576).

Holland, Henry, *The Historie of Adam, or the Foure-fold State of Man* (London, 1606).

Holinshed's Chronicles of England, Scotland, and Ireland (London: J. Johnson et al., 1807–8).

Holland, Peter, '"The Interpretation of Dreams" in the Renaissance,' in Peter Brown (ed.), *Reading Dreams: The Interpretation of Dreams from Chaucer to Shakespeare* (Oxford: Oxford University Press, 1999), pp. 125–46.

Holmyard, E.J., *Alchemy* (Harmondworth: Penguin, 1957).

Hopkin, Charles Edward, *The Share of Thomas Aquinas in the Growth of the Witchcraft Delusion* (Philadelphia: University of Pennsylvania Press, 1940).

Hussey, Maurice (ed.), *The Canon's Yeoman's Prologue and Tale* (Cambridge: Cambridge University Press, 1966).

Hutchinson, Francis, *An Historical Essay Concerning Witchcraft* (London, 1718).

Hutchinson, Keith, 'What Happened to Occult Qualities in the Scientific Revolution,' *Isis* 73 (1982), pp. 233–53.

Hyperius, Andreas [Gerhard], *Methodi Theologiae, sive Praecipuorum christianiae Religionis* (Basel, 1563).

Hyperius, Andreas [Gerhard], *Two Common Places taken out of Andreas Hyperius* (London, 1581).

James, R., *Daemonologie, in Forme of a Dialogue, Divided into Three Bookes* (Edinburgh, 1597).

Jeffrey, David Lyle (ed.), *A Dictionary of Biblical Tradition in Literature* (Grand Rapids, Michigan: Eerdmans, 1992).

Jensen, Peter, 'Calvin and Witchcraft,' *The Reformed Theological Review* 34 (1975), pp. 76–86.

Johnstone, Nathan, *The Devil and Demonisn in Early Modern England* (Cambridge: Cambridge University Press, 2006).

Jones, Norman, 'Defining Superstitions: Treasonous Catholics and the Act against Witchcraft of 1563,' in Charles Carlton (ed.), *State,*

Bibliography

Sovereigns & Society in Early Modern England (Gloucestershire: Sutton Publishing, 1997), pp. 187-203.

Keck, David, *Angels & Angelology in the Middle Ages* (New York: Oxford University Press, 1998).

Kittredge, George Lyman, *Witchcraft in Old and New England* (Cambridge, Massachusetts, Harvard University Press, 1929).

Klaassen, Frank, and Christopher Phillips, 'The Return of Stolen Goods: Reginald Scot, Religious Controversy, and Magic in Bodleian Library, Additional B.1.' in *Magic, Ritual, and Witchcraft* 1 (2006), pp. 135-76.

Kratz, Dennis M., 'Fictus Lupus: The Werewolf in Christian Thought,' *Classical Folia* 30 (1976), pp. 57-79.

Lavater, Ludwig, *Of Ghostes and Spirites Walking by Nyght* (London, 1572).

Lavater, Ludwig, *Of Ghostes and Spirites, Walking by Nyght* (London, 1596).

Lea, Henry Charles, *Materials Toward a History of Witchcraft* (New York: Thomas Yoseloff, 1957).

Linden, Stanton J., *Darke Hieroglyphics: Alchemy in English Literature from Chaucer to the Restoration* (Lexington, Kentucky: The University Press of Kentucky, 1996).

Lumby, Jonathan, *The Lancashire Witch-Craze: Jennet Preston and the Lancashire Witches, 1612* (Lancaster: Carnegie, 1995).

Macfarlane, Alan, 'A Tudor Anthropologist: George Gifford's *Discourse* and *Dialogue*,' in Sydney Anglo (ed.), *The Damned Art: Essays in the Literature of Witchcraft* (London: Routledge and Kegan Paul, 1977), pp. 140-55.

Macfarlane, Alan, *Witchcraft in Tudor and Stuart England* (London: Routledge and Kegan Paul, 1970).

Mackay, Christopher S. (ed. and trans.), *Malleus Maleficarum* (Cambridge: Cambridge University Press, 2006).

[Marnix van St. Aldegonde, Philips van], *The Bee Hive of the Romishe Churche* (London, 1579).

Marsden, J.H., *Philomorus: A Brief Examination of the Latin Poems of Sir Thomas More* (London: Pickering, 1842).

Marsh, Christopher W., *The Family of Love in English Society, 1550-1630* (Cambridge: Cambridge University Press, 1994).

Marten, Anthonie (trans.), *The common Places of the most famous and renowned Diviner Doctor Peter Martyr* (London, 1583).

Martin, Randall, *Women, Murder, and Equity in Early Modern England* (New York: Routledge, 2008).

[Mascall, Leonard], *The Country-mans Recreation, or the Art of Planning, Graffing, and Gardening, in three Bookes* (London, 1640).

McKerrow, Ronald B., *The Works of Thomas Nashe* (London: A. H. Bullen, 1904-10).

Miller, William E., 'Abraham Fleming: Editor of Shakespeare's Holinshed,' *Texas Studies in Language and Literature* 1 (1959), pp. 89-100.

Monter, E. William, 'Inflation and Witchcraft: The Case of Jean Bodin,' in Theodore K. Rabb, and Jerrold E. Seigel (eds.), *Action and Conviction in Early Modern Europe* (Princeton: Princeton University Press, 1969), pp. 371-89.

Monter, E. William, *Witchcraft in France and Switzerland: The Borderlands during the Reformation* (Ithaca and London: Cornell University Press, 1976).

Mora, George (ed.), *Witches, Devils, and Doctors in the Renaissance: Johann Weyer, De Praestigiis Daemonum* (Binghamton, New York: Medieval and Renaissance Texts and Studies, 1991).

Muenster, Sebastian, *A Brief Collection...Gathered out of the Cosmographye of Sebastian Munster* (London, 1572).

Nicholson, Brinsley (ed.), *The Discoverie of Witchcraft by Reginald Scot, Esquire* (London: Elliot Stock, 1973).

Notestein, Wallace, *A History of Witchcraft in England from 1558 to 1718* (Washington: American Historical Association, 1911).

P[aget], E[usebius] *A Harmonie upon the Three Evangelists, Matthew, Mark, and Luke, with the Commentarie of M. John Calvine* (London, 1584).

Patterson, Annabel, *Reading Holinshed's Chronicles* (Chicago: University of Chicago Press, 1994).

Perkins, Williams, *A Discourse of the Damned Art of Witchcraft* (London, 1608).

Porta, John Baptista, *Natural Magic* (London, 1658).

Price, S. R. F., 'The Future of Dreams: From Freud to Artemidorus,' *Past and Present* 113 (1986), pp. 3-37.

Probes, Christine McCall, 'Calvin on Astrology,' *Westminster Theological Journal* 37 (1974), pp. 24-33.

Pumfrey, Stephen, 'Potts, Plots and Politics: James I's *Daemonologie* and *The Wonderfull Discoverie of Witches* in Robert Poole (ed.), *The Lancashire Witches: Histories and Stories* (Manchester: Manchester University Press, 2002), pp. 22-41.

Rawski, Conrad H. (trans.), *Petrarch's Remedies for Fortune Fair and Foul* (Bloomington & Indianapolis: Indiana University Press, 1991).

Bibliography

Robbins, Robin (ed.), *Sir Thomas Browne's Pseudodoxia Epidemica* (Oxford: Clarendon Press, 1981).
Roberts, Alexander, *A Treatise of Witchcraft* (London, 1616).
Roper, Lyndal, *Witch Craze: Terror and Fantasy in Baroque Germany* (New Haven: Yale University Press, 2004).
Rosen, Barbara, *Witchcraft* (London: Edward Arnold, 1969).
[Roussat, Richard], *The Most Excellent Profitable, and Pleasaunt Booke of the Famous Doctor and Expert Astrologian Arcandum* (London, 1578).
Russell, Jeffrey Burton, *Witchcraft in the Middle Ages* (Ithaca and London: Cornell University Press, 1972).
Ryan, Granger, and Helmut Ripperger (trans.), *The Golden Legend of Jacobus de Voragine* (New York: Arno Press, 1969).
Salisbury, Joyce E., *The Beast Within: Animals in the Middle Ages* (New York and London: Routledge, 1994).
Schaff, Philip (ed.), *Saint Chrysostom: Homilies on the Epistles of Paul to the Corinthians* (Grand Rapids, Michigan: Eerdmans, 1969).
Schreiner, Susan E., 'Exegesis and Double Justice in Calvin's Sermons on Job,' *Church History* 58 (1989), pp. 322–38.
Scot, Reginald, *A Perfite Platforme of a Hoppe Garden, and Necessarie Instructions for the Making and Mayntenaunce thereof* (London, 1574).
Scot, Reginald, *The Discoverie of Witchcraft* (London, 1584).
Scott, Randy A. (trans.), *On the Demon-Mania of Witches* (Toronto: Centre for Reformation and Renaissance Studies, 1995).
Sharpe, James, *Instruments of Darkness: Witchcraft in England 1550–1750* (London: Hamish Hamilton, 1996).
Sharpe, James, *Witchcraft in Early Modern England* (Harlow: Longman, 2001).
Shaw, Jane, *Miracles in Enlightenment England* (New Haven and London: Yale University Press, 2006).
Slusser, Michael (trans.), *St. Gregory Thaumaturgus: Life and Works* (Washington, D.C.: The Catholic University of America Press, 1998).
Smelik, K. A. D., 'The Witch of Endor: 1 Samuel 28 in Rabbinic and Christian Exegesis till 800 A.D.', *Vigiliae Christianiae* 33 (1979), pp. 160–79.
Stearne, John, *A Confirmation and Discovery of Witchcraft* (London, 1648).
Stein, Claudia, 'The Meaning of Signs: Diagnosing the French Pox in early modern Augsburg,' *Bulletin of the History of Medicine* 80 (2006), pp. 617–48.
Stephens, Walter, *Giants in those Days* (Lincoln and London: University of Nebraska Press, 1989).

Stephens, Walter, *Demon Lovers: Witchcraft, Sex, and the Crisis of Belief* (Chicago: The University of Chicago Press, 2002).

Summers, Montague, *The Geography of Witchcraft* (London: Kegan and Paul, 1927).

Summers, Montague, *The Discoverie of Witchcraft by Reginald Scot* (London: John Rodker, 1930).

Summers, Montague (ed.), *Francesco Maria Guazzo: Compendium Maleficarum* (New York: Dover, 1988).

Summers, Montague, *The Discoverie of Witchcraft by Reginald Scot* (Mineola, New York: Dover, 1972).

Teall, John L., 'Witchcraft and Calvinism in Elizabethan England: Divine Power and Human Agency,' *Journal of the History of Ideas* 23 (1962), pp. 21–36.

Thomas, Keith, *Religion and the Decline of Magic* (Harmondsworth: Penguin, 1984).

Torijano, Pablo A., *Solomon, the Esoteric King: From King to Magus, Development of a Tradition* (Leiden: Brill, 2002).

Tschacher, Werner, *Der Formicarius des Johannes Nider von 1437/38* (Aachen: Shaker Verlag, 2000).

Walker, Ralph, *A Learned and Profitable Treatise of Gods Providence* (London, 1608).

Walsham, Alexandra, *Providence in Early Modern England* (Oxford: Oxford University Press, 1999).

Watt, Diane, *Sectaries of God: Women Prophets in Late Medieval and Early Modern England* (Cambridge: D.S. Brewer, 1997).

Webster, John, *The Displaying of Supposed Witchcraft* (London, 1677).

West, Robert H., *Reginald Scot and Renaissance Writings on Witchcraft* (Boston: Tayne Publishers, 1984).

Whatmore, L.E., 'The Sermon against the Holy Maid of Kent and her Adherents, delivered at Paul's Cross, November 23rd, 1533, and at Canterbury, December the 7th,' *The English Historical Review* 58 (1943), pp. 463–75.

Whiston, William (trans.), *Flavius Josephus, The Antiquities of the Jews*, http://www.gutenberg.org/files/2848/2848-h.

White Robert J. (trans. and comm.), *The Interpretation of Dreams: Oneirocritica by Artemidorus* (Park Ridge, New Jersey: Noyes Press, 1975).

Wood, Anthony A., *Athenae Oxonienses* (London, 1691).

Wootton, David, 'Reginald Scot/Abraham Fleming/ The Family of Love,' in Stuart Clark (ed.), *Languages of Witchcraft: Narrative, Ideology*

Bibliography

and *Meaning in Early Modern Culture* (Hampshire: Macmillan, 2001), pp. 119-38.

Wordsworth, Christopher (ed.), *Horae Eboracenses: The Prymer or Hours of the Blessed Virgin Mary, according to the Use of the illustrious Church of York* (Durham: Surtees Society, 1920).

W.W., *A True and Just Recorde, of the Information, Examination and Confession of all the Witches, taken at S.Oses in the Countie of Essex: Whereof some were Executed, and other some Entreated according to the Determination of Lawe* (London, 1582).

Zilboorg, Gregory, *The Medical Man and the Witch during the Renaissance* (Baltimore: The Johns Hopkins Press, 1935).

Index

Adam 189, 220 n. 105
Ady, Thomas 2-3
Agrippa, Cornelius 7, 144, 221 n. 106
alchemy 173-7
Ambrose 101
Anabaptists 221 n. 106
angels 155-77
  angelology and 74-6
  alchemy and 175
  corporeality of 76-7, 124-5, 179
  see also free will
Anglo, Sydney 182
Apollo, temple of 126
Apuleius 100-101
Aquinas, Thomas 76-7, 79, 102-3, 105, 113-14, 132, 142
  causation 132
  corporeality and 76-7
  demonic intervention 113-14
Aristotelianism 102, 165-6, 185
Aristotle 74, 77, 103, 114, 140, 142
Artemidorus of Ephesus 140
astrology 136-9
atonement, Ransom theory of the 67-8, 135
auguries
  casual, divine and natural 142-3
augury 21-2
  Johann Weyer and 141
Augustine 76-7, 79, 101-103, 113, 128, 142, 147, 180, 212 n. 88, 218 n. 48

demons and 76
Platonism and 76-7
transformation of humans and 101-103
see also 'sons of God'
Avicenna 140, 177, 226 n. 58

baptism 58, 93
Barton, Elizabeth 16, 121
Basson, Thomas 6, 188
see also Family of Love
Bernard, Richard 4, 86
bewitchment 14, 28, 36, 42-3, 107, 124
Bible, the 46, 49
  as source 97, 103, 113, 119, 142
  authority of 118, 140, 148
  categories of 20-5, 146, 155
  interpretation of 104, 117-18, 180-2, 184, 188
Bodin, Jean 18, 33, 80, 82, 87-9, 96, 128, 147, 169, 197 n. 63, 202 n. 76, 209 n. 33
  Brian Darcy and 41-2, 44
  Reginald Scot and 47-8, 99-103, 138
  transportation 88-9
  witchcraft and melancholy 63-5
  see also melancholy; Scot, Reginald; transportation; Weyer, Johann
Brandon 169-72
Briggs, Agnes 123

241

Brome, William 5, 8
Browne, Thomas 59

Cabalism 144-5, 221 n. 106
Calvin, John 49-51, 98, 137-9
  astrology and 137-9
  scepticism of 49-51
  see also Devil, the; transportation
cannibalism 48, 143
  see also Mass, doctrine of
Cardano, Girolamo 64-5
casting of lots 143
categories of the criminal 48
  see also Bodin, Jean
Catholicism 45-6, 89, 131, 148-9, 190-1
  demonology and 32-3, 91
  doctrine of transubstantiation 103, 148
  magic and 143, 149, 160
  Protestantism and 46, 131, 190
  witchcraft and 14-16, 45
causation 132
  see also Aquinas, Thomas
Cautares, John 8, 169
Chaucer, Geoffrey 173-5
Christ 46, 130, 143, 148, 152, 161
  miracles 133, 135, 191
  ransom paid by 67-8, 135
  second coming of 25-6
  transportation of 97-8
  see also atonement, Ransom theory of the
Chrysostom, John 114, 125, 217 n. 35
Clark, Stuart 179, 186
Cokars, John 156-7, 159
compact, Satanic 15, 59-60, 65, 72, 79-80, 83-7, 93-4, 108, 208 n. 27, 224 n. 11
confessions 66-9, 87, 94, 115
conjuring tricks 2, 7, 8, 108, 109, 158, 161
conjurors 155, 157, 159, 161, 168, 170
  see also Brandon; priests

Constantius of Lyon 92
Cotta, John 4, 32
Cranmer, Thomas 25, 122
creation, doctrine of 91, 148

Dalton, Michael 84-6
Daneau, Lambert 33, 80, 82-4, 102, 200 n. 26
Darcy, Brian 17, 40, 42, 45, 55
Daston, Lorraine 132-3
Davies, Owen 145
Della Porta, Giambattista 95-7, 113, 164, 168
della Spina, Bartolomeo 80-1, 91, 93, 209 n. 32
Delphic Oracle, the 125-7
demonology 2, 18, 30, 61, 69, 109, 114-15, 178-80, 185
  Catholicism and 32
  Continental (European) 21-2, 37, 71-2, 74, 78
  John Knox and 83
demons 76, 89, 101, 108, 112-13, 161
  corporeality 4, 76-7, 105, 110-11, 114-16
  illusions of 101-2, 109-11, 128-9, 211 n. 57
  impersonation by 93, 95, 97
  melancholy and 61-2
  possessed by 123-7, 217 n. 35
  power of 31, 198 n. 61
  transportation by 93, 97
  see also Devil, the; incubi
Devil, the 19, 30, 48-9, 54, 58-68, 99, 135, 153-54, 160-1, 181, 209 n. 33, 224 n. 153
  eschatology and 25
  illusions created by 118-20, 128
  mark of 83-7
  possessed by 16, 39, 123-4
  Protestantism and 186
  sex with 104-7, 112-14, 203 n. 82
  transportation by 97-8
  women and 59, 61, 65-8, 80-1, 155

Index

see also compact, Satanic
de Voragine, Jacobus 92
Diana, goddess 82, 90, 92, 94, 99
disease 27–8, 43, 46, 138
 explanations of 62–3
 incubi and 111–12
 punishment by 43
 symptoms and 27–8
divination 7, 136–9, 143, 145, 161
divine providence 29–30, 76
Dove, John 25
dreams 89, 91, 94, 98, 139–42
Duffy, Eamon 149
During, Simon 8

Elizabeth I 14, 18, 82, 129, 135
 threats to 35
enchantments, secular 168–69, 181
 see also magic, natural; magic, secular
Erastus, Thomas 65–6, 205 n. 132
Estes, Leland 32, 182
Eugenius IV, Pope 71
European, see Continental
Eve 59, 180–1, 189

Fall of Man 180–2, 189
familiars 37–38, 44–5, 84–5
Family of Love 187–9
Featés, Bomelio 129, 169, 170–1
fixity of species, doctrine of 102–3
Fleming, Abraham 4–5, 140, 147, 188
fortune telling 141–2
free will 75, 137
 see also angels
Freud, Sigmund 19

Galen 60–4
 humoural physiology of 60, 115, 138, 167
Galis, Richard 34, 36–40, 55
Garden of Eden 59
Gaule, John 57, 79
Germain, St. 92, 95

Gibson, Marion 41
Gifford, George 3, 30–1
Glanvill, Joseph 4
God 27, 87, 122–3, 127–8, 139, 142, 180
 glory of 165
 interventions of 79, 97, 132, 133
 Job and 51–2
 justice of 31, 138
 powers of 29–31, 192
 providence of 68, 166
 relationship with 137
 sovereignty of 54, 148, 200 n. 27
 spirit of 184–90
 treason against 47–9
 Word of 131
Gratian 89–90
Gregory Neocaesariensis, St.
 see Thaumaturgus, St. Gregory
Gregory of Nyssa 126
Grillando, Paolo 210 n. 55
Guazzo, Francesco Maria 62

Handley, Richard 38
Harsnett, Samuel 3
Harvey, Gabriel 3
Heaven 75–6
Hemingius, Nicolaus 33, 147
Henry VIII 14, 121–2, 135, 170
heresy 15, 21, 26, 32, 48, 53, 71, 84
Hill, Thomas 140
Holland, Henry 52, 59
Holy Spirit 187–91
Hooper, Bishop John 131
Hutchinson, Francis 4
Hutchinson, Keith 166
Hyperius, Andreas 113–14, 200 n. 27

imagination 102, 110–11
 melancholy and the 60–2
 transportation by the 88, 93–4, 96–7
 see also demons, illusions of
incubi 111–12, 114–16

James VI (James I) 1–2, 8, 19, 64, 71–2, 86, 98, 104
Jewel, John 14
Job 51–2, 54
Johnstone, Nathan 186
Josephus 118, 159, 160
juggling 168-169, 171, 173

Keck, David 74
Kempe, Ursley 41–2, 44–5
Kingsfield, of London 8, 169, 172
Kramer, Heinrich 8, 33, 58, 73, 80–1, 108, 114, 198 n. 65

Lambarde, William 121
Lavater, Ludwig 111, 128
law 15–17, 89–99, 95
legerdemain 148, 169, 171
Lyly, John 52

Macfarlane, Alan 41, 56
madness 50, 70, 79, 113
magic 54, 72, 79, 146, 148–9
  angelic and demonic 155–8
  image 37
  in the Bible 20, 146, 159–61
  medical 150–1, 153–4
  natural 163–6, 168, 174–5, 185–6
  secular 2, 8, 168–9
  verbal (word) 151–2
magical charms 146–55, 168, 173
magicians 7, 19, 49–50, 95–6, 113, 159–60, 168–69, 194 n. 12
  see also Solomon
manifest qualities 165–66, 185
  see also Aristotelianism; Aristotle
Manwood, Sir Roger 9–10
Margaret, St. 160–1, 224 n. 153
Mass, doctrine of 103, 143, 148
  see also cannibalism
melancholy 11, 50, 60–9, 80, 104, 205 n. 119

delusions of 21, 60–5, 67, 104
  see also demons, illusions of; madness; witches
Merlin 113, 214 n. 121
miracles 22, 130–35, 139
More, Henry 184
Moses 20, 139, 159, 168
Muhammad 225 n. 27

Nashe, Thomas 3
natural philosophy 95, 134, 178
Nebuchadnezzar, King 103–4, 180, 198 n. 74
neo-Galenicism 64
  see also Galen
neo-Platonic 76
  see also Platonism
Neopolitanus, Johannes Baptista
  see Della Porta, Giambattista
Nevell, Sir Henry 35, 38–9
Nider, Johannes 58, 72–3, 92, 105

oracles 130, 135–6
  see also Delphic Oracle, the; Pythonism
Ovid 103

Paris, University of 74
Park, Katherine 132
Peck, Francis 5
penises 108–10
Perkins, William 4, 31
Petrarch 177
Platonism 77, 142
  see also More, Henry; neo-Platonism
Pneumatochi, the 187
poisoners 117–20, 215 n. 2
Ponzinibio, Giovanni Francesco 210 n. 55
Potts, Thomas 206 n. 3
Pratensis, Jason 112
priests 15
  lasciviousness of 104, 108, 113

Index

magical practices of 148, 153, 155
prophecies 130, 135-7, 139
Protestantism 15, 51, 143, 186, 190
pseudo-Augustine 89
punishment 47-8, 66
  by God 31, 97
  capital 118
  eternal 87
  familiars and 43
  of witches 63, 65-6,
    100, 154
  threat of burning 44
  see also witchcraft, prosecutions of
Puritanism 32
Pythonism 121-7

Roberts, Alexander 58
Robin Good-fellow 115, 214 n. 135

Sabbath, Satanic 50, 72-4, 81-2,
  87-90, 193, 195
  see also transportation
sacrifice 153
salvation 32
  of Christ 67, 135
  of witchcraft collaborators 32
  see also atonement, Ransom
    theory of the
Samuel 3, 127-30, 134
Satan
  see demons; Devil, the
Saul 3, 51, 127-30, 218 n. 45
Scot, Reginald 9-13, 21-3, 48-50
  Bible and 103-4
  demonology and 71-2, 78, 109
  four Biblical categories 117-61
  intent of 57, 61, 88, 117
  Saduceeism and 182-3, 187
  scepticism of 1, 29-30, 78-9,
    135, 145-6, 191
  sources for 4, 18-19, 34, 44, 73,
    87, 95, 98, 113
Selles, Henry 202 n. 69
Sennert, Daniel 165

Shakespeare, William 3, 103, 214
  n. 35
Sharpe, James 182
Simons, Margaret 16, 26-8
'sons of God' 113-14
Solomon 159-60, 163, 166
soul 183-4, 227 n. 82
  see also More, Henry
spirits 23, 92, 132, 158-9, 164
  corporeality 111, 114-16,
    179-84, 186-91
  exorcism of 152
  intervention by 132-4, 136
  see also miracles
Stearne, John 59
Stephens, Walter 77
Stile, Elizabeth 36-40
Summers, Montague 177-8
Sylvanus, St. 112-13

Thaumaturgus, St. Gregory 126
theology 30, 183, 185
  of Spirit 23-4,
  of Reginald Scot 185-91
  Puritan 32, 83
Thomas, Keith 66, 139
Torijano, Pablo 159
T.R. 155, 157, 159
transformation into animals 22,
  72, 99-103, 108
transportation 50, 88-9, 93-7, 210
  n. 55
transubstantiation, doctrine of 99,
  102-3
Trevor-Roper, Hugh R. 198
  n. 68
trickery 3-4, 7-8, 49, 171, 175,
  194 n. 12
Trinitarianism 187
Turner, Robert 7

Vairus, Leonardus 147, 167, 169,
  224 n. 11
vehicles of the soul 4

ventriloquists 121-6
visions 91, 93-4

Webster, John 13
Weyer, Johann 3, 19-21, 112, 117, 120, 125, 152-7, 211 n. 57
  melancholy and 61-6, 104
  Pythonism 125
  Sigmund Freud and 19
  transportation 95-7
  witches and the Bible 19-21
  see also Della Porta, Giambattista
wise women
  see witches
witchcraft 1-4, 17, 21, 23, 25, 51-3, 72, 79, 83-4, 114, 189
  accusations of 10, 27, 44, 54-5, 57, 65, 19
  acts of 34, 36, 38, 41, 107
  confessions of 66, 83
  legislation against 14-16, 71
  prosecutions of 4-6, 14, 39-40, 82, 96

women and 58-9, 63
  see also compact, Satanic; demonology; melancholy; scepticism; transportation
witches 17-19, 26-7, 34, 61
  'black' and 'white' 31-3
  cults of 71-4
  evil eye 167-8
  four kinds of 20-2, 33, 49
  of St. Osyth 40-9
  of Windsor 35-40
  origin of 114
  powers of 29-32, 47, 53-4, 66-7, 69, 128, 141, 148
  women and 58-9, 64-5, 167
  see also compact, Satanic; familiars; transportation; Sabbath, Satanic
Witch of Endor, the 3, 51, 127-30
Wood, Anthony 12
Wootton, David 187

Zilboorg, Gregory 62-3

www.ingramcontent.com/pod-product-compliance
Ingram Content Group UK Ltd.
Pitfield, Milton Keynes, MK11 3LW, UK
UKHW020819240326
469204UK00019B/93